RELIGION AND THE FAMILY:
WHEN GOD HELPS
Laurel Arthur Burton, ThD
Editor

𝕮𝕳𝕻𝕻

SOME ⸍

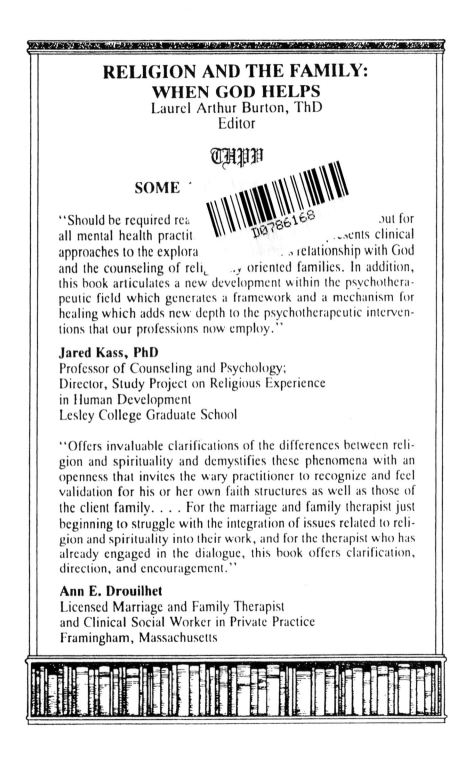

"A sophisticated yet readable book that deals with central issues at the interface of theology and the social sciences. The book is sound theologically and rich practically. It is a contribution to the emerging re-named area of practical theology. It should become required reading not only in introductory courses in pastoral care, but in advanced courses in both pastoral and secular family therapy. [It] invites dialogue between clergy and secular therapists in learning both the theory and practice of assessing religious dynamics in the therapeutic changes invited by each."

Peggy Way, PhD
Professor of Pastoral Theology
Eden Theological Seminary

"Offers a guide for the counselor/therapist on the necessary importance of the God construct in assessing the client's model of reality. Several models are offered for assessing and intervening in a family system, incorporating the powerful influence of religion/spiritual beliefs. This volume includes theories and applications of value to the humanist or spiritualist, the family therapist, individual psychotherapist, pastoral counselor or anyone working with people in conflict and in need of change."

Marco De La Cruz, MD
Family Physician and Family Therapist
Rush Anchor HMO, Chicago, Illinois

Religion and the Family
When God Helps

THE HAWORTH PASTORAL PRESS
William M. Clements, PhD
Senior Editor

New, Recent, and Forthcoming Titles:

Growing Up: Pastoral Nurture for the Later Years by Thomas B. Robb

Religion and the Family: When God Helps edited by Laurel Arthur Burton

Victims of Dementia: Services, Support, and Care by Wm. Michael Clemmer

Horrific Traumata: A Pastoral Response to the Post-Traumatic Stress Disorder by N. Duncan Sinclair

Religion and the Family
When God Helps

Laurel Arthur Burton, ThD
Editor

𝕿𝕳𝕻𝕻

The Haworth Pastoral Press
An Imprint of The Haworth Press, Inc.
New York • London • Norwood (Australia)

Published by

The Haworth Pastoral Press, an imprint of The Haworth Press, Inc., 10 Alice Street, Bingham-
ton, NY 13904-1580.

Library of Congress Cataloging-in-Publication Data

Religion and the family : when God helps / Laurel Arthur Burton.
    p. cm.
   Includes bibliographical references and index.
   ISBN 1-56024-192-6 (hard : alk. paper). — ISBN 1-56024-197-7 (pbk. : alk. paper)
   1. Family—Religious life. 2. Family—Psychotherapy. I. Burton, Laurel Arthur.
BL625.6.R46 1991
291.6′1—dc20
                                        91-23285
                                          CIP

CONTENTS

Preface   xi

INTRODUCTORY ISSUES

**Chapter One: Does "God" Enter the System? A Review
and Introduction**   3
Laurel Arthur Burton, ThD

Religious Issues in Therapy?   3
Some Possible Explanations   4
Religion and Weltanschauung   6
Weltanschauung and Therapeutic Stance   7
An Editor's Preference   9

**Chapter Two: A Hermeneutical Approach to Religion
and Family Therapy**   13
Laurel Arthur Burton, ThD

Introduction: Approaching Religion   13
Spirituality   14
Religion   15
Multiple Religious Realities   19
Values and Models of Therapy   22
A Proposed Hermeneutic Model for When God Enters
the System   26
Conclusion   36

**Chapter Three: Foundations for a Spiritually Based
Psychotherapy**   41
Charles Verge, PhD

What God? Whose God?   42
In Search of Truth   42
Theory of Change   44
Healing and Curing   47
A Bridge of Love   47
Wholeness and the Integration of Our Two Selves   51
Goals of Therapy   52

The Practice of Spiritual Psychotherapy   53
Family Therapy and the Art of Healing   56
Contexts for Grace   57

APPLICATIONS

**Chapter Four: Therapeutic Change in Religious Families:
Working with the God-Construct**   **63**
     James L. Griffith, MD
     Melissa Elliott Griffith, MSN

Introduction   63
The God-Construct and Its Epigenesis   64
A Language Systems Approach to Working
   with the God-Construct in Psychotherapy   70
An Illustrative Psychotherapy   74
Summary   83

**Chapter Five: Spirituality and Systems Therapy:
Partners in Clinical Practice**   **87**
     Douglas A. Anderson, PhD

An Illustration   87
Introduction   88
Paradigm One: Spirituality   89
Paradigm Two: Systems Theory   91
Some Commonalities and Differences   92
Convergence   93
Three Implications for Counseling   94
Another Case Study   96

**Chapter Six: Mixing Oil and Water Religiously:
Counseling Interfaith Families**   **103**
     Lucinda S. Duncan, MDiv

Introduction   103
Approaching Faith Structures: Boundaries and Coordinates   106
Judaism As Affect   111
Christianity As Meaning   114
Unitarian Universalism As Power   115

The Impact of Family   118
Specific Dynamics of Interfaith Consultations   132
The Job Ahead: Gatherings, Grief Work, Possibilities   135

Chapter Seven: Family Therapy with the Faithful:
Christians As Clients   **139**
    Anne F. Grizzle, MS

Assessment Models for Natural and Spiritual Relationships   140
Biblical Relationship Principles   142
Typical Tangles of Natural and Spiritual Relationships   147
Spiritual Family Resources   156
Therapeutic Goals for the Faithful   159
Conclusions   161

RESEARCH

Chapter Eight: Assessing the Role of Religion in Family
Functioning   **165**
    Melvyn C. Raider, PhD

Conceptual Frameworks   166
Family Systems Theory   166
Religious Commitment   168
Religious Commitment and Family Style   169
The Assessment Model   171

Chapter Nine: Religion in Family Therapy Journals:
A Review and Analysis   **185**
    Eugene W. Kelly, Jr., PhD

Introduction   185
Method   186
Extent of Religion in Family Therapy Journals   187
Religion As Theme or Subtheme   188
Religion in Family Therapy Practice and Research   196
Conclusion   201

Index   **209**

ABOUT THE EDITOR

Laurel Arthur Burton, ThD, is Bishop Anderson Professor of Religion and Medicine and Chair of the Department of Religion, Health, and Human Values at Rush University in Chicago, Illinois. A Clinical Member and Approved Supervisor in the American Association for Marriage and Family Therapy, Dr. Burton is the author or editor of six books and more than 25 articles. He has taught at Millikin University, Boston University's School of Theology and Schools of Medicine and Public Health, and The Divinity School of Harvard University. Dr. Burton is a member of the American Association of Pastoral Counselors, the College of Chaplains, the Society for the Scientific Study of Religion, the Society for Pastoral Theology, and the Society for Health and Human Values.

CONTRIBUTORS

Douglas A. Anderson, PhD, is Executive Director, Presbyterian Counseling Service, Seattle, Washington.

Laurel Arthur Burton, ThD, is Bishop Anderson Professor of Religion and Medicine, and Chairperson of the Department of Religion and Health at Rush University, Rush-Presbyterian-St. Luke's Medical Center in Chicago, Illinois.

Lucinda S. Duncan, MDiv, is Associate Pastor of the First Unitarian Universalist Parish in Cambridge, Massachusetts.

James L. Griffith, MD, is Director of the Family Therapy Program at the University of Mississippi Medical Center in Jackson, Mississippi.

Melissa Elliott Griffith, MSN, is a Clinical Instructor in Psychiatry, Department of Psychiatry and Human Behavior, University of Mississippi School of Medicine, Jackson, Mississippi.

Anne F. Grizzle, MS, is a therapist in private practice in Houston, Texas.

Eugene W. Kelly, Jr., PhD, is Professor of Counseling and Human Services at The George Washington University in Washington, DC.

Melvyn C. Raider, PhD, is Associate Professor at the Wayne State University School of Social Work in Detroit, Michigan.

Charles Verge, PhD, is Co-Director of the Family Institute of Cambridge and a lecturer in psychiatry at Harvard Medical School. He has a private practice in Newton, Massachusetts.

Preface

I have a fond memory of my first day-long seminar at the Kantor Family Institute in Cambridge, Massachusetts. Having recently completed my doctorate I had been encouraged by friends to spend the next year studying family therapy. Since pastors and pastoral counselors have been involved in working with families prior to the formal organization of the discipline, and since my own history had involved me in "natural family therapy" from a very young age, this seemed a fine idea. So there I sat, along with clinical psychologists, social workers, a couple of nurses, and a reasonably well-known author. I was the only "religious" person in attendance.

That first day was exciting. I participated in group exercises and discussions. I was becoming a true believer. Systems thinking was what I had been doing all along, but I did not know it. Imagine, then, my surprise and confusion when one of the supervisors suggested that I, of all the students, would have the most difficult time with systems theory. The reason, he said, was that I was religious! (Rabbi Edwin Friedman's *Generation to Generation* had not come along yet, obviously.)

There are still folks who believe that religion and family therapy do not mix, or that spirituality is not an appropriate category for reflection and intervention. A friend once shared the following story: "I was part of a supervision group. It was my turn to present and when I started to give information about the couple's religious practices, the supervisor stopped me. 'That's not important,' she said. 'Let's skip that and get to the meat of the case.' Well, I thought it was important and said so. The supervisor said, 'Let's ask the rest of the group.' One by one my peers shared little ways that spirituality was important to them personally, and in their work as therapists. It was amazing. I don't know who was more surprised, the supervisor or me. She then confessed, 'I'm not comfortable with this and I don't know much about religion, but if you think it's important, let's hear about it.'"

More and more we in the field are "hearing about it." At the AAMFT meeting in New York City a few years ago, the networking luncheon seats at tables labeled "spirituality" had to be increased twice. Many of the therapists present were not orthodox Christians or Jews, but did identify themselves as spiritual and claimed spirituality as part of their practice. There is an entire journal, *Common Boundary*, devoted to issues of spirituality and therapy, and in 1990, *The Family Therapy Networker* devoted its cover story to psychotherapy and spirituality. We are hearing about "it."

The idea for this book evolved from countless stories told at professional meetings, in class, through supervision or in the process of doing therapy. When I suggested the topic to The Haworth Press, there was recognition of the need to hear more from the stories. The contributors are folks who regularly work to make sense of the spirituality/religiosity they hear in their work as family therapists.

The first section, *Introductory Issues*, includes three chapters. The first is a simple introduction to the "problem," and the second, in addition to seeking some definition of spirituality and religion, offers a working model I have devised for integrating spiritual issues into therapy. Charles Verge, who is a Co-Director of the Family Institute of Cambridge (MA), offers a sophisticated and powerful framework for thinking about a spiritually-based therapy.

In the second section, *Applications*, the Griffiths demonstrate an approach to working with the God-Construct in therapy. Douglas Anderson, a pastoral counselor, links two paradigms (spiritual and systemic) in his model of counseling, and Lucinda Duncan raises significant issues about and offers some helpful understandings for working with interfaith couples. Then, Anne Grizzle shows how she uses "spiritual genograms" with her clients.

Finally, the last section is *Research*. Here Melvyn Raider reports on some of his research with families around religious issues, and Eugene Kelly surveys the family therapy journals with regard to issues related to religion.

This volume has some self-imposed limits. First, it has a western, anglo, Judeo-Christian bias. Second, it is not systematic in its dealing with religious issues, beliefs, or practices. Its great strength, from my perspective, is that all the contributors are practicing therapists, supervisors, and teachers, who approach spirituality and/or religion in sensitive yet different ways.

I must express my gratitude to the contributors for their generosity and patience. Randy Doyle, my research assistant here at Rush University has been a remarkable help, and indeed all the staff of The Haworth Press have provided care-full attention and unflagging good humor.

In the next ten years, I believe we will hear clients speak of spiritual issues with increasing frequency and confidence. Pollster George Gallup, Jr. projects that the "American population that will emerge in the 1990s will be more Catholic, more non-Western, more Mormon, more unaffiliated, and less Protestant than it is today" (Gallup, G. and Castelli, J. (1990) *The People's Religion: American Faith in the 90s*). Faith issues will need to be further understood as significant aspects of family evaluation, therefore, as much for their resourcefulness as for their potential pathology.

Laurel Arthur Burton, ThD

INTRODUCTORY ISSUES

Chapter One

Does "God" Enter the System?
A Review and Introduction

Laurel Arthur Burton, ThD

Most of us from experience know what real hospitality feels like. It means being received openly, warmly, freely, without the need to earn your keep or prove yourself. An inhospitable space is one in which we feel invisible — or visible but on trial. A hospitable space is alive with trust and good will, rooted in a sense of our common humanity. When we enter such a space, we feel worthy because the host assumes we are.

Parker Palmer

RELIGIOUS ISSUES IN THERAPY?

"Where does God enter the system?" I asked.

"God? What's religion got to do with it anyway?" responded the therapist I was supervising.

The family being interviewed turned out to be active in their religious community. Their congregation and the teachings of their faith were a significant part of the family's value system and its basis of operation. The parents, assuming the importance of their religious orientation, did not bother to mention it. The therapist, experienced but new to marriage and family therapy, traditionally trained and seeking to maintain objectivity, did not want to contaminate the therapy with religious issues. She said, "I mean, religion just shouldn't be a part of the clinical picture . . . should it?"

This supervisee was expressing what many therapists and researchers believe, namely, that the issue of religion is irrelevant at best, detrimental at worst. Sociologists Darwin Thomas and Gwendolyn Henry confirm this with the following observation:

> In the research and theory rush of the 1960s and 1970s the place of religion in the study of the family went almost unnoticed. Of the 1,006 pages in Christensen's *Handbook of Marriage and the Family*,[1] "religion and the family" appears in only three entries of the index, as does "religious groups." This separation of religion and family is also seen in the two volumes of *Contemporary Theories About the Family*.[2] These two volumes were designed to summarize research and theory in important substantive areas in family study, and they have no religion chapter or even an extended discussion of religion within a chapter. There are only two insignificant references to religion in the index in each of the two volumes.[3]

Another supervisee, working on her doctoral research in this field, reported that when she conducted a seminar session on "religion and family therapy," the majority of the class members — all therapists — expressed a good deal of negative feeling about religion in general and their own experiences in particular, with one firmly stating that "the only reason to deal with religion in therapy is to help clients get over it!" Indeed, a number of psychologists, psychiatrists, social workers, and even some pastoral counselors of my acquaintance focus on the adverse effects of religion and express suspicion of any religious material in therapy. Why is this?

SOME POSSIBLE EXPLANATIONS

There are several possible responses to this question. One of my own teachers, Orlo Strunk, whose work has been in psychology and religion, once suggested that psychoanalytic approaches to religion seemed "more promising" at one time. Further, Strunk believed that complex human behaviors, as a focus of study, fell into neglect in some circles under the influence of behaviorism.[4] Writing in the *Annual Review of Psychology 1988*, Richard Gorsuch suggests two ways of understanding the history of the study of the relationship between psychology and religion. The first is "The Scholarly Distance Hypothesis,'' which suggests that the ideal of objectivity, as part of training in the social sciences, is responsible for the apparent decline of interest in psychology and religion. Indeed, Beit-Hallahmi says "As early as 1912 . . . it was shown that scientists, especially psychologists, were less religious than most of the American population. Scientists in the 30s might have felt that the long war between science and religion was won by science and there was not much left to study in religion.''[5] Shafranske and Gorsuch claim:

> The relative inattention to the religious or spiritual and the eschewing of the study in this area may have its root in the historical precedents of the profession. In its urgency to dissociate itself from philosophy, to earn its credentials and respectability as an empirical science as opposed to a speculative discipline, the dimension of spirituality was ushered out of the legitimate purview of psychology.[6]

"The Personal Relevance Hypothesis," the second way of understanding psychology and religion according to Gorsuch, claims that those who study religion do so because they find it personally meaningful while others, such as psychologists, do not. Given the growing awareness of the problems with "objectivity," as well as research that points to the "personal relevance of understanding client's worldviews,''[7] neither of these hypotheses seems to be born out.

A third possibility is raised by Lovinger, who contends that the scientific worldview, humanistic orientation, and liberal political orientation of therapists has influenced the minimal attention to religious issues in therapy.[8]

Whatever the reasons for this relative inattention previously, there are signs that religion and spirituality are not so much at odds with therapy as they perhaps once were. A. E. Bergin writes, "The emergence of studies of consciousness and cognition which grew out of disillusionment with mechanistic behaviorism has . . . set the stage for a new examination of the possibility that presently unobservable realities — namely, spiritual forces — are at work in human behavior.''[9] When Shafranske and Malony studied members of the American Psychological Association with regard to religious and spiritual orientation, they found that the "subjects, in general, appeared to view religious beliefs and questioning as valuable," with 53% rating religious beliefs as "desirable for people in general," 14% rating religious beliefs as undesirable, and 33% taking a neutral position. A total of 65% of the subjects indicated that spirituality was "personally relevant." Almost three-quarters of the respondents disagreed with the statement that "religious or spiritual issues are outside the scope of psychology."[10]

Bergin and Jensen, reporting on a national survey of clinical psychologists, marriage and family therapists, social workers, and psychiatrists, found that:

> The results confirm other findings in that psychologists show low rates of conventional religious affiliation and participation; but we also discovered a substantial amount of religious participation and spiritual involvement among all groups of therapists beyond or in addition to traditional conventions. There may be a reservoir of spiritual interests among therapists that is often unexpressed due to the secular framework of professional education and practice. This phenomenon, which we termed "spiritual humanism," could provide the basis for new dimensions of practice that might bridge the cultural gap between a secular profession and a more religious public.[11]

Of particular interest for marriage and family therapists is the finding that members of this profession "consistently manifested the highest level of religiosity," and that "the religiosity profiles of Marriage and Family Therapists and Clinical Social Workers are more similar to those of the public at large." The authors conclude their article by saying, "The potential for a change in the direction of greater empathy for the religious client is underscored by the surprisingly significant levels of unexpressed religiosity that exists among mental health professionals."[12]

RELIGION AND WELTANSCHAUUNG

It may seem obvious to most marriage and family therapists, but it still bears repeating, that *who* we are colors *what* we see. Whether therapist or client, one's *Weltanschauung*, or worldview, is an important aspect or expression of the system. Centuries ago the Greek philosopher Pindar said that ethics is the study of what we should do by virtue of who we are. Implicit in this view is the recognition that our own preferences, viewpoints, family stories, etc., help determine the conclusions we draw from experience.

In her "Foreword" to *Feminist Family Therapy*,[13] Rachel Hare-Mustin claims that

> . . . all social organization is politics, just as all meaning is semantics; every position involves "taking a standpoint." The question is not whether the standpoint is right or wrong, an unanswerable question in a post-modernist society, but what are the consequences of a particular standpoint.

Thomas and Henry seem to agree "since, for us, any acquisition of knowledge simultaneously involves a reading of meaning *into* the data as well as reading of meaning out of the data, it becomes important for social scientists to look carefully at the presuppositions."[14] P. H. McNamara, writing in the *Journal of Marriage and the Family*, points out that when behavioral scientists study conservative Christian families, they have a tendency to view them according to their own beliefs about the nature of religious institutions. This leads to a selective use of data that, when seen more broadly, provides a very different understanding of the family.[15]

WELTANSCHAUUNG AND THERAPEUTIC STANCE

The worldview of the therapist makes a great deal of difference in how a couple or family is assessed and what interventions are made. Too often this stance is acted on without adequate appreciation for the worldview and stance of the clients. Kantor and Neal say:

> [C]rucial is whether the therapist recognized and pays attention to validity of the client's model of reality, particularly if it is in conflict with the therapist's view. Jackie Hoover, a black psychiatric social worker and family therapist who trains and treats black and white students and clients in Boston, insists that "all therapy in America, even therapy conducted by whites with whites, is influenced by the slave mentality — which is an integral component of the American model of reality." Hoover argues that clients are put at risk when they must

subordinate their reality to that of the therapist. Reiss' theory and research on the disorganization process of families in crisis is consistent with this assertion and shows how a family's own sense of history and bounded identity can be sacrificed when its reality is subordinated to that of a larger social community, psychiatric hospital, or we will add, the temporarily powerful community of the therapy system.[16]

At his Cambridge, Massachusetts based training program, Kantor noticed that some therapists seemed to work better with some families than with others. As he began to research this observation, he saw an emerging pattern. Therapist's models for doing therapy are based, in part at least, on their own "boundary profiles," that is, the therapist's personal givens, grounded in family of origin scripts, training experiences, and cultural experiences. For example, therapists have differing preferences in matters of personal closeness or distance, whether they operate out of their heads or hearts, their ideas about change, health and pathology, gender roles, etc. As an illustration, recall the supervisee mentioned earlier. She was a non-religious Jew from an upper-middle class, suburban family, who seemed to have difficulty working with a very religious Roman Catholic, Hispanic family from the inner city. It was not that this supervisee *could not* or should not work with that particular client, but rather that her current lenses select out certain factors and impose others as their model for therapy is bounded by the elements of her history and culture. "If modern physics emphasizes an observer-created reality, social scientists ought not to back away from questions about how their own conceptual systems along with measurement devices combine to influence the meaning they see in their data."[17] Kantor's methodology for training couples and family therapists stresses the importance of constructed realities. Describing his approach, journalist Christina Robb writes:

> Kantor's students are not allowed to filter their information through a single metaphor like medicine or crime. They are also not allowed to regard as failures the cases that don't respond. If something doesn't work or someone doesn't fit a

theory, they have to figure out why and come up with an expanded theory that does work.[18]

Kantor himself says "when you're building a model, you have to have the utter conviction that everything you find is explainable by the model or alters the model." Religion and spirituality are thus understandable in terms of one's model for therapy, or they must alter the model in some way. Salvador Minuchin has an elegant way of putting it:

> We live our lives like chips in a kaleidoscope, always part of patterns that are larger than ourselves and somehow more than the sum of their parts. Our individual epistemology usually blinds us to this kaleidoscopic self, and that is unfortunate because, when we look at human beings from this perspective, whole new possibilities open up for exploring behavior and alleviating pain.[19]

AN EDITOR'S PREFERENCE

It should be clear by now that the model being developed here is influenced by the idea that reality is, in part at least, socially constructed.[20] While some religiously conservative therapists may experience difficulty with this claim, I believe that the relativizing impact of this position can be helpful to both religionists and secularists alike, to the extent that either equates a particular construct with Truth. Therapists exercising a traditional or orthodox Judeo-Christian perspective tend to believe that Truth is determined by God and revealed through certain sacred texts providing rules for right behavior. Other therapists, influenced by the philosophers of post-modernism, prefer a stance that sees all truth claims as relative. (Houston Smith says of post-modernism, "Not only does it lack an embracing outlook; it doubts that it is any longer possible — or even desirable — to have one."[21]) Surely my former colleague Alan Slobodnik is correct when he says:

Realistically, it is virtually impossible to be a pure determinist or constructivist. While the constructivists are correct in alerting us to the dangers of believing we see reality, the determinists remind us that everyone always believes in something. Carried to the logical extreme, a constructivist would be unable to choose between the infinite, multiple realities to even ask a question. At the other extreme, a determinist would only make statements and not ask questions once reality was determined. Clearly a mix of both is required for effective family therapy to occur.[22]

The question "What's religion got to do with therapy, anyway?" finds its response in two other questions: "Whose religion are we talking about?" and "What *doesn't* it have to do with therapy?" The worldview and stance of both the therapist and the client make a difference. If religion is part of that stance, explicitly or implicitly, it alters the system, and therefore is of strategic importance to the process of therapy within the system.

Being male, I write and think from the perspective of my maleness. Carol Gilligan[23] is correct to describe much of my moral thinking as operating according to a pattern of "competing rights," since I am arguing that spiritual and religious values in both clients and therapists should at least be given a fair hearing and not dismissed out of hand. I must note, however, another model that Gilligan has observed in women; one she calls "responsibility and care," where it is simply assumed that everyone in the system will be responded to and included. It is this latter valuing behavior that I would hope for if and when God enters the systems with which each of us works.

REFERENCE NOTES

1. Christensen, H.T. ed. 1964. *Handbook of Marriage and the Family*. Chicago: Rand McNally.

2. Burr, W.R., R. Hill, R.I. Nye, and I.L. Reiss, eds. 1979. *Contemporary Theories About the Family*, I and II. New York: The Free Press.

3. Thomas, D.L. and G.C. Henry. 1988. "The Religion and Family Connection: Increasing Dialogue in the Social Sciences," *The Religion and Family Connection*, ed. D.L. Thomas. Provo, UT: Brigham Young University.

4. Strunk, O. 1975. "The Present Status of the Psychology of Religion." *The Journal of Bible and Religion*, 25:287-292.

5. Beit-Hallahmi, B. 1974. "Psychology of Religion in 1880-1930: The Rise and Fall of a Psychological Movement." *Journal of the History of the Behavioral Sciences*, 10:84-94.

6. Shafranske, E.P. and R.L. Gorsuch. 1984. "Factors Associated with the Perception of Spirituality in Psychotherapy." *The Journal of Transpersonal Psychology*, Vol. 16, No. 2, 231-241.

7. *See* McGoldrick, Giradono, and Pearce. 1981. *Ethnicity and Family Therapy*. New York: Guilford, for example.

8. Lovinger, R.J. 1984. *Working with Religious Issues in Therapy*. New York: Jason Aronson.

9. Bergin, A.E. 1980. "Psychotherapy and Religious Values." *Journal of Consulting and Clinical Psychology*, 48(1):95-105.

10. Shafranske, E.P. and H.N. Malony. 1990. "Clinical Psychologists' Religious and Spiritual Orientations and Their Practice of Psychotherapy." *Psychotherapy*, Vol. 27, No. 1:72-78.

11. Bergin, A.E. and J.P. Jenson. 1990. "Religiosity of Psychotherapists: A National Survey," *Psychotherapy*, 27:3-7.

12. Ibid.

13. Goodrich et al. 1988. *Feminist Family Therapy*. New York: W. W. Norton.

14. Thomas and Henry, *op. cit.*

15. McNamara, P.H. 1985. "The New Christian Right's View of the Family and Its Social Science Critics: A Study in Differing Presuppositions." *Journal of Marriage and the Family*, 47 (May):449-458.

16. Kantor, D. and J. Neal. 1985. "Integrative Shifts for the Theory and Practice of Family Systems Therapy." *Family Process*, Vol. 24, No. 1, March 1985, 13-30.

17. Thomas and Henry, *op. cit.*

18. Robb, C. 1988. "Counseling with a Difference." *The Boston Globe Magazine*, May 1, 1988.

19. Minuchin, S. 1987. *Family Kaleidoscope*. Cambridge, MA: Harvard University Press.

20. Berger, P. and T. Luckmann. 1966. *The Social Construction of Reality*. Garden City, NY: Doubleday.

21. Smith, H. 1989. *Beyond the Post-Modern Mind*. New York: Crossroads Publishing Co.

22. Slobodnik, A. 1990. "Family Therapy as Healing." *The KFI Newsletter*, Vol. 2, No. 1, Winter 1990.

23. Gilligan, C. 1982. *In a Different Voice: Psychological Theory and Women's Development*. Cambridge: Harvard University Press.

Chapter Two

A Hermeneutical Approach to Religion and Family Therapy

Laurel Arthur Burton, ThD

INTRODUCTION: APPROACHING RELIGION

A colleague of mine was administering a questionnaire about spirituality and religion. As she was reviewing some of the returns, she came across a response that, while incomplete, was illuminating. Among the early questions, the term "spiritual" was linked with "religious." The respondent had written in bold print: "Well, which is it: spiritual or religious? It makes a difference, you know! I can't answer these without that information." The rest was blank, but the experience serves to demonstrate the importance of making distinctions early on.

How are we to distinguish between the two? Are some people spiritual without being religious; or religious without being spiritual? I practice and teach in a healthcare institution. On a daily basis I talk with people who say they are not religious, but who evidence some form of spiritual practice (a good luck charm, meditation, self-help books or tapes, and positive imaging to name a few). Some of these people also report a religious affiliation, but many do not. Another example: among my therapist friends around the country there are people who are interested in Tarot cards, the I Ching, Runes, crystals, channeling, goddess devotion, and other non-traditional practices. Are they religious or spiritual? I have come to operate with the assumption that all people have some form of spirituality, but not everyone will express that spirituality in terms of a religion.

Both spirituality and religion can be important to the process of family therapy, since both influence – and are influenced by – choices made within the system. In this chapter I am going to briefly discuss and define both spirituality and religion from one perspective and look at some of the ways religion has traditionally been approached in sociology, psychology, and theology. I will then explore the relationship between "values" and religion, leading to a working model for dealing with spiritual and religious issues in therapy.

SPIRITUALITY

Several assumptions come into play as the concept of spirituality is explored. First, I believe that, at least in western culture, spirituality finds its genesis with what Tillich called ". . . the existential awareness of nonbeing."[1] This awareness may be triggered by or manifest itself in terms of loss (or threatened loss) of relationship with self, God, or others. Such awareness of nonbeing is described by Tillich, who was an existentialist theologian, as "ontological anxiety," undifferentiated fear around the possibility of loss of being. This anxiety, then, gives rise to some construction of what is "ultimate" in one's life. Clearly, then, spirituality is grounded in the midst of history where messy life events are being experienced and interpreted; for one cannot "be" without being somewhere nor experience anxiety about not being without some sense that there is somewhere one will not be.

The second assumption involved in an overall definition of spirituality is that human beings (a) seek interpersonal connection and (b) at the same time seek safety in/from connection. This is a way of saying that everyone, then, is a self-in-relation.[2] This "relation" may appear different to different people and finds its expression in different ways, including solitude. Further, whatever or whoever is construed as the Ultimate will be a part of this relation. Here the role of family history of belief, community, cultural patterns of belief, etc., must be acknowledged as having a part in this relational development.

A third assumption involves embodiment. That is, spirituality is experienced and expressed in the context of physical structure, social class, ethnicity, gender, age, and sexual orientation. Each of these may be an important variable in spirituality in that each offers both possibility and limitation. Each is a potential source of creativity as well as a reminder of personal finitude. This is not to say spirituality is necessarily limited by embodiment, but rather that embodiment (and its potential limitations) is a primary context for the development and expression of spirituality.

Spirituality is a non-linear, dynamic process of complex interactions between and among these various factors in relation to historical events. Therefore, these assumptions lead to the following working definition:

> Spirituality is a dynamic construction, exploration, and expression of self-in-relation to the dynamic construction of the Ultimate, growing from experience of and reflection on the tension between possibilities and limits of human existence in history.

RELIGION

The root meaning of the word "religion" is "to bind together." A former colleague, Michael Vickers, once told me, "I always thought the function of religion was to keep people from experiencing too much randomness."[3] Religion, I believe, binds together the ontological anxiety experienced in the threat of randomness and non-being, thus allowing some degree of confident, personal functioning.

I understand religion to be secondary to spirituality though, in true non-linear form, it interacts with spirituality in such a way that each participates in the ongoing formation of the other. By "secondary" I mean that religion is an organized expression of spirituality, and therefore is more specific and defined in its structures.

Three Approaches to Religion

Scholars have long debated the proper approach to the study of religion. Sociologists, beginning with Durkheim,[4] have generally understood religion as a social phenomenon related to the needs of a particular social group. Religious rules and doctrines, according to some sociologists, are actually a representation of the order needed by the society to govern itself. Here one might focus on the function of religion in culture.

Psychologists, on the other hand, have tended to emphasize inner, emotional factors in the approach to religion, sometimes focusing on religion as a way to deal with conflicting "drives," and other times understanding religion as a way of working out personal meaning and identity. Here the focus may be on the intra- or interpersonal dynamics of religion.

The theological approach begins with God or the Ultimate as a given and works from there. Whether working from ancient, sacred texts or current human experience, the focus is on discerning the relationship between God/Ultimate and persons/creation. Usually there is a normative and ethical dimension to this task as theologians ask what is it to be in "right relation" with God and others and the earth and cosmos?

Determining Stance

Sociology, psychology, and theology are stances taken by observers in the study of religion. Stance clearly plays an important part in determining what one sees. If I stand up and look down, I get a picture that is very different from the person who lies down and looks up. Stance is further defined in terms of what has been called the constructivist-determinist split.

> Since the 1970s there have been two competing views about family therapy: determinism and constructivism. The earliest family therapists were determinists, such as Don Jackson, Nathan Ackerman, and Salvador Minuchin. Determinists believe that reality exists, and observers can become increasingly skilled at discovering that reality. They believe that systems have internal structure like biological organisms and are homeostatic. Determinists often have equally strong views about causation and outcome. The original Milan group were the first family therapists to adopt an almost pure constructivist view. Constructivists believe that all reality is constructed, with each system or part of a system having its own unique reality. Internal structure is not considered fixed. Reality can

therefore be easily reframed by the introduction of new information.[5]

The stance I am taking is both determinist and constructivist, combining theories, methods, and insights from sociology, psychology, and theology. That is to say that this approach takes seriously the outer structures of religion as constructed by social groups, as well as the inner meanings of religious faith for individuals, in light of the Ultimate.

Images and meanings can be constructed and deconstructed and reconstructed. For some this may be experienced as heresy, but for me it is more like "taking on the Gods."[6] "In psychotherapy, when God changes, we change. The process of therapy usually accomplishes multilevel goals simultaneously. Clients with deeply religious convictions often experience what they call 'progress toward God' as therapy unfolds."[7] That is, when previous constructs of God are altered, clients change. It is also my experience that when individuals, couples, or families change, their constructions of God — or the Ultimate — change. This is then a systemic process in which a variety of fields mutually affect each other.

Religion and Cultural Systems

Talcott Parsons claimed that "the cultural system structures commitments vis-à-vis ultimate reality into meaningful orientations toward the rest of the environment, and the organismic system similarly adapts itself and the other systems to the physical environment."[8] Human life, he said, can be understood within four interactive subsystems. The first of these is *the cultural system* of "meanings, intentions, norms, and patterns of human behavior." The second is *the social system* of patterned interaction and order, while the third is *the personality system*, which considers individual factors and goals. Finally, the fourth subsystem is *the organic system* focusing on biological needs. Parsons places these into the context of two "environments," that of *physical nature* and *ultimate reality*. He means that people structure their behaviors in ways that are validated by constructions of that which they believe to be ultimate.

Lessa and Vogt provide an additional comment about the ultimate:

> Religion may be described as a system of beliefs and practices directed toward the "ultimate concern" of a society. "Ultimate concern," a concept used by Paul Tillich, has two aspects—meaning and power. It has meaning in the sense of ultimate meaning of the central values of a society, and it has power in the sense of ultimate, sacred, or supernatural power which stands behind those values.[9]

One further element in the approach to religion: it is a symbol system that expresses itself via myth and ritual. As such, Clifford Geertz's definition of religion must be noted along with that of Anthony Wallace. For Geertz, religion can be defined as: "(1) a system of symbols which acts to (2) establish powerful, pervasive, and long-lasting moods and motivations in men [sic] by (3) formulating conceptions of a general order of existence and (4) clothing these conceptions with such an aura of factuality that (5) the moods and motivations seem uniquely realistic."[10] Here, then, religion is a cultural-linguistic system, which is then maintained, according to Wallace, "by a set of rituals, rationalized by myth, which mobilizes supernatural powers for the purpose of achieving or preventing transformations of state in [people] and nature."[11]

These many considerations and definitions all play a part in an approach to religion for a systemic family therapist. This approach is intentionally broad enough to include both those who would consider themselves as religious and those who would not. My working definition, then, is:

> Religion is a cultural phenomenon, involving mutually interacting systems, whereby symbol, myth, and ritual serve to organize and bind personal and group anxiety about non-being, and to validate norms and behaviors via reference to and in relation to some conception of the Ultimate.

MULTIPLE RELIGIOUS REALITIES

I was at a party once, given to introduce me to the members of a college religion department where I was going to give a series of presentations. Everyone knew of my religious orientation (I am an ordained clergyman), and as my hostess took me from group to group, there were some very interesting responses. The apparent spokesperson for one circle of people greeted me with the words "I hope you have come to give us the decisive word, my friend. Most religion professors these days do not seem to stand for anything." Another group included a faculty couple who, as they extended their hands to me, laughingly said, "No religion please, we're Unitarian." Yet a third group was deeply embroiled in a discussion as we approached. As we interrupted the debate, one woman explained the topic and the differing positions and asked, "So what do you think?"

Each of these groups had a particular perspective on reality; each represented a different epistemology and related assumptions about structure. Therefore, each of these groups can also serve as an illustration of differing faith paradigms.[12] A paradigm contains both the theory and the practice of a particular Weltanschauung or world view which an individual or group believes to be normative. Constantine claims:

> The image or images comprising a family paradigm are not themselves visible to us, and may not even be in the conscious awareness of family members. What we see are particular patterns of behavior that, by their redundancy, become recognizable as characteristic of a particular family's way of dealing with life.[13]

Berger has pointed out that we live in the midst of modernity, having traveled the road from "fate to choice."[14] Whereas there was a time when constructs of reality were "determined" so that people assumed and accepted that "things are as they are and we can do nothing about them," now most folks would agree with the position of a small town mayor who once said to me, "If people don't like it here they can just move somewhere else." This points, of course, to the social construction of reality.

Thomas Kuhn has called this process of multiple realities "paradigm shifts," noting how it has operated in the world of science.[15] In the area of family therapy, Kantor and Lehr[16] explored these multiple, constructed realities, and Hans Kung[17] has employed the idea of paradigm shifts to describe and explain the variety in theological systems. As described here, these paradigms — which integrate family systems and approaches to religion — are grounded in the work of Kantor and Lehr[18] who based their conclusions on the results of a major field study. They observed three different family types, each with its own structures and rules and each coexisting with full knowledge of the others.

The first of these types is *Traditional-Closed*[19] and its motto is "Stability through Tradition." It is a hierarchical structure with a deductive epistemology, having received knowledge from a higher source. At the other end of a imaginary continuum is the *Individualistic-Random* type, whose motto is "Variety through Innovation." Anarchy can aptly describe the structure here, and the epistemology is reductive, centered entirely in what the individual knows from personal experience. Finally, somewhere in the middle is the third type, *Negotiating-Open* whose motto is "Adaptability through Negotiation." Structures tend to be more democratic and knowledge is inductive. When a couple or family enters the office of a family therapist, there may be a collision of worldviews, with the family operating from one type and the therapist another.

An Illustration

When Harold and Maggie* came to see me several years ago, we were headed for just such a collision. Harold and Maggie were members of a conservative, Christian congregation (operating from the Traditional-Closed paradigm) and had been referred to me by their pastor who, knowing I was a Christian, expected understanding treatment for his parishioners. What he did not know was that I did not share that congregation's conservative approach to religion.

---

*In all illustrations or examples, names have been changed and situations altered to protect the confidentiality of the people involved.

(Like many pastoral therapists, I tend toward the Negotiating-Open paradigm.) Therein lay the potential clash.

Harold and Maggie were having trouble with their son, they said, who was acting out in school and church. They wanted me to see the boy and "make him behave." Though Maggie did much of the talking, especially when it came to using feeling language, she deferred to Harold for authoritative explanations. Harold seemed sincere when he spoke of "sparing the rod and spoiling the child," and about "raising up the child in the way in which he should go," both proverbial sayings from scripture. He concluded by indicating that the more they "cracked down" on the boy, the worse things got.

When I asked how all of this was affecting them as a couple, the look on Maggie's face indicated a lot of pain as she turned to Harold once more. Harold, too, looked grim, as he told of Maggie's desire to return to work as a school teacher. He continued, "But it's not right that a woman should be out of the home when there is a child who needs her, so I told her she couldn't go back to teaching until Roger was much older. The husband *is* the head of the house, like it says in scripture."

It was a struggle to listen and make joining moves. My own faith paradigm was (and is) considerably more liberal, and I wanted to oppose this couple's beliefs and actions one, two, three. Fortunately, I did not and managed to engage all three in relating personal views of what was going on. Later that day I shared the experience with a colleague and indicated it was clear to me that the problem was with the couple and conflict around the hierarchy, reinforced by their Traditional-Closed religious paradigm. It made sense to me to try to change their beliefs and to restructure their relationship so that it was more equal. While my friend was sympathetic — even enthusiastic — about my goal, she wisely noted that all our work would seem so much easier if our clients would only conform to our particular worldviews. "But not everyone sees the world through the same liberal lenses you do, Larry."

She was right, of course. So, in subsequent sessions, instead of imposing my paradigm, I joined the couple and began to work with them as they struggled to be faithful to their religion, their child, and their relationship. This did not mean that I ignored my own convictions. Rather, I took one step at a time, honoring the worldview of the clients so that I could find resources within the therapy system (including the client's beliefs and my own) to help the family with their painful concerns. The task, then, was not *either* therapeutic *or* religious, it was both. Krasner, a "contextual therapist," writes:

> The pain that people suffer in their relationships with each other must be as old as life itself. Religion, like psychology, has struggled to identify the sources of that suffering and to offer options for health and healing. It may be that the primal scream for healing through meeting was first heard when God called out, "Adam, where art thou?", a cry that eventually was met with "man's fearful and ambivalent response: '. . . I was afraid because I was naked, and I hid myself.' (Gen. 3:10) . . . Martin Buber argues that the justice of the human order can be rebalanced in the I-Thou relationship where "deep calls to deep." In clinical terms it has been argued that the distribution of justice can be reworked when people can reassess the balances and imbalances of fairness in their relationships on a periodic basis — that is, when they can discover sufficient trust to join in a dialogical assessment of the assets and debits, the burdens and benefits, and the healing and injury that lie between them.[20]

VALUES AND MODELS OF THERAPY

Every therapist has a model of therapy. It may be implicit, derived pragmatically from what has worked; it may be explicitly aligned with that of a particular teacher, theory, or school. Any model will exhibit values. Rokeach defines a value as "an enduring belief that a specific mode of conduct or end-state of existence is personally or socially preferable to an opposite or converse mode of conduct or end-state of existence."[21] Dienhart claims two kinds of values in therapy:

Therapeutic values are those which a therapist holds in virtue of subscribing to a particular theory of counseling. *Therapist values* are those to which a therapist subscribes independently of his [or her] official theory. There will very likely be overlap and conflict between therapeutic and therapist values.[22]

A value system, according to Rokeach, is "an enduring organization of beliefs concerning preferable modes of conduct or end-states of existence along a continuum of relative importance."[23] Researchers have identified three values systems related to therapeutic models. These are (1) theistic, (2) clinical-humanistic, and (3) clinical-humanistic-atheistic.[24] Each of these suggests a somewhat different epistemology (the theistic may have more deductive elements in it while the clinical-humanistic-atheistic may be more reductive) and hermeneutic (see below). Given the possibility that a therapist may hold values that are positive toward religion (model #1 for instance) yet employ a model that tends more toward models #2 or #3, Worthington comments:

> . . . *any* therapeutic interaction might be perceived in one of five ways — as involving (a) detectable (by the client) religious values similar (but not necessarily identical) to his or her own values (*religious counseling*), (b) detectable antireligious values aimed at changing important tenets of the client's faith (called *antireligious counseling* regardless of the religiosity or lack of religiosity of the counselor), (c) detectable nonreligious values (*nonreligious counseling*), (d) detectable mixtures of salient religious, antireligious, or nonreligious values (*conflictual counseling*), and (e) undetectable (or undetected) religious, antireligious, or nonreligious values (*secular counseling*). No counseling is completely uniform; all involves a mixture of the five approaches.[25]

Such epistemological tension can become outright values conflict. Worthington goes on to point out that the approach of Freud (acting as a blank screen) and Rogers (unconditional positive regard for the client and her/his point of view) are two ways of dealing with this values complexity in therapy. A third strategy is to rationally reveal personal values as a part of therapy.[26] This is part of the reason Liddle suggested that therapists make some sort of "episte-mological declaration" for themselves, "our own idiosyncratic statement of what we know and how we know it, what and how we think, and what and how we make the clinical decisions we do."[27] Since in marriage and family therapy we generally believe that "the knower and what is known are inseparable and influence one an-other,"[28] at least as clinicians we will know something of our foun-dational assumptions about therapy.

I was conducting a workshop once about religion and therapy where several experienced therapists indicated they held a very pos-itive view of spiritual practices, and that they themselves meditated, participated in 12-step programs of some sort, or found meaning in Native American practices. Four of these same folks, however, were either skeptical or outright hostile to organized religion, sug-gesting that it "does more harm than good." By the same token, I know many Christian therapists who believe that organized religion is an important part of healthy family life and who are highly suspi-cious of what they call "this New Age stuff." It is entirely possible for there to be such differences between different faith groups *within* organized religion as well (Christians vs. Jews, Protestants vs. Roman Catholics, fundamentalists vs. liberals, etc.).

Based on his own research, Worthington has proposed three propositions to help understand religious clients: (I have added, in parentheses, what I believe to be the equivalent understanding with regard to spiritual orientations.)

Proposition 1: People highly committed to religion usually evaluate their world on at least three important value dimen-sions: The role of authority of human leaders, scripture or doc-trine, and religious group norms. (Spiritually oriented people will focus on locus of control, source of teaching or practice, and relationship to others.)

Proposition 2: Each individual can be represented (in theory) by a point in a three-dimensional space defined by the three dimensions important to highly committed religious people. (This might be internal to external locus of control, human-esoteric-spiritual source of teaching or practice, and solitary,

teacher/student, or communal with regard to human relationships.)
Proposition 3: People differ in the amount of toleration that
they have for the values of others on the three critical value
dimensions. (Same)[29]

He offers this example: ". . . suppose an orthodox Jew and a
fundamentalist Christian were in relationship with each other. Although they might disagree vociferously over many (perhaps most)
specific beliefs, they could converse with mutual respect because
both might believe that (a) high authority be accorded to human
leaders and defiance of leaders is discouraged, (b) high authority be
given to scriptures, and (c) there is strong identification with their
'in group' and separation from non-'in group' members. Despite
their agreement on all three dimensions, there would be complete
disagreement on the specific values of *which* human leaders deserve
fealty, *which* scriptures were authoritative, and *which* people con-
stitute the 'in group.'"[30]

The different dimensions in Worthington's model might be trans-
lated into structure, epistemology, and boundaries. The three
types (Traditional-closed, Negotiating-open, and Individualistic-
random)[31] described above are clear, religious options with regard
to these dimensions and can serve as descriptive markers when
working with this model within a therapy setting. Further, as therapists we might assess ourselves as to where we stand as spiritually
or religiously oriented people in this model. This would provide
some sense of our own preferences and values. For instance, we
might ask ourselves (1) Who or what has power and authority in our
lives and in the lives of others? As a therapist, do I believe in God
or a Higher Power or some other spiritual figure or guide? (2) How
do we image human beings? Are people basically good, bad, or
neutral; determined or free? (3) How do we view change? Is it continuous or discontinuous; developing or converting; who or what
are the agents of change; what are the goals of change?

Even in this quick and dirty assessment we have covered three
major theological categories (the nature of the Ultimate, the nature
of human beings, and the nature of hope), which have profound

implications for the way people live their lives and the way therapists approach therapy.

Values and Hermeneutics

Therapeutic values plus therapist values equals the hermeneutic
for therapy. "Hermeneutics" is a technical word from religious
studies that concerns principles for interpreting texts.[32] All human
beings have stories that are subject to interpretation, especially in
therapy. In fact, one early scholar of psychology and religion called
patients "living human documents."[33] For instance, a "Freudian
hermeneutic" will rely on interpreting a patient's stories vis-à-vis
belief in the unconscious, whereas a "behaviorist hermeneutic"
will interpret the narrative's cause and effect in terms of positive
and negative reinforcement. One can easily see how closely values
are related to hermeneutics because one's therapeutic values, as
well as personal (therapist) values, greatly influence how one goes
about the process of interpretation. I choose to use the word "hermeneutics" because it holds within it the idea of difference. That
one has a hermeneutic for doing therapy suggests, in this age of
modernity, the existence of other hermeneutic principles used by
other therapists, not to mention the hermeneutic principles operative in the lives of clients. This is in part what Ricoeur called "a
surplus of meaning."[34]

A PROPOSED HERMENEUTIC MODEL
FOR WHEN GOD ENTERS THE SYSTEM

For several years I have been working on a model for therapy that
respects spiritual and religious belief and practice as a resource for
healthy living, and at the same time recognizes that sometimes
these beliefs and practices may be involved in disabling life strategies and structures and therefore become part of the goal setting for
therapeutic change.[35] Like all systemic models it is, and will remain, in process, and I offer it here with that caveat.

To understand the context for this model, it is helpful to imagine
a quadraplex of constraints and opportunities[36] that surround and
constantly interact with—effecting and being effected by—the process of therapy.

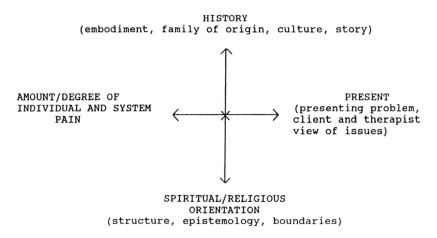

HISTORY
(embodiment, family of origin, culture, story)

AMOUNT/DEGREE OF
INDIVIDUAL AND SYSTEM
PAIN

PRESENT
(presenting problem,
client and therapist
view of issues)

SPIRITUAL/RELIGIOUS
ORIENTATION
(structure, epistemology, boundaries)

Each of these presents limitations (constraints) and at the same time offers potential opportunities (resources) for the healthful operating of the various subsystems involved in the larger, interconnected system. Therefore, we cannot forget that both therapist and clients are subject to these limitations and opportunities.

History is the context of physiological, psychological and cultural "givens." History is what has happened in our past—even long before we were born—to help shape our personal and family story; it contains our sex, race, and other genetically transmitted features, our gender identification, age, developmental status, ethnicity and cultural heritage, features of the dominant culture, social class, and so on.

The *Present* is the current re-presentation of history, where the presenting problem/issue has emerged. Views of the present may be divergent or shared within the family, religious community, or therapy system. For instance, the clients may view the problem as resulting from punishment by God or perhaps a lack of obedience to the prescribed structure on the part of a child or spouse. The therapist, on the other hand, may see the present as resulting from a disabled parental hierarchy (this is, of course, yet another way of describing the human/Ultimate relational system) and marital conflict. Whether the same or different, these representations of the present must be negotiated as part of the context of therapy.

The *Spiritual/Religious Orientation* includes the various subsystem's beliefs and values about structure, epistemology, and boundaries. This may be similar to or very different from the historical spiritual/religious orientation. A child's participation in a sect or cult at odds with the family's spiritual/religious values may in fact be part of the clients' presenting problem. Therapists may have chosen a very different spiritual path from that of their families of origin, or may have continued historical commitments.

Finally, *The Degree of Individual and System Pain* impacts the model. "Enduring psychological pain usually restricts the person's zone of toleration and defines the boundaries of the zone sharply."[37] Amounts of pain may severely constrain certain interventions and facilitate others. For example, working with a conservative Christian couple who have very recently lost their only child to SIDS (Sudden Infant Death Syndrome), I felt constrained from introducing any suspicion of their belief that this was somehow God's punishment for their pre-marital sexual activity, and at the same time was able to call on "hymn theology" (the beliefs expressed and reinforced by the texts of favorite religious songs) as a source of temporary comfort in the joining process.

In the midst of these limitations and opportunities the process of therapy is worked out. The model presented below can accommodate, I believe, the majority of systemic therapies. What it offers are four hermeneutic stages, that is, four interpretative lenses through which both therapist and clients view the clients' story at different points in the therapy process.

These stages are:

1. RISK AND HOSPITALITY
2. SUSPICION AND DE-CONSTRUCTION
3. IMAGINATION AND RE-CONSTRUCTION
4. GENERATIVITY AND CONFIDENCE

Risk and Hospitality

I have a sense of risk every time I meet new clients. Indeed, since I operate from a systemic (non-linear) perspective, I know that everyone in that consulting room is at risk in some way. We wonder, "What does the other know about me? What does the other expect? Is there danger here?" As a therapist, I risk being inducted into a system that is apparently disabled and thereby becoming disabled myself. Or, I may risk experiencing some threat to or change in my own beliefs and values. (This latter may be especially true around spiritual/religious material in therapy.) Clients, of course, also risk something. While they come to therapy seeking relief, there may not be much interest in personal or systemic change. This apparent preference for homeostasis is so well documented that it appears as a "given" in almost all MFT training. It is in part because of this sense of risk, particularly for clients, that this stage also includes "hospitality."

"Joining" is a central task of hospitality. While the various joining techniques[38] are both important and helpful, research has shown that the person of the therapist and the therapist's relational skills are often even more important for therapeutic effectiveness.[39] With hospitality the therapist evidences more than sympathy or even empathy for the clients. This "something more" is "interpathy."[40]

> Interpathic caring awaits the discovery of how caring is given and received within that culture before initiating caregiving on patterns from one's own tradition. Interpathic identification prizes the meeting of humanness in which universals of life experience coincide, but without assuming that the interpretation or the emotional savoring of these universals will overlap or necessarily even touch. Interpathic presence enters another world of human energies and risks, making the self available to entertain what was formerly alien, to be hospitable to what is utterly new.[41]

This adds a qualitative dimension to joining techniques that makes this initial stage hospitable.

Hospitality shares its roots with words such as hospice, hospital, and hostel. One of the essentials of Jewish Law has been to provide hospitality to strangers. Early in the Common Era—that is, the last 2,000 years—Christian religious orders established places of shelter and sanctuary for travelers, the sick, poor, and others who might be suffering. Indeed, the origin of the word "patient" is associated with the meaning of "one who suffers." Hospitality, then, is a relational process of providing a safe space for people—and systems—who are suffering.

More often than not, religious couples or families who are in psychological pain believe that some aspect of their faith system will offer comfort or a solution. I believe that is why so many Americans turn to clergypersons as a first line helper when they are in trouble. Hospitality engages these beliefs in an accepting and non-judgmental way. Jewish mystic Martin Buber wrote:

> What [people] want is a being not only whom [they] can trust as a person trusts another, but a being that gives [them] now the certitude that "there *is* a soil, there *is* an existence. The world is not condemned to deprivation, degeneration, destruction. The world *can* be redeemed. *I* can be redeemed because there is this trust."[42]

"It is precisely the delivery of care that is the common thread between religious reality and psychotherapy," says Krasner. She continues, "Each of these modalities has a vision of human potential that offers viable paradigms of healing and the conviction that people can be healed."[43]

Hospitality takes care-full notice of the contexts of constraint and opportunity, especially History and Spiritual/Religious Orientation. As Minuchin and Fishman point out, "The structural family therapist, knowing how people select observations in order to reinforce their beliefs, can direct [him/herself] to notice positives. After all, people coming for therapy are doing their best, as we all are."[44]

Harold and Maggie, the couple mentioned earlier, were doing *their* best. They held a view of family life that required each member of the family to play a pre-determined role, distinguished by age and gender. In this view, they were following their particular religious community. They did not believe that theirs was a family or couple's problem, but rather a problem of discipline for their son, whom they wanted me to treat. This couple needed to feel that they had an ally and safe space in which to deal with their son. In the second session I offered hospitality first by empathically joining with each member of the family, listening to how each viewed the problem. Next I asked each "where it hurt," so that individuals had an opportunity to name their pain. Then I asked what they thought God was doing about the problem. In each of these interventions, I sought and found material that could be positively connoted, and at the conclusion of the session asked them, as a family and individually, to pray daily for a solution to their problem. Each person was to listen for what personal change he/she believed God was directing, reporting the results at the next session. The goal here was not only to be hospitable with regard to their religious orientation, but to call attention to a resourceful structure in which people are empowered. When asked by the parents when I would start working with the boy alone, I suggested that I needed their help to make the timing just right, and so invited them to come alone the following session so that we could "talk privately." (This last was to provide an opportunity to further assess the marital dyad.) Meanwhile, they were to pray for strength and guidance from God.

Suspicion and De-Construction

It was my hope that by indicating my belief that through prayer the family would be empowered and by suggesting that I needed the parents' help in directing the care of their son, they would at some level begin to question their sense of powerlessness.

Philosopher Paul Ricoeur coined the phrase "hermeneutics of suspicion" to describe a process whereby the relationship between text and reader is altered so that what was once taken at face value is now questioned. Ricoeur attributes the initiation of this process (in Western culture at least) to Marx, Nietzsche, and Freud.[45]

Many of us of a certain age, having had the opportunity to go to college, may remember "Introduction to Religion" classes where the professor began to point out internal contradictions in sacred texts, leading us to question childhood teachings. Or, in psychology classes we learned to question motivation. (This is much in evidence in the popularity of codependence books which have made literally thousands of people suspicious of their motives to help or serve.) When I was sharing the experience of the first session with Harold and Maggie, my colleague's remark about lenses created suspicion about my own model. In the work of suspicion, something new is introduced into our way of viewing things that raises questions about previously unexamined beliefs or values. This, in turn, can lead either (1) to a redoubling of efforts to maintain previous explanations (we might call this a manifestation of resistance or experience it psycho-politically as opposition) or (2) to the de-construction of those explanations.

Often people fear that this suspicion and de-construction is too risky and, from a religious point of view, perhaps bad or sinful. Therefore, the first stage (Risk and Hospitality) is of necessity an ongoing therapeutic activity in this second stage so that there is sufficient safety to tolerate the anxiety prompted by de-construction. Religion as "binding-up" takes on an even deeper dimension of resourcefulness in this context. It is like holding on with one hand as one reaches with the other. I often use the metaphor of Moses and the Jews in the Exodus story. Things were not as the Hebrews had thought they would be, and many wanted to go back into slavery in Egypt rather than venture further. God gave them manna to eat and provided a pillar of cloud by day and a pillar of fire by night to remind them that they were not alone. As therapists we know that in this stage lie important elements of healing. Ricoeur says "Destruction . . . is a moment in every new foundation. The 'destruction' of hidden worlds is a positive task."[46]

For Harold and Maggie it did not feel very positive. When I asked them to report on the previous week, there was an air of confusion. As I had rather expected, the IP confessed he hadn't actually prayed, except at meals with his parents, and he'd acted pretty much the same as before.

"But," he added, "I'd feel a lot better if Dad and Mom would stop fighting."

"What do they fight about?" I asked.

Before he could answer, Maggie hastened to correct him. "We don't really fight, Roger." Turning to me she said, "Really, we don't."

I thanked Roger for his information, smiled at Maggie, and asked, "What did God suggest about your behavior, Maggie?"

"Nothing. It was odd. I kept thinking I should just go along with Harold—he *is* the head of the house—and do what he wants, you know, stay home, but . . . ." Maggie stopped.

"But, it sounds like you don't want to, and you didn't hear God tell you to," I remarked. "What *did* God say to you?"

"You know," Maggie answered, "I was so worried about not

wanting to be a disobedient wife, I'm not sure I even listened to God."

I nodded. "Seems a very difficult place to be, caught in the middle. You and Roger have something in common."

Maggie looked at me sharply. "What do you mean about Roger?"

"I only meant that it seemed to me you and Roger are both struggling with how to be faithful, loving, and responsible."

After a few moments of silence, Harold said, "It looks like I'm the only one who's been listening during the prayers." With some trepidation I asked what he had heard. "At first not much. Guess maybe I was doing the talking, telling God what I wanted Him to say. But I quieted down and . . . I don't know . . . I think I heard 'Be still, be still. I am God. Be still.'"

I looked at him, smiled, and asked softly, "How was that?"

"Weird! How can I be the head of the house and be still? It doesn't make any sense," he said.

From this experience of suspicion, we would move care-fully into de-construction. Harold had come up against the limits of his style of being "head of the house," and Maggie was becoming suspicious of her overt following/covert opposing. Roger, by breaking the silence about the marital discord, had raised suspicions about this being his problem alone. During the next couple of sessions we worked with a kind of "hospitable de-construction" as disabled and disabling structures were explored.

Imagination and Re-Construction

As Harold and Maggie began to work together on the issue of Maggie's returning to work, Roger's behavior returned to acceptable limits. Here we have entered the third step of therapy where much of the actual healing takes place.

Imagination is a quality, a context of freedom. Disabled and disabling structures often have the consequence of imprisoning folks so that they act like victims and victimizers. Sometimes the process of therapy itself can perpetuate this belief. Where hospitality has not genuinely valued differences—of gender, class, ethnicity or spiritual/religious orientation for instance—clients may rely on negative feedback about themselves and therefore have difficulty participating in the creation of new structures.

Clearly I have a point-of-view that values and seeks to promote therapeutic co-creation. While I do not doubt for a moment that there are times when it is appropriate for the therapist to act decisively (as the most powerful one in an hierarchical structure), I believe this to be an instrumental—to use Rokeach's distinctions[47]—rather than terminal therapeutic (and therapist) value. Indeed, for me, this sense of co-creation is very much at the heart of my personal therapeutic values.

Imagination builds on the idea of risk and de-construction and both grows from and contributes to the exercise of each. Imagination is active in the process of circular questioning, for instance.[48] It goes on, then, to re-construct the family story in ways that are empowering for everyone. Some hermeneutical scholars have linked this to the idea of "parable" in which the story frees itself "from the limitations of the immediate situation" and discloses a larger world.[49] Capps points out that "this world-disclosure, however, can only be gotten at through the story of human interaction, and it is accessible through the different perspectives ('guesses') listeners bring to the story."[50]

Instead of reading the family story as a fixed narrative which can have only one outcome, Imagination helps family members to Reconstruct the story, using ideas, images, feelings, and so forth, that were previously unavailable. Like positive connotation or reframing, Imagination gives new meanings that in turn construct a somewhat different world in which the family can live more effectively.

This is especially important when working with spiritually or religiously oriented families. Often the resource of belief has become a burden, which can be reframed as a resource once again. For example, Roger's behavior was reframed as an act of concern for his parents, allowing them to see their struggle over family control more clearly. Harold's role as head of the house—derived from a cultural-religious heritage of hierarchy and patriarchy—had become defined, under pressure, as absolute and arbitrary. His role, too, was labeled differently. This time it was re-constructed by religious images of a God who hears complaints and shares power with women as well as men. This last is of special interest and importance, given the gender implications of power distribution in many of the world's religions. Goldner has pointed out:

> By ignoring the complex interpenetration between the structure of family relations and the world of work, family therapists tacitly endorse the nineteenth century fiction that the family is a domestic retreat from the market place economy . . . . The dichotomization of these social domains is a mystification and a distortion that masks a fundamental organizing principle of contemporary family life. The division of labor (both affective and instrumental) and the distribution of power in families are structured not only according to generational hierarchies but also around gendered spheres of influence that derive their legitimacy precisely because of the creation of a public/private dichotomy. To rely on a theory that neither confronts, nor even acknowledges, this reality is to operate in the realm of illusion.[51]

One cannot avoid confronting the interface of gender and power when working with spiritual/religious families. The process of Imagination and Re-construction may well involve work that reframes traditional religious understandings.

Generativity and Confidence

I believe that enabled families show some care for the future and display some trust in the present. When spiritual and religious practices are most enabling, they engender this sense of confidence; they bind-up ontological anxiety and seek to positively influence the future. This is Generativity and Confidence, the "end point" of therapy. (It is likely that the breakdown of generativity and confidence through some crisis experience is what prompts behaviors that eventuate in problems and lead people into therapy.)

As Erikson describes generativity, it

> . . . is primarily the concern for establishing and guiding the next generation . . . the concept of generativity is meant to include productivity and creativity, neither of which, however, can replace it as designations of a crisis in development.

For the ability to lose oneself in the meeting of bodies and minds leads to a gradual expansion of ego-interests and to a libidinal investment in that which is being generated.[52]

Reading Erikson can be somewhat problematic, given his gender and cultural assumptions. Therefore, the idea of generativity must be understood relationally (not autonomously) and as potentially different for men and women (not just based on male experience). Harold's idea of generativity for Maggie was apparently different from that for himself. As a result of the re-construction process, Harold and Maggie were able to recast generativity for Maggie as including her teaching work outside the home, and for Harold as shared parenting.

Confidence, especially as it relates to spiritually and religiously oriented people, is an expression of a sort of "basic trust" or "object confidence" (to relabel an object relations term) regarding the process of living in relation to the cosmos. This may be articulated through absolute-trust-in-God-no-matter-what (Traditional-Closed paradigm) or through some degree of acceptance of uncertainty or ambivalence about the universe (Negotiating-Open or Individualistic-Random paradigms).

Harold and Maggie retained their Traditional-Closed faith paradigm. Though the hierarchy had been challenged, God remained in place, framed as the initiator of changed understandings within the family. To some therapists this might be insufficient. In fact, I would have preferred that they had altered their faith paradigm more in the direction of my own. My model requires that both therapist and clients risk some change, and the change for me was to accept — with confidence — the empowering choices the couple *did* make.

CONCLUSION

In this chapter I have explored issues/definitions of spirituality and religion in the context of systems theory with particular attention to the structural-analytical theory of Kantor and Lehr. A discussion of spirituality and religion as values systems in relation to therapy and therapist values led to a Hermeneutic Model for therapy with spiritual or religious clients.

It has been my purpose to show how spirituality and religion are aspects of human life that influence and are influenced by the process of therapy. As such, these are as much potentially enabling factors as they may be disabling. The late Buckminster Fuller once said, "Don't oppose forces, use them. God is a verb, not a noun."[53] When God enters the system, hospitality, while potentially risky, may clearly lead to generativity and confidence on the part of therapist and clients alike.

REFERENCE NOTES

1. Tillich, P. 1952. *The Courage to Be*. New Haven: Yale University Press.

2. Self-in-relation is the term used by the scholars at The Stone Center at Wellesley College to indicate the relational matrix that is understood to be central to the psychological development of women.

3. Vickers is a family therapist and Approved Supervisor in AAMFT who practices in Cambridge and Framingham, MA.

4. Durkheim, E. 1915. *The Elementary Forms of Religious Life*. London: G. Allen.

5. Slobodnik, A. 1990. *The KFI Newsletter*, Volume 2, No. 1. Cambridge, MA: Kantor Family Institute.

6. I refer here to Merle Jordan's book (1986) *Taking on the Gods*. Nashville: Abingdon.

7. Rossi, A. 1985. "Change in the Client and in the Client's God." *Psychotherapy and the Religiously Committed Patient*. New York: The Haworth Press, Inc.

8. Parsons, T. 1966. *Societies*. Englewood Cliffs, NJ: Prentice-Hall.

9. Lessa, W. and Vogt, E. eds. 1965. *A Reader in Comparative Religion*. New York: Harper and Row.

10. Geertz, C. 1966. "Religion as a Cultural System." *Anthropological Approaches to the Study of Religion*, ed. M. Banton. London: Tavistock Publications.

11. Wallace, A. 1966. *Religion: An Anthropological View*. New York: Random House.

12. Burton, L. 1986. "Three Sources of Pastoral Identity." *Quarterly Review*, Winter; 1989. *Pastoral Paradigms*. Washington, DC: The Alban Institute; and in press, *Journal of Religion and Health*.

13. Constantine, L. 1986. *Family Paradigms*. New York: Guilford Press.

14. Berger, P. 1979. *The Heretical Imperative*. New York: Anchor.

15. Kuhn, T. 1962. *The Structure of Scientific Revolution*. Chicago: University of Chicago Press.

16. Kantor, D. and Lehr, W. 1975. *Inside the Family*. San Francisco: Jossey-Bass.

17. Kung, H. and Tracy, D. 1989. *Paradigm Change in Theology: A Symposium For the Future*. New York: Crossroads Publishing Co.

18. Kantor and Lehr, *op. cit.*

19. What follows is my own adaptation of Kantor and Lehr, integrated with the work of Peter Berger.

20. Krasner, B. 1986. "Trustworthiness: The Primal Family Resource." *Family Resources*. ed. M. Karpel. New York: Guilford Press.

21. Rokeach, M. 1973. *The Nature of Human Values*. New York: The Free Press.

22. Dienhart, J.W. 1982. *A Cognitive Approach to the Ethics of Counseling Psychology*. Washington, DC: University Press of America.

23. Rokeach, *op. cit.*

24. See: *Journal of Consulting and Clinical Psychology*, 48:
Bergin. A.E. 1980. "Psychotherapy and Religious Values."
––––– 1980. "Religions and Humanistic Values: A Reply to Ellis and Walls."
Ellis, A. 1980. "Psychotherapy and Atheistic Values: A Response to A.E. Bergin's 'Psychotherapy and Religious Values.'"
Walls, G.B. 1980. "Values and Psychotherapy: A Comment on 'Psychotherapy and Religious Values.'"

25. Worthington, E. 1987. "Understanding the Values of Religious Clients: A Model and Its Application to Counseling." *Journal of Counseling Psychology*.

26. Ibid.

27. Liddle, H. 1982. "On the Problem of Eclecticism: A Call for Epistemological Clarification and Human-scale Theories." *Family Process*, 21, 243-250.

28. Nichols, W. and Everett, C. 1986. *Systemic Family Therapy: An Integrative Approach*. New York: Guilford Press, p. 58.

29. Worthington, *op. cit.*

30. Ibid.

31. *op. cit.*: Kantor and Lehr, 1975; Burton, 1986, 1989; Constantine, 1986.

32. See for instance, Ricoeur, P. 1974. *The Conflict of Interpretations: Essays in Hermeneutics*, ed. Don Ihde. Evanston, IL: Northwestern University Press. Or Ricoeur, P., 1976. *Interpretation Theory: Discourse and the Surplus of Meaning*. Fort Worth: Texas Christian University Press.

33. Anton Boison, the founder of the clinical pastoral training movement, coined this phrase early in this century to emphasize the human dimension of the data being studied by clinicians.

34. Ricoeur, *op. cit.*

35. An earlier version of this model appears in (1989) *Pastoral Paradigms*. Washington, DC: The Alban Institute.

36. This idea of constraint was first suggested to me by my colleagues at The Kantor Family Institute in Cambridge, MA, where the second stage of training

centers on understanding therapeutic constraints. I have taken the idea and developed it somewhat differently, but I am grateful for its original source.

37. Worthington, *op. cit.*

38. See Minuchin, S. and Fishman, C. 1980. *Family Therapy Techniques.* Cambridge, MA: Harvard University Press.

39. Kniskern, D.P. and Gurman, A.S. 1980. "Clinical Implications of Recent Research in Family Therapy," in *Group and Family Therapy*, ed. by Wolberg and Aronson. New York: Brunner/Mazel.

40. Augsburger, D. 1986. *Pastoral Counseling Across Cultures.* Philadelphia: Westminster Press.

41. Ibid.

42. Buber, M. 1965. *The Knowledge of Man.* Trans. Friedman and Smith. New York: Harper and Row. (As quoted in Krasner, *op. cit.*)

43. Krasner, *op. cit.*

44. Minuchin and Fishman, *op. cit.*

45. Ricoeur, P. 1978. "The Critique of Religion," trans. DeFord, in *The Philosophy of Paul Ricoeur: An Anthology of His Work*, eds.: Reagan and Stewart, Boston: Beacon Press.

46. Ricoeur (1974), *op. cit.*

47. Rokeach, *op. cit.*

48. See Fleuridas, Nelson and Rosenthal. 1986. "The Evolution of Circular Questions: Training Family Therapists." *Journal of Marital and Family Therapy*, 12(2).

49. Capps, D. 1984. *Pastoral Care and Hermeneutics.* Philadelphia: Fortress Press.

50. Capps, *op. cit.*

51. Goldner, V. 1985. "Feminism and Family Therapy." *Family Process* 24(1).

52. Erikson, E. 1968. *Identity: Youth and Crisis*, New York: Norton and Company.

53. As quoted by Beavers (1986) in "Foreword," *Family Resources.* Ed. Mark Karpel. New York: Guilford Press.

Chapter Three

Foundations
for a Spiritually Based
Psychotherapy

Charles Verge, PhD

When I was asked to contribute a chapter to this book, I became intrigued with the [editor's working] title. I thought to myself, *When God Enters the System* . . . Now there's something to contemplate! For if God were truly to enter the system in such a way that the members were indeed aware of this presence, the business of "therapy as usual" might come to a grinding halt. Indeed, we all might forget that we had come together for the business of therapy, and instead stand in awe of the immediate experience before us. Of course it is also possible that we might be so intent on our preoccupation with the family process, the language and metaphors of the members, etc., that we might use some kind of intervention to block this presence: "Excuse me, God, you're trying to be helpful, I know, and you *are* very helpful, but Mary and Mom didn't get to finish their conversation . . . Go ahead, Mom, you were saying that you didn't feel her love for you . . . ."

In this chapter I wish to address the question of where we place our attention, and how our awareness can dramatically alter the domain of conversation in family, as well as all modes of psychotherapy. I will refer to this focus upon the entrance of God into the system as spiritual awareness or consciousness. And I will describe how within such spiritual awareness the goals of therapy, the perception of problems, the function of symptoms, the view of change, and the therapist's role in that change are distinct and complementary to those of psychotherapies that do not hold this awareness. Moreover, the introduction of this awareness may very well enrich both the families we serve and ourselves who have chosen (or as Maya Angelou states, ". . . have been chosen *for*") this path of service.[1]

WHAT GOD? WHOSE GOD?

What God? Whose God? A good place to start. Surely there are myriad views of God and many differences between them, including agnosticism, atheism, the major world religions, Native American spirituality, mysticism, and the Goddess devotions, to mention only a few. The view here does not depend on any particular spiritual practice or path. It only refers to the redirection or reorientation in the *awareness* of the observer and the consequences for the doing of psychotherapy. Specifically, for the purpose of this chapter, spiritually oriented psychotherapies are herein defined by the presence of spiritual awareness in the therapist, and the set of inner actions that correspond to the presence of this awareness. Let's first understand what spiritual awareness entails.

IN SEARCH OF TRUTH

Fundamental to spiritual awareness is either a faith in, or an experience of, some greater consciousness that I will call the Divine, Spirit, or God. However we define or conceptualize that consciousness, it includes the notion of that which goes beyond all limitations, conditions, and impermanence. This consciousness is simply not bound by qualities of time and space. Thus, for those on conscious spiritual journeys, faith often serves as the motivator to seek an experience of this greater consciousness, this greater truth, for oneself.

In this search it is important to focus one's awareness on those qualities of spirit or divinity within one's own life. Thus, we cannot locate this awareness in any aspect of ourselves that is conditional, transitional, or contextual. Clearly, our physical bodies are subject to all kinds of change and decay, but so are our emotions and thoughts. They come and go with the vicissitudes of life. And since they are subject to change with the shifting conditions and contexts in life events, they are subject to cure by the shifting of conditions and contexts. Indeed, much of contemporary family therapy rests on this very premise — that a problem is embedded within a matrix of contexts and conditions (i.e., meanings, metaphors, structures, and interpersonal strategies) and that facilitating shifts of these contexts and conditions will result in resolutions or dissolutions of the problems presented. Likewise, the shifting of the context and condition of the body, such as the application of medicine or radiation, can result in dissolutions of cancer.

However, healing, which requires the presence of that which is not bound by contexts and conditions, certainly cannot be brought about by that which *is* bound by contexts and conditions. In short, a spiritual awareness is not brought about by changes in the body, mind, or emotions, not by changes in organization and language patterns, nor by insight into the negative consequences of change. It is brought about through the direct experience of that consciousness of unconditionality itself.

This consciousness of unconditionality is a consciousness of complete acceptance of what is, and a personal alignment to it. It emerges from a faith or belief in the divine perfection of the moment, and thus does not judge a circumstance as "bad" or "wrong." Rather, each moment is seen as holding a gift within itself. This gift is in the choice to free oneself from fear, judgment, and blame, and to usher forward one's love, acceptance, and forgiveness. Each time such a choice is made the inner source is nourished, and our capacity for such choices expands.

However, herein lies an important distinction: the choice to move our awareness to those unconditional qualities within ourselves is not to be misconstrued as a denial of our feelings. A consciousness of unconditional acceptance includes ourselves, i.e., our bodies, minds, and emotions. This spiritual awareness does not stop our need to mourn the loss of a loved one. In fact, it allows it fully. Nor does it block the outrage one may feel when first learning they have cancer. Rather, it brings compassion to the feelings of rage, allowing them full voice and making room for their expression and release. So, being spiritually aware does not require acceptance of intolerable human conditions; we can and must always react appropriately. Rather, it allows us to view these difficult conditions from a perspective that accepts their existence in our lives as part of the total human state, from which all spiritual development is possible.

Essentially, spiritual awareness allows us to keep our hearts open to pain so that we will not close down on it or deny it. Keeping our hearts open allows us to move through our emotions fearlessly and without judgment. This is not easy. As Steven Levine says, "It's easy to keep our hearts open in heaven. It's hard to keep our hearts open in hell."[2] Yet it may well be that our inner freedom and joy lie before us on this hard road through hell.

Now let us turn to the most fundamental notion in all psychotherapies—the nature of change. How does a spiritual view complement other perspectives in the field? And how may these separate views be integrated for a more comprehensive approach to human suffering?

THEORY OF CHANGE

A central notion of spiritual awareness is the idea of perfection within a severely imperfect world. Indeed, the world as most of us know it is dramatically unjust: Parents lose children to accidents and illnesses; whole communities of people starve by famine while others throw away unwanted food; and children are born into families torn apart by conflict, only to be subjected to physical, emotional, and sexual abuse. Each of these circumstances demonstrates all too clearly the injustice inherent in life. Life's inequities are a fact, and are indeed the basis for our pain and suffering. It is these injustices and the resulting sufferings that people bring to psychotherapy. More clearly stated, it is the *perception of life's injustice and the meaning made out of it* for which we seek psychotherapeutic assistance.

The client who experiences some life injustice typically places a judgment on the circumstance as "wrong" or "bad," and this immediately closes off his or her awareness of spiritual love and acceptance. Sometimes the hurtful event is an infidelity, sometimes a painful relationship, such as a neglectful parent or a disrespectful child. Or it may be an inner experience like depression and the seemingly endless inability to take pleasure in life. Whatever the circumstance, the client's experience includes a fundamental belief in the wrongness of some aspect of life. He or she then operates out of several possible beliefs: either that the universe or God is unkind, that they themselves are being punished, that the cosmos is uninterested or disconnected from them, that there is no God, or that some other form of spiritual relationship exists that is less than generous or loving. Not too many people are walking into therapists' offices claiming how grateful they feel for the problems at hand. Yet it is precisely the client's resistance to the problem and the meaning and judgment he or she creates concerning it that produces the client's suffering.

This is not a notion held exclusively in spiritual psychologies. It is shared by many schools of therapy, including strategic and systemic family therapies, as well as some cognitive and psychodynamic orientations. However, there are very important differences between these schools concerning the "real meaning" of the problem, and thus the perception of health and the conduct of change.

Unlike other models of change, a psychotherapy guided by spiritual awareness includes two fundamental assumptions about the meaning of an injustice. The first is that it does have a spiritual function. This is just as other theories contemplate the functions for the ego, the personal self, the homeostasis of the body, the metaphorical material unexpressed, the family, the generations that went before, loyalties, etc.*

The second assumption, and this may distinguish between schools even more, is that the "problem" need not change at all. Indeed, from a spiritual consciousness, the "injustice" can simply be embraced as it is, in its perfection — certainly not the perfection of justice, but perfection in its *presence; perfection in its very exis-*

---

*Some systemic and strategic therapies that follow a strict constructivist doctrine explicitly avoid the idea of symptom functions, preferring to focus on the facilitation of new (and hopefully more satisfying) meanings for the client. This places these schools outside the domain of spiritually based psychotherapy. However, it should be pointed out that this does not preclude the possibility of using these approaches from a spiritual consciousness. It simply states that the assumptions stated by the major writers about these approaches do not include spiritual dimensions. Remember, the presence of spiritual psychotherapy is determined by the particular awareness of the therapist. My belief and experience with many therapists who practice these schools is that many of them do indeed work within that awareness.

tence. For there is no other anything. There is no other life, no other universe, no other past, no other present. *This is what is, and that is all there is.* And since the place of spirituality within the person is a place of impersonal unconditionality, we are allowed from this center to let our source of unconditional acceptance bear directly on the injustice. *No matter what.* So, regardless of the condition before us, and before our client, from our spiritual heart there is room for this injustice . . . space for this condition, just as it is, with no need for it to be any different in order for us to bear our forgiveness, acceptance, and love upon it. (Again, this does not imply tolerance for an outer circumstance that we can and should change. Rather, we are speaking of acceptance and an inner state of peace with regard to the problem's existence because we see it as an opportunity for spiritual growth.)

In this place of unconditional relatedness we find our spiritual source, our essential being, or "God in me." Call it whatever you will, this is the place that is the fact of our life . . . the place that transcends, through its very nature of unconditionality, all that is impermanent, allowing us to dance more easily through the unending mystery of life with awareness and grace.

Thus, the very presence of injustice calls forward our awareness of perfection in this and all moments. It humbles us before the Great Mystery, and ushers forth our spiritual love. Indeed, the moment will not need to change before we can find this perfect love. Rather, it is the very presence of the injustice itself that serves to awaken and kindle the fires of our eternal heart.

This is the spiritual function of the symptom that we addressed above. For whenever injustice brings us to a judgment on life which imbues our experience with wrongness, fear, hate, or a rejection of life as it is, we are thrust into our conditional relationship with ourselves. In this relationship we separate ourselves from our own heart, contract from aliveness, and move our awareness away from our spiritual source. When we thus move out of a full participation in the Dance, we find ourselves alone, and the Dance finds no place to be fully expressed within us. Grace and divine intervention may very well require our willingness to dance. Our suffering is the call to the Dance. And the Dance never stops; we simply forget.

HEALING AND CURING

The goal of a spiritually based psychotherapy is now defined as "awakening the center of our unconditionality in the presence of conditions of injustice." Put another way, it is to bring our spiritual love to bear upon otherwise unbearable circumstances. Or said even more simply, it is to bring light into darkness. This is what is traditionally called healing. Healing is a change of perception. It is *not necessarily* a change in the circumstance (the problem), and as noted above, it distinctly does not primarily seek a change of circumstances. Rather, healing requires a change in focus away from a view that demands changing of the circumstance, or that the circumstance be removed, to a perspective that *embraces* the circumstance from another inner source.

Curing, on the other hand, *does* seek change at the level of the problem, and is the direction of most psychotherapies. This distinction can be made clear by the often used scenario of the cancer patient whose physical symptoms seem to have been cured by chemotherapy, yet who continues to live in the same angry and depressed state they were in prior to treatment. This contrasts with the patient whose perception of life is dramatically altered by having the cancer, and yet dies of it young and spiritually whole. In both cases the circumstances of illness were identical, but their perceptions were completely dissimilar. This leads us to define curing as the action of change upon any aspect of life that is subject to change, and healing as the action of the unchangeable applied to any aspect of that which changes.

What is meant by "aspects of life subject to change," and "the unchangeable?" An exploration of these separate domains and their relationship to the art of spiritual psychotherapy can highlight some very fundamental problems in the field of family therapy.

A BRIDGE OF LOVE

Figure 1 is a diagram that outlines one of the ideas basic to this model of spiritually-oriented therapy. Moving across the diagram from left to right, we begin with the experience of injustice in the world, for example, physical hardship, painful childhoods, divorce, etc. When fed through the human, mental, and emotional faculties,

FIGURE 1: Chart showing features of a spiritually based psychotherapy.

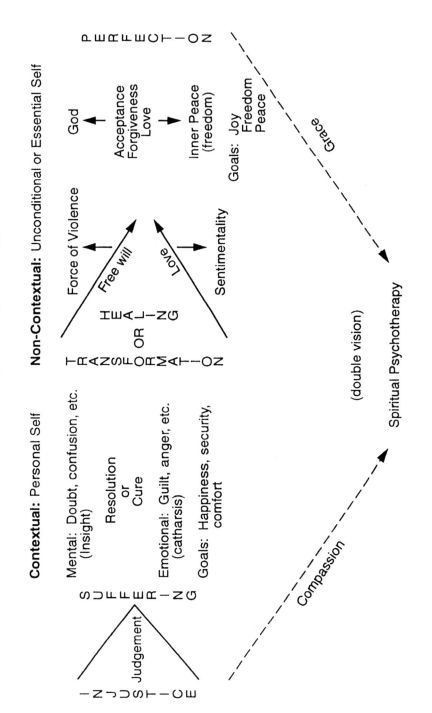

these injustices inspire judgments on creation *as it is* and create pain and suffering in our lives. Our minds, struggling to comprehend injustice, fail to find reason or method in the experience and therefore compute the events as "wrong" or not as they should be, making comparisons to either better or worse outcomes as a way to digest the experience.

Correspondingly, our emotions follow in line with parallel feelings of anger, fear, guilt, resentment, and so forth, as our minds move forward and back in attempted understanding. The tragedy of sudden loss is instructive here. When a child dies, the parent's experience is far too big for the mind to wrap itself around. It simply makes no sense. What often happens is that the experience gets broken down into little bits and pieces upon which the bereaved parent focuses, going over and over them in his or her mind countless times. With each retracing of steps the heart aches, the rage swells, the guilt envelops, and the empty pain prevails. Simply, grief takes over. Try as you may, the mind will not rest, stirring the emotions to levels of intensity perhaps never before experienced. This process continues until a decision must be reached, a choice made. Often that choice is only perceptible in hindsight, but a vital choice has been made all the same. It is a life choice that often sets in motion a fundamental position or attitude about living. This is the choice to live in love or fear, to expand or contract, to open or close the heart, to embrace life in it entirety or fear its unpredictable nature.

Although it is well known that the stages of grief move toward "acceptance," this state of acceptance shows two faces: (1) the humble embrace and (2) resignation. One accepts reality as part of the life process and opens up to come into accord with it, while the other fears and resists it. One forgives God, life, or fate for its sword of injustice, and the other resents them. One surrenders control before the vicissitudes of life or God's will, and the other seeks protection or acts in defiance of them. One seeks wisdom, the other understanding.

This choice may indeed be the human demonstration of free will—to disconnect our internal experience from external events, i.e., to transform injustice and human suffering into forgiveness, acceptance, and love simply by exercising our free will to embrace them as they are, not as we think they should be. For systems thinkers, we might see this as a kind of spiritual negentropy, changing energy of a certain psychospiritual nature to a higher form, much like our bodies ingest food with a certain chemical structure and transform it into a significantly more complex molecular composition.

In the autobiographical account of her personal journey through grief and pain, Paula D'Arcy, in *Song for Sarah*, writes the following letter to her deceased husband and child:

> Everyone dies. I mean, no one lives forever. So then why do we live? What is it all for? How easy to focus alternately on either our joys or our fears, as I have done . . . . And though they were important to the individual lives, none of the brief joys and tears have ultimate meaning. Pain would defeat men if it did. No, all those circumstances around which I measured my life were impermanent . . . . All those moments hung one day in the same closet with your empty clothes . . . all that remains, from all that we were, is the love. Love did not move and does not change. So the question in life, every day, for every person, is not what can I enjoy, or who will I please? . . . The question is, how do I love? . . . . I am sure of one thing, my little one. Emptiness is all around us. But if one chooses to look for God, he will not be empty, and his life will never be the same . . . . And no one avoids that choice, for to ignore it is to decide.[3]

Referring again to Figure 1, we see that this transformation is what I have called healing, and what has been described earlier as the experience of unconditionality in the presence of conditions of injustice and suffering. I suggest here that three experiences of the unconditional are found in forgiveness, acceptance, and love.

It is important to emphasize that the bringing to bear of these inner "eyes of perfection" is not designed to change the reality of the event or its cognitive and emotional content in any way. This non-contextual self is in no way to supplant or replace the mind or emotions, the head and heart of our living. Rather, it embraces those with a certain awareness, a spiritual awareness that originates from a different inner source — from one's essential beingness, or divine center. And it stands side by side with the suffering of the contextual self. Indeed, it is often the pain of our lives which awakens our unconditional qualities for ourselves and for others. Both sides of living are needed for wholeness.

The bereaved parent mentioned earlier is often brought directly into this choice in a most compelling manner. To stay indefinitely in the throes of grief is unbearable. So a choice is made. To resolve the pain, the bereaved can work to relieve the heartache. But if these efforts are disconnected from forgiveness and love, the heart eventually turns in on itself and moves toward resignation. Too often in grief counseling this form of "acceptance" is called "working through the grief." But in fact the grief has *not* been worked through.

It is equally incomplete to move the awareness only to the spiritual center of unconditional love, denying grief's pain and thus divorcing oneself from compassion for the very real heartache of the experience. This results in a kind of denial of self and an insensitivity to others. In grief work it tends to produce physical symptoms.

Wholeness is found in embracing both selves: our personal self and our divine Self. To view life through this "double vision," as Jacob Boehme suggests, is to be fully alive.[4] To bring to bear on human suffering the compassionate heart together with the inner eyes of grace may be the fine art of a spiritually based psychotherapy.

WHOLENESS AND THE INTEGRATION OF OUR TWO SELVES

As shown in Figure 1, the personal self emerges out of our physical, emotional, and intellectual senses, and ushers forth our empathy, compassion, and understanding of human suffering in all of its circumstances. The personal self holds all of our hopes and cries, as well as the courage for change when our lives are in pain. The spiritual self (essential or unconditional self) emerges from our divine center within. It brings forth unconditional acceptance for the way things are, forgiveness for ourselves and others, and the kind of love that will not be thwarted by suffering. In this model of human coordination of both these selves is the art of living. A personal self divorced from the spirit within is either all too prone to depression over the seemingly meaningless waves of change in the course of living, or to hatred over the injustices present in life. In short, the personal self alone is dependent on the nature of outer things, and its best defense is self actualization, or the development of ego strength.

Similarly, the spiritual self which is divorced from the personality and all its needs, wishes, and dreams is too vulnerable to surprise attacks from the denied aspects of the cognitive-emotional system. Unavoidably, the unconscious will have its day sooner or later.

Wholeness is thus conceptualized as the full expression of our psychospiritual nature, bringing both acceptance and feeling to all aspects of our lives. Such full expression of the total self ensures the capacity to live both lovingly and politically in a world of injustice and pain. Our personal self moves us into action in order to change intolerable human conditions for ourselves and others, while our spiritual self keeps our love in the action so we may avoid falling into inner violence. The inner harmony of the two selves is the peace required for effective social activism. Likewise, both selves need full acknowledgment in a spiritually-based psychotherapy — the process of healing requires their simultaneous expression. This process is best described by the concept of matching and will be detailed later in the section of the practice of a spiritually based psychotherapy.

GOALS OF THERAPY

The goals of a contextual psychotherapy are indeed radically different from a non-contextual (unconditional) therapy. As stated earlier, contextual therapy is about the alleviation of personal pain, the resolution of problems or simply, cure. It seeks to provide a way out of mental and emotional distress by helping the person *feel* better about their situation, and perhaps themselves, as well as helping them to think differently about the problem they are bringing to therapy. Thus, the goals of contextual therapy are happiness, security, and comfort (see Figure 1). These qualities are attributes of the physical, emotional, and cognitive domains of life and are based on one's *human condition*. We feel secure when there's enough money in the bank, happy when our children love and respect us, and comfortable when we possess the things in life we think we should have. The attainment of these states of mind are indeed partially dependent on psychological dynamics such as assertiveness, autonomy, goal directedness, empathy, and relatedness. These, in turn, may be related to childhood experiences, parenting, biology, family history, and many other psychodynamic and systemic influences. Yet again I emphasize that these qualities are based on one's conditions and are quite transitory. Tomorrow the stock market may dive, children may enter junior high school and no longer be respectful, or an earthquake may destroy one's home.

In contrast, the goals of an unconditional view of life are those qualities which by definition are based solely on the inner action of healing, not on the shifting conditions of life. These qualities are joy, freedom, and inner peace (see Figure 1). Spiritual development can be defined as the nourishment of these inner qualities, and the hallmarks of its presence are demonstrated at those very moments in which the presence of conditional goals such as happiness, security, and comfort are not available. We cannot fully know our inner peace until we are disturbed, nor our freedom until our security is stripped. Nor can we know our capacity for joy until the conditional reasons to be happy are nowhere to be found. The irony of life is that we are set free by our suffering. (Or at least the possibility is always there.) The Chinese hexagram for crisis means danger plus opportunity. This age-old wisdom has been known to most religions and cultures throughout the ages. It may only have been lost in our contemporary psychotherapies. When God enters the system, wisdom is restored.

THE PRACTICE OF SPIRITUAL PSYCHOTHERAPY

A central premise of this paper is that a spiritually based psychotherapy lies in the awareness of the therapist (team, consultant, etc.) and not in the presence of absence of any particular set of techniques, stances, or actions. However, since action often follows thought, we might expect that a therapy guided by this awareness may indeed focus on some of these qualities in the discourse of the

therapy. *This need not be so.* The qualities of joy, peace, and freedom are inner experiences and not words. We can be talking about
anger, betrayal, or frustration while speaking from inner peace. For
example, a spouse may confront an alcoholic partner with force, or
even walk out, from a place of love and forgiveness. There is an
essential difference between confronting or leaving a partner in anger or doing so from a place of love and forgiveness. Similarly, it is
possible to confront abuse, resentment, or hatred while staying accepting, forgiving, and loving inside oneself. (These three uncondi-
tionals are not feelings, and should not be confused with feelings.
They are inner actions.) And this is precisely the task of the therapist in a spiritual psychotherapy. *The practice of a spiritually based
psychotherapy is defined by the particular joining process wherein
the therapist's personal self meets the client's personal struggle
with compassion, and the therapist's spiritual self remains fully
aware of unconditional acceptance.*

This joining process can best be described by the concept of
matching. One of the ways we understand another's experience is
through referencing a similar experience inside ourselves. Indeed,
our depth of empathy rests on how closely we can match another's
experience. The therapeutic power of support groups and healing
communities, such as 12-Step Programs, grief groups, and adult
survivor networks is in large measure a result of the deep empathy
and compassion available from people who have similarly suffered.
Thus having one's personal pain understood by another is in itself
therapeutic. Good psychotherapy rests on this foundation of joining
and empathizing.

However, it may matter more how well the individual who is
joining the client relates to the internal match or reference point
than how similar their experiences have been. For misery does love
company, and merely understanding another's suffering may lead
to nothing more than identification and countertransference. Thus,
the power of the support communities noted above rests not only on
the available compassion, but also on the compassion of others who
have indeed been healed. Within such communities there are available reference points for the pain and reference points for the transformation of pain. To know that others have walked the path before
you (and found light at the end of the tunnel) provides hope. To see
that some other parent who also lost a child eventually found inner

strength awakens inspiration. To talk to another alcoholic who found a new relationship to her life by "letting go and letting God" can instantly provoke intense questions and soul searching. Indeed, to sit with one who knows your personal pain and has been *healed by having that pain* sets a context that maximizes the opportunity for your healing to unfold.

The process of spiritual psychotherapy works very much the same way. The therapist joins with the client or client system from his or her place of empathy within the personal self. It is not essential that the therapist have a very close match to the client's point of pain. It is essential that the therapist join in an authentic and fully compassionate manner such that their own reference point is experienced. Then, as the therapist enters into that reference point, he or she will also enter into whatever degree of healing is present within them with regard to that point. Thus, to fully join with a client's grief touches not only my grief, but also my relationship to my grief at that time. *It is precisely this relationship to my own pain, triggered by joining with you, the client, that is my first task in a spiritually based therapy.*

Healing begins with oneself. So the therapist must access the source of unconditional love, acceptance, and forgiveness within him or herself and bring it to bear on the mutual pain held within the therapist-client system. This does not necessitate that the client will be healed. There is no cause and effect here. *Nor do we necessarily prevent our clients from healing their pain, even if ours is not. But the kind of joining which enters into full personal compassion for ourself and others, provides a context generously fertile for healing.*

This is no easy task and requires that the therapist makes this task a central part of his or her personal and professional development. Thus, the therapist makes the life work of being a therapist his or her primary path of psychospiritual growth. Each session can become a new opportunity for self-healing as both client system and therapy system come together for a mutual healing process to unfold. For just as a client's pain can elicit our own pain when we sit in compassion with them, unconditional love can elicit the same experience in another when we sit in acceptance with them. When this unconditional love awakens in both ourselves and our clients, grace is possible. Even fate can be changed as we once again participate in the Dance. This may provide a new meaning to Jesus' words, "whenever two or more of you are gathered together in my name." Perhaps the "name in which we gather" is a relationship defined by compassion and love for ourselves and each other. The creation of such a context for healing is the art of spiritual psychotherapy. Now let us look at a few ingredients that go into the making of this context in family therapy.

FAMILY THERAPY AND THE ART OF HEALING

Although it was unintended, the field of family therapy has developed some remarkable ingenious methods for creating contexts wherein the therapist can be actively engaged in the discourse of a session while remaining centered in the spiritual self. This is known as therapeutic neutrality and has a rather long and interesting history in the psychotherapy literature. The concept of neutrality has taken on new meanings and emphases with the birth of family therapy due to the intense scapegoating and blaming that often prevail when family members are brought together in the therapy session. This presents a rather unique challenge to the therapist's empathy, for he or she must remain empathic to all sides as well as being accepting of various points of view. Training in "seeing the system," constructivism, cybernetic theory, circular causality, structural analysis, and therapeutic conversation can all be very important in the maintenance of therapeutic neutrality. Family therapists have even gone so far as to build walls with one way mirrors where groups of therapists (often larger in number than the family) caucus in order to preserve neutrality.

It is widely accepted that if the therapist is in some state of judgment and blame, it is quite likely that the therapy relationship can replicate the family dynamics, and a therapeutic impasse will occur. From a spiritual point of view, neutrality is more importantly the access route to the therapist's inner life of unconditional love, acceptance, and forgiveness. It is the road to his or her divine source, for one cannot be simultaneously in a state of judgment and a state of acceptance. One state closes the heart, the other opens it. So here is a key to the practice of spiritual psychotherapy: any communication that takes place in an attitude of judgment carries that judgment as part of the message. In other words, our hearts become the medium through which we converse therapeutically. And this medium is ultimately the message. So even if "cure" were to result from whatever technology we employed in working with families, healing may not.

From a spiritual perspective, neutrality is a necessary inner state and is not defined by any outer action. Therefore, it is possible to be outwardly confronting one part of the system while maintaining inner peace. And the nourishment of that inner state is not achieved by all the particular models, methods, and mirrors designed to produce it. They are only attempts to safeguard against judgment and blame; and to the extent that they do this for a particular individual or group, their tools are invaluable to both the process of curing and healing. In fact, it is possible to review the history of family therapy methods as an evolving spirituality, i.e., the training of therapists to access their unconditional love in the presence of judgment and blame. In a spiritual psychotherapy, this process is taken as the central goal of the therapy, and therapy begins with it. Rather than safeguard against judgment and blame, it is possible to use these internal states as information signaling the need for healing or transformation of these states by the simultaneous action of compassion and unconditional love.

We still can ask if there are any contexts for therapeutic interaction which might facilitate this inner process for the therapist and the family members. I will mention only a few here, but my hope is that in the development of the art of spiritual psychotherapies, many approaches will be proposed with this same goal in mind. Again, the goal which needs to be constantly remembered is that of embracing whatever situation we find before us *as it is* with both compassion for the suffering and unconditional acceptance for the way it presently exists. The rest is left of Grace.

CONTEXTS FOR GRACE

So how are forums for the transformation of judgment and blame into acceptance, forgiveness, and love created? Or more properly stated, how do we create forums for the awakening of our acceptance, forgiveness, and love in the presence of judgment and blame? First, as stated above, the therapist joins the system with this goal in mind both for him or herself and for the family. All questions, directions, frames and conversations would be directed toward this process. Personal and interpersonal block and/or limits of this process would be explicitly seen as such, and thus would become the subject of therapeutic dialogue.

The function of the symptom would now be viewed as presenting an opportunity for this spiritual progression by the therapist and possibly by the family, if appropriate. Certainly questions that focus specifically on the effect the problem is having on each person's inner life regarding him or herself and others would be central to the interview. History-taking could surely focus on family of origin teachings, as well as modelings of acceptance, love, and forgiveness. Specific explorations of the history around conditional versus unconditional relating and its impact on current relationships could provide the context for interventions that might facilitate this process.

Many additional techniques from other non-spiritually oriented schools may be employed, yet now with a different goal in mind. Circular questions now locate the place of judgment and the particular ways in which the family is stuck acting out conditional contracts. Strategic interventions can free these conditional contracts from their hold on family members. Rituals may be designed to facilitate the process of acceptance and forgiveness. The negative consequences of change are now the missed opportunities to break long histories of self-blame and scapegoating, and positive connotations are found in the imminent possibilities for truly new ways to relate to self and others. Indeed, family therapy could become a forum for much more than the alleviation of symptoms. It would be a context for fundamental healing. Over the 15 years I have practiced and supervised the work of therapy with families, I have been amazed at the power of this forum for exactly that kind of life healing, even when it wasn't intentional. I wonder what could happen if the field made it the heart of what we do.

REFERENCE NOTES

1. This quotation comes from Maya Angelou's opening remarks in her address to the March, 1989 Family Therapy Networker Conference in Washington, DC.

2. This quotation by Stephen Levine, author of *Who Dies* and *Healing Into Life and Death*, is often used when he lectures about working with the dying.

3. From Paula D'Arcy, *Song for Sarah*, Harold Shaw Publishers, 1979, p. 105.

4. The term "double vision" is used throughout the writings of Jacob Boehme, the sixteenth century mystic. An excellent review of these ideas can be heard on audiotape by Howard Thurman, "The Grapple of the World: Jacob Boehme," available from Howard Thurman Educational Trust, San Francisco, CA.

APPLICATIONS

Chapter Four

Therapeutic Change in Religious Families: Working with the God-Construct

James L. Griffith, MD
Melissa Elliott Griffith, MSN

INTRODUCTION

From our coins that proclaim "In God We Trust" to our public invocations of God's aid before football games, to the prayer breakfasts of governors and presidents, there are constantly visible tokens of our commitment as a culture as we offer homage to a suprahuman Being who provides an orienting point for our meaning as a nation, a football team, or a state. For millions of individual Americans, the power of these public rituals pales before his or her personal relationship experienced with a God who is known through a very private, unique set of images, beliefs, prayers, and feelings. For religious persons, parenting and one's relationship as a spouse must be lived in harmony with one's personal relationship with God. Personal relationships with God often hold a dominating influence upon family behaviors.

Few argue that this description fits millions of American families. Yet systemic family therapists have explored this context of family life relatively little. Few words have been written as guides for working therapeutically within this context when addressing family problems.[1]

For many years we have conducted family and individual therapies from within the context of client relationships to God when that relationship was counted as significant by a family member or client. We have developed methods that enable us as therapists to enter respectfully into this personal reality of the client while maintaining integrity as a therapist. We will discuss our work by describing a clinical theory that coordinates our observing, thinking, and interacting during therapy, then by illustrating our actions with clinical examples.

THE GOD-CONSTRUCT AND ITS EPIGENESIS*

Leslie: "I can't tell you all this — I need to stop or just leave. I am afraid it is too overwhelming."

Therapist: "Is there anyone you would not worry that you would overwhelm?"

Leslie: "Only God. Only God could listen to all this."

Therapist: "Tell me about what it is like to tell it to God. How would you describe God in those moments? Is God as close as we are sitting now?"

Leslie: "He is not so close. It is more like He is up on something — maybe a throne — on the other side of the room."

Therapist: "What does God's body look like? Is He sitting on the throne or standing?"

Leslie: "Not standing. I can only see His face. It is concerned, with kind eyes."

Therapist: "What I'm curious about is what happens in your mind's eye if you imagine this face of God and begin to tell Him as much as you can, as long as you wish — just go on and on in the fantasy — watch the face and tell me what you see."

Leslie: [After a few moments] "I think His face got tired, sad — too tired. I couldn't see the eyes anymore. I had to quit and leave. I felt like it was too much for God. That's crazy, and I know it is not right, but that is what I saw."

---

*This transcript is based upon a dramatization of the K. family produced together with LuAnn Fischer Bross, MS and Jenny Freedle, MSW.

Leslie is describing a very personal experience of God. We refer to this privately perceived and experienced image of God as her *God-construct*, a mental construct existing as an autonomous cognitive structure. A God-construct is specific and unique for each individual. It arises developmentally, grounded in deeply emotional and nonverbal processes of early life, and is typically described not only as a visual image but in auditory, tactile, olfactory, proprioceptive, or other sensory terms as well.[2,3] Its features do not bear any necessary relationship to the person's stated beliefs, doubts, dogma, or theology.

We have adapted Piaget's notions about cognitive development to provide an explanation for how a God-construct arises. Piaget suggested that a person utilizes organized patterns of behavior, or *schemes*, as cognitive structures for organizing personal experience in the world.[4,5] Schemes can be thought of as deeply ingrained "mental habits" that govern how perceiving, thinking, and acting are done. Schemes, from their earliest origins in simple reflex activities, are few in number and undifferentiated in the very young child. In response to environmental perturbations, however, a child over time steadily reworks his or her schemes by making new distinctions within the experience of living that renders behavior more effective. For example, a simple scheme may govern the cognitive processes of an infant so that the baby, cooing and gazing wide-eyed, responds in like manner to all adults who reach out to hold her. At about seven months of age, however, schemes for "mother" and "not-mother" have differentiated so that the aunts and uncles are suddenly greeted by a rejecting scream when trying to pick up their niece who once was so friendly. Stranger anxiety becomes evident for the first time.

Evidence from studies in developmental psychology suggests that a young child chooses among schemes used for perceiving and relating to intimate parenting figures (usually but not necessarily mother and father) in constructing God-schemes.[6] Intimate relationships with each human parent and observations by the young child of parents' language and behavior about God, such as their reverent tones when speaking about God and their worshipful manner at church or synagogue, seem to provide the primary sources.[7] The God-scheme then organizes how the child responds to perturbations from life, whether private and intrapersonal perturbations, such as day fantasies and night dreams involving God, or public and interpersonal perturbations such as admonitions to behave in a Godly way or to offer petitions to God in prayer.

As with other schemes, a God-scheme is steadily revised over time in directions that enable the child to operate more effectively in the world, according to the child's personal judgment. Experiences with parenting persons appear to contribute most prominently, but influences from teachers, Sunday School, other beloved or feared adult friends — experiences both secular and sacred — also contribute to this reconstruction.

During the latency years of childhood, a God-scheme typically becomes an autonomous cognitive structure, the *God-construct*.[8,9] A God-scheme may show an organizational drift in which, influenced by the child's experiences in living, its organizational pattern shifts until a key developmental event, *organizational closure*[10-12], occurs. The organization of a God-scheme achieves organizational closure when the God-scheme influences the child's behavior in a manner that creates environmental conditions inadvertently reinforcing the God-scheme's stability. Stated in more technical cybernetic terms, an external observer studying the child notes that interactions between the child's self and God-scheme have begun to generate recursively the initial structure of the God-scheme in self-reflexive, closed feedback loops, thereby stabilizing the structure of the God-scheme. This reflexive process is now termed the God-construct. Figure A contrasts how this process may lead to a God-construct who is soothing and comforting in one case, but to a God-construct who is harsh and abusing in another case.

These processes are similar to those that govern the formation of other stable intrapersonal images, such as those of "mother" and "father," referred to as "internalization of primary objects" in psychoanalytic literature.[13] Ana-Maria Rizzuto, writing in the psychoanalytic tradition, found evidence in her research that the steps leading to an autonomous God-construct ("internalization of the God-representation") were part of a continuous process throughout the early years of life. She described this process as reaching completion typically at about age nine, which is three to four years after representations of the human parents.[14]

> In the case of Leslie (above), she mentioned a wish, weeks later, that she have her deceased granddaddy with her to tell about her troubles. Due to chronic leukemia, he had moved in with Leslie's family when she was three years old. Leslie would go upstairs to his bedroom, but there was a gate across the door. Granddaddy wanted to be with the children, although he could not risk exposure to their childhood illnesses. But he loved for them to come to the door and talk to him. He was a kind, wise, good listener, but very sick and quick to tire. Leslie used to plan her visits in the morning so he wouldn't be so tired, but still he sometimes wore out, nodding off before she could finish. When he was in the bed across the room, only his pink face peeked out from beneath the covers.

Rizzuto further noted that a child gradually creates an inner image of God from a variety of sources. The parental contribution was the most influential, usually with one parent having a greater impact than the other. Not only the "real parent," but the wished-for ideal parent and the feared parent of the imagination appeared on equal footing in contributing to the construction of an image of God.[15]

This process describes how a child comes to a felt relationship with a stable inner presence named "God," but it does not account for beliefs about God, including beliefs as to whether a personal God-construct does or does not exist in objective reality. Rizzuto found in her work that the influence of official religion comes after a stable, autonomous God-construct has already formed.[16] She describes belief or unbelief in God as arising after the formation of the God-construct. An unbeliever is a person who has decided, consciously or unconsciously for reason based on his or her own personal history, not to believe in a God-construct he or she nevertheless holds. Maturity and belief are therefore not related issues.[17] A client's doctrinal beliefs and theological explanations may therefore imply little for therapeutic work involving his or her God-construct.

FIGURE A

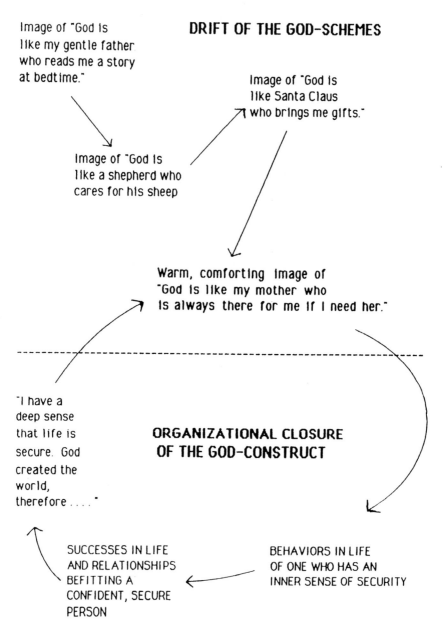

DRIFT OF THE GOD-SCHEMES

Image of "God is
like my gentle father
who reads me a story
at bedtime."

Image of "God is
like Santa Claus
who brings me gifts."

Image of "God is
like a shepherd who
cares for his sheep

Warm, comforting image of
"God is like my mother who
is always there for me if I need her."

"I have a
deep sense
that life is
secure. God
created the
world,
therefore . . . ."

**ORGANIZATIONAL CLOSURE
OF THE GOD-CONSTRUCT**

SUCCESSES IN LIFE
AND RELATIONSHIPS
BEFITTING A
CONFIDENT, SECURE
PERSON

BEHAVIORS IN LIFE
OF ONE WHO HAS AN
INNER SENSE OF SECURITY

Image of "God is
like my father who is
frightening when he
gets angry."

DRIFT OF THE GOD-SCHEMES

Image of "God is
like our rich neighbor
who laughs at poor people."

Image of "God is
like the flood that
drowned all the people
on TV."

Fearful, resentful image of
"God is strong enough to help
me but doesn't care."

"God created
the world this
way. God is
powerful and
could change it
if He wished,
therefore . . . . "

ORGANIZATIONAL CLOSURE
OF THE GOD-CONSTRUCT

DISAPPOINTMENTS IN LIFE
AND RELATIONSHIPS
BEFITTING ONE WHO
IS PESSIMISTIC AND
DISTRUSTFUL

BEHAVIORS IN LIFE
OF ONE WHO DOUBTS
AND LACKS BASIC TRUST

A LANGUAGE SYSTEMS APPROACH
TO WORKING WITH THE GOD-CONSTRUCT
IN PSYCHOTHERAPY

We have directed the focus of our psychotherapeutic work involving the God-construct upon the conversational domain that emerges between self and God-construct, rather than at the client's religious beliefs about God.[18-20] As an autonomous cognitive structure, the God-construct engages through language in the private conversations that occur within the self. Probably every person can recall having conversed with God at some time in his or her life. For many persons this is a regular, ongoing conversation arising spontaneously many times a day throughout life.

Recent work regarding language systems has studied characteristics of conversational interactions among autonomous systems.[21-25] From this perspective, one way to understand problems and suffering within relationships is to focus upon how stable, recurrent conversations can maintain the viability of problems — both interpersonal conversations among those interacting around the problem, as well as intrapersonal conversations within each participant. Such problem-engendering discourse is typically characterized by participants speaking from monological perspectives — participants ask the same questions over and over and hear the same answers over and over, leading to the same selection of problem-solving behaviors, etc. In this stagnant state, new meaning, innovative ideas, and alternative behaviors seldom emerge.[26,27] When dialogue stops between the God-construct and the self, the consequences are much the same as when dialogue stops in other relationships, in which the two parties from their monological perspectives continue nevertheless to impact one another despite the absence of dialogue.

Some religious persons thus have regular conversations between self and God-construct that have become problematic. For example, one person may address God on a daily basis, "I know that whatever I do, it can never be enough for what you expect." Even non-religious persons who express publicly their disdain for religious beliefs may nevertheless sustain an ongoing intrapersonal dialogue between self and God-construct that brings forth suffering (e.g., to God: "I don't even believe you exist. Why do you torment me with guilt?'' or ''Even though I know you don't exist, I can't stop rebelling against what I think you would want.'') Further, God-constructs within persons involved in a relationship may so organize reciprocal behaviors of both partners that suffering is a regular by-product, as in the following vignette:

> Margaret was a highly skilled special-education teacher, embarrassed that her own son had been referred for school-related behavioral problems. Her husband, Tom, was a computer programmer.
>
> In couples therapy, Margaret described her visual image of God as a kind, patient, wise, old man, standing above her and looking down. She felt God expected her to be patient, quiet, and obedient, which she tried hard to do.
>
> Tom likened God to his father who would watch Tom from the athletic field sidelines, caring and encouraging, but also scrutinizing and shaming him if he did not take charge, make sharp decisions, and run with determination.
>
> In the interview, Margaret would always turn to Tom, even when asked questions directly. When questions about family and children arose, Margaret would silence herself, denying the family her wisdom as a gifted teacher. She insistently followed Tom, who, despite feeling incompetent and unsure of himself, would doggedly lead on, trying without success to devise reasonable plans for parenting and for organizing the household.
>
> For Margaret to show competent leadership or for Tom to support the leadership of another were behavioral patterns alien to the dialogue of their respective self/God-construct relationships.

A therapist can act by joining a client — or joining the relationship between clients — in therapeutic conversation that includes conversation with the involved God-constructs. From this position, the therapist can facilitate authentic dialogue between self and God-construct in which new linguistic distinctions arise that can become the source of new meanings and creativity. This represents a shift from a monological perspective to a dialogical perspective in the conversation between self and God-construct.[28] With this creation of a new conversational domain between self and God-construct, a context is provided in which creative new solutions may emerge for life problems that led the client to seek psychotherapy.[29-31]

In psychotherapy, elements of this clinical theory of the God-construct can be employed through a variety of therapeutic strategies. Our initial work with the God-construct arose out of our work utilizing psychodramatic techniques to embody private, inner realities of clients. In our experience, psychodramatic techniques, such as doubling, role reversal, and sculpture,[32,33] are unequalled in their effectiveness for rendering a person's God-construct external and visible to therapist and/or other family members. One can then work "hands-on" with both God-construct and interpersonal relationships.[34-36]

More recently we have focused upon how to utilize the God-construct within the process of questioning in the psychotherapeutic interview. These efforts seek therapeutic change through working systemically with the client's systems of language and meaning.[37-41] The participation of the God-construct in creating the client's description of reality becomes an avenue for the introduction of new systemic information.

Asking a question to trigger therapeutic change — rather than making a behavioral assignment, exploring for insight, or even seeking the question's specific answer — has provided a creative focus for some of the most significant contributions family therapists have brought to the broader psychotherapeutic community. Termed "interventive interviewing" by Tomm, systemic therapists have brought a rational organization to the art of asking questions and have introduced guidelines for asking questions that facilitate, rather than inhibit, therapeutic change.[42] Rather than seeking to draw out specific answers, these questions are simply "loosening moves" that provide an opening for new distinctions and a conversation within the client between the God-construct and the self.[43] This provides a context in which creative change can occur in unexpected ways first within the client, then secondarily in family and other relationships.

We have used the systematic approaches to questioning offered by Karl Tomm[44,45] and by Michael White[46] as a method for designing questions that invite fresh dialogue and new linguistic distinctions in the conversations between self and God-construct.

Some typical examples of interventive questions useful for this work include:

1. Circular Questions[47-49]
   a. About which relationship in the family do you think God would express the most satisfaction? About which relationship do you think God would express the least satisfaction?
   b. If you worked out your sexual relationship with your husband so that you both found it to be satisfying, would you feel closer or further away from God?
   c. With whom in the family can you talk about God? With whom would it feel awkward?

2. Future Questions[50-52]
   a. If your daughter were to grow up, marry, and divorce, how would you hope her relationship with God might be different from your own relationship with God? How would you hope it might be similar?
   b. If you were to find your relationship with God changed at the end of this therapy, in what aspect of the relationship would you most hope you might see the change? What aspects might you hope would remain unchanged?

3. Reflexive Questions[53,54]
   a. Had you possessed the relationship you now have with God when you first married, how do you suppose your different behavior might have altered the way the relationship evolved?
   b. If God were to restructure this interaction, how do you think it would go?
   c. If God were to see worth in this relationship which the two of you might not be able to see, what might that be?
   d. If you were to discover that God had in fact been present and active in this situation all along, where might that have been?

4. Unique Outcome and Unique Account Questions[55]
   a. Has there ever been even a brief moment when, contrary to

your expectations, you did sense approval coming from God?

b. Can you recall a time when your husband might have criticized your relationship with God but didn't?

c. In view of all the betrayals you experienced in your life growing up, are you surprised to discover that you have learned to trust God?

5. Unique Redescription and Unique Possibilities Questions[56,57]

a. What difference will your having learned how to trust God make in your learning how to trust your wife?

b. If you see yourself as the person God sees, what new possibilities might you imagine for this relationship?

c. If you were to agree with the outcome you believe God wants for this relationship, what might be the next step in getting there?

AN ILLUSTRATIVE PSYCHOTHERAPY

A case summary and transcripts from a psychotherapy session will illustrate how psychodrama and questions that explore the patterning of relationship among self, God-construct, and human others can be employed to bring forth new solutions to old problems.

Case Example: Martha K., soft-spoken with a troubled face, came with her 20-year-old daughter, Deborah, for family therapy. Deborah, brightly-clad and angry, initially said nothing. Martha's pastor had called saying that she had requested he refer her to a "Christian psychiatrist" for depression, but the pastor, sensing the likely source of her distress suggested she come together with her daughter to our family therapy program instead.

Martha told how she and Deborah had lived alone since Deborah's father died ten years earlier. Now Deborah wanted to move out with her boyfriend, an act that would sin against God and shame Martha. Interrupting her mother's account, Deborah stated emphatically that they had been in an unending fight over boy friends and career plans since Deborah graduated from high school. Now Deborah was determined to move out and set her own life course. As the conversation began drifting into another fight, the therapist

(JLG) inquired about how things might have been had their hopes, rather than disappointments, been realized:

Therapist:	"Well, how should this have gone with the two of you? Both of you probably have a sense that when a girl reaches those years between 17 and 22, more or less, it is a good time for leaving home. I'm wondering, if things in your family had gone smoothly and happily, how would that story have been told?"
Martha:	"Well, I guess every mother has ideas in her head, mine was that—you know—she graduate from high school, perhaps meet someone there, fall in love, and get married. And she tried college for a little while. I don't know if it was the college or what, but her lifestyle changed. We've always been church people and she just got away from it."
Therapist:	"You mention church and that Deborah's moving out and living with someone would be sinful. I gather that God has been important in your life?"
Martha:	"He has been to me. I have always considered God to be the center of our home."
Deborah:	"He's . . . that's been about it. It's been Mama, me, and the church. We'd go to church every time the church doors were opened."
Therapist:	"Oh, even now? Or until recently?"
Martha:	"She doesn't go quite as much, but I encourage her as much as I can."

A shift occurred in the interview, as God entered onto the stage of the dialogue, a focus of mother and daughter's conflict over separation, autonomy, and responsibility:

Therapist:	"The two of you are talking about this decision as if it has been structured just between the two of you. You haven't mentioned conversations with friends or other people. It does sound as if you have had conversations about it with God."
Martha:	"I have."
Therapist:	"Can you tell about your conversation with God?

	And . . . have the two of you had a discussion about this before?"
Martha:	"She doesn't call it a discussion. She calls it a lecture."
Therapist:	"Okay. Would it be alright if we brought God into the room, since God has been a very important presence?"
Martha:	"I consider Him here."
Therapist:	"Okay, I'll show you a way that I've often used in therapy if you can feel comfortable playing along with me . . . . Let me stand and do something with you that you have probably never done before. For a moment, come and be God."
Martha:	"You want me to be God?"
Therapist:	"Yes. Could you come sit here?"

Martha moved from her chair, across the room to another seat henceforth designated as God's chair. Standing behind her, the therapist began a psychodramatic character enrollment,[58] speaking softly, using Martha's description of her inner image of God as a guide:

Therapist:	"For a moment I would like you to be God. Now, I'll bet that deep within you there is some image of what God might look like, of what God might be like. There may be a face, or some physical feature, or some particular characteristic that would help you to get into the character of the God with whom you have a relationship. And—for the sake of the therapy—could you speak as if you were that Presence? Could you be God just for a moment and say 'I am _____,' and describe yourself as known by Martha?"
Martha:	"You mean, just say, 'I am God,' and describe myself?"
Therapist:	"What does God look like?"
Martha:	"God doesn't really have a face to me. It's strange—I do see a beard, but I think that is from all the paintings by artists."
Therapist:	"Just stay with that image. It's okay. It may have a

	beard. And we'll separate your theological beliefs from this picture that feels to be God."
Martha:	"I always see Him sitting down, kind of pondering — I'm pondering and thinking over and worrying about . . . ."
Therapist:	"Can you show me that posture of the thinking and pondering and worrying? Where are your feet placed? And where are your arms placed?"
Martha:	"I think my feet are flat on the ground. I am out of doors. I am wringing my hands — not necessarily out of worry all the time — just wondering, just feeling a lot of concern."
Therapist:	"Now, as you look toward this mother and her daughter, where do your eyes go? What do you notice?"

[Martha, as God, gazed at the empty chair Martha had earlier occupied and at Deborah.]

Martha:	"I notice the mother and her strong belief. I see a lot of anguish, a lot of pain. The daughter is lost, doesn't really know her way. Where is she going? What is she going to do? Her life has no pattern. There are no real goals ahead of her, and the mother knows and worries about this and what will become of her daughter."
Therapist:	"As God, what are some of your fears?"
Martha:	"I am afraid that she is going to get with people who will further take her away from the beliefs that she used to believe, away from Me, getting into trouble."

With Martha merged into the character of God, her God-construct, until now known only privately to Martha, could speak openly in full view of both Deborah and the therapist. Then, through a series of role reversals[59] back and forth as Martha and as God (physically moving each time to Martha's chair or to God's chair), the therapist directed Martha's portrayal of a typical conversation between her self and God-construct:

Therapist: "Could I ask you to go back and be Martha again and I will sit in and be God?" [Martha moved back to her original chair, as the therapist sat in God's chair.]

Therapist: [as God speaking to Martha] "I am so worried about Deborah, afraid that she will get away from the beliefs. Worried that she will be lost."

Therapist: [now standing to reassume identity as therapist and speaking to Martha] "Now when you hear that from God, how do you feel inside?"

Martha: "I really feel like a failure. I feel like I have failed God in some way. Supposedly, you bring up the children in the way that they should go . . . and she is not in the way that I think she should go and the way I think God would want her to go. I place that fault on me. I don't know if that is punishment from God or something that I have done, but I think that it is my fault. I feel very guilty at times for failing."

Therapist: "Could you come back and be God for a moment?" [Martha returns from her chair to God's chair.] "As God, I would like you to speak the expectations to Martha that she is hearing."

Martha: [speaking as God to Martha] "Martha, I expect you to teach your daughter. I expect you to pray for her, to teach her to pray. I expect you have her in church, to keep her on the right path."

In order to draw out explicitly the unspoken meanings within Martha's religious language, the therapist employed doubling, a psychodramatic technique in which the therapist stands behind or to the side of the client and adopts the client's body postures while speaking, as if to be the client's alter ego stating out loud the client's inner, private dialogue:[60]

Therapist: "I wonder if I could double something for you. As your double, I will speak what I think may be your unspoken thoughts, if you will agree to correct them if I am wrong or to put them in your own words if I am right."

Martha:	"Okay."
Therapist:*	[speaking sternly, doubling as Martha's inner voice of God] "Martha, if you fail to teach your daughter I will hate you!"
Therapist:	[speaking to Martha and no longer doubling] "Can you correct that, or else put it in your own words?"
Martha:	[as God] "Martha, I am very disappointed in what you have done. It doesn't mean I don't love you, but I expected so much more from you because you have been such a devoted servant."
Therapist:	[again doubling as God] "Martha, I was counting on you and you let me down."
Martha:	[restating the double's statement] "Martha, I did count on you and you let me down."
Therapist:	[motioning] "Can you now be Martha again?" [Martha moves from God's chair back to Martha's chair, and the therapist sits in God's chair.]
Therapist:	[role-playing as God and speaking Martha's own words back to her] "Martha, I was counting on you and you let me down." [Then standing and stepping out of the role] "Now what is happening inside as you hear those words from God?"
Martha:	"It tears me up. My stomach feels tight, kind of panicky feeling. It is an awful feeling to know that you have disappointed God. A terrible burden."
Therapist:	"If you were to speak from that panicky feeling in your stomach, what would it say?"
Martha:	"I am sorry. I tried, but I don't know what else to do. I have tried to do what I was taught to do and to be what I was taught to be. It scares me as to what is going to happen to me, but mostly what is going to happen to my child. To fail God—as a mother, to

---

*As a technical point, the power of doubling as a technique for deepening the intensity lies not in whether the therapist has accurately stated the client's inner thoughts, but in how the client corrects or restates the double's words. The client's restatement is typically an intrapersonal statement that would not otherwise have been revealed explicitly in the interpersonal world. Ideally, the therapist-double's words prompt, but do not coach or interpret.

fail—it's scary. It hurts.''

Therapist: [now standing behind mother, assuming her posture, doubling for the voice of her inner Self] "God, I don't know if You expected too much, but I don't feel that You have revealed to me enough to know how to be a good parent. I look to You as the sole provider of information. I really feel let down by You.''

As the therapist guided the unfolding of the conversation between Martha and her God-construct, Deborah watched silently from the side. During the last minute, she inched closer and closer to her mother. Then she suddenly interrupted the interchange between mother and therapist, grasping her mother's arm:

Deborah: [weeping and agitated] "Mama, I love you so much. I love you so much. I know you were a good mama. You are a good mama.''

While a powerful catharsis between mother and daughter had been evoked, its pattern of anger-then-remorse felt old and well-trodden. Rather than following its affect, the therapist continued the questioning:

Therapist: "Deborah, what do you believe your mother would have needed to have known so that the expectations she felt from God would not have seemed too impossible?''

Deborah: "I think that she just needed to know that she was enough and that one parent was enough. That she has been the best to me. That I don't mind sacrificing for her.''

Martha: [to therapist] "I really don't want her to feel so guilty about leaving. I didn't realize that was what I was doing.''

In the immediacy created by Martha's new perspective, the therapist wondered whether she might also experience God in a new way:

Therapist:	"Let me ask you one more question before we stop. Martha, come back and be God for a moment." [Martha moved back to God's chair.] "Look at this mother." [Therapist sat in Martha's chair, role-playing her.]
Therapist:	[as Martha] "You know that I have tried in every way that I know how. I have done what I could and I feel like it hasn't been enough, and I feel like You are disappointed in me. I feel that I have failed in Your eyes."
Martha:	[as God] "Martha, you haven't failed. You have made a great effort. You judge yourself too harshly, much harsher than I would ever judge you."
Therapist:	"Switch with me." [Martha moves back to her original chair, and therapist moves to God's chair.]
Therapist:	[to Martha, repeating Martha's words as God] "You judge yourself more harshly than I would ever judge you."
Therapist:	[moving out of Martha's chair, assuming his own identity] "What about that? What do you think really is the case?"
Martha:	"I think it is probably true, but I hadn't really thought about it. I always think of God as a forgiving God — except when it came to me. I am probably my own worst enemy."
Therapist:	"Do you think that with one more role-play you could speak for the forgiving God that you refer to?"
Martha:	[having moved back into God's chair] "Martha, you have talked to Me often, more than most people ever think about. You have asked for forgiveness, and I have granted it. But you haven't forgiven yourself. And sometimes you ask for forgiveness for things that are not even wrong, that you didn't need forgiveness for. You have been faithful to Me. You are not a disappointment.

[Martha and therapist switch places, now Martha in her own chair and therapist in God's chair.]

Therapist:	[speaking as God, paraphrasing Martha's own words] "Martha, you have prayed far more than most people have ever imagined. You have been faithful to Me. You are not a disappointment. You have not forgiven yourself."
Therapist:	[moving out of God's chair, assuming own identity] "Martha, I wonder how it feels to hear those words?"
Martha:	"It feels like a relief. I also feel very close to God at this particular moment."
Therapist:	"You know, at a moment like this when you are feeling close to God, do you see your relationship with Deborah in any different way?"
Martha:	"I do. I really do."
Therapist:	"What?"
Martha:	"I just see my need to back off and let her be an adult. She is going to make mistakes, and I have been trying to prevent that in an effort to protect her. I feel that I need to trust her with what I have taught her. I don't think it will be easy. I can sit here and say this, but I think it will be a struggle on my part to do this. That's normal, I think. But I have taught her well. Maybe we just need to — or I need to — trust her more. Because I feel like I have done all that I can do as far as teaching her. She has a mind of her own now that she is an adult. I can't hold her with me forever. I think that may have been what I tried to do." [Now turning to Deborah] "It wasn't intentional."

Case Summary: God is an intrapersonal reality, and only secondarily a social one. Hence, this consultation is a working-in-the-presence-of kind of psychotherapy in which psychodrama offers therapist and daughter a window through which the conversations between Martha's self and God-construct can be seen. These conversations enter the mother-daughter system as new information. In the reflexivity between the Martha-Deborah interpersonal relationship and Martha's self/God-construct intrapersonal relationship, both are transformed. A new pattering of each relationship and a new conversation are seen at the end.

The work illustrated here can be clearly distinguished from psychotherapeutic approaches organized to further a particular religious dogma, such as Christian counselors who utilize scripture to prescribe to clients correct Christian role behavior as husband, wife, mother, or daughter. As psychotherapists we claim expertise in utilizing language to create contexts in which previously unsolvable problems can become solvable. As in this case, we do not have in mind one correct path that we believe the relationship impasse should follow in its resolution. We work instead to provide conditions under which participants in the problem can create a solution that is acceptable to each participant.

One can see in this example the power of psychodrama to offer multiple vantage points from which a client can see new perspectives. One can also see how interventive questions, incorporated into the psychodrama dialogue, invite surprise and creativity into stale conversations that have heretofore led nowhere. A starting point appears from which a new story can be told, a story whose constraints upon the relationship present invite healing rather than pain. In many psychotherapies, as with Martha and Deborah, this story of healing can be anchored upon the God-constructs residing within those languaging about the problem at hand if the psychotherapist so chooses to inquire.

SUMMARY

The intrapersonal image of God, or *God-construct*, holds therapeutic possibilities that have been relatively unexplored in family therapy. We propose that a family member's relationship with his or her God-construct provides a readily available resource for a family therapist working to catalyze change in a family.

As a universal cognitive structure, a God-construct develops in an analogous manner to that of other stable, intrapersonal presences of parenting figures (internalized objects). Its epigenesis can be explained using Piaget's concept of a cognitive *scheme* whose organization drifts along with a child's life experiences. When *organizational closure* occurs, the God-scheme becomes a stable, autonomous inner presence that participates in intrapersonal conversations with the child. Yet, in the same way that the earliest images of parents that have been constructed by a small child can change over time as relationship with parents mature, so it is possible for a primitive God-construct of childhood to change and mature.

Change in the quality of dialogue between God-construct and self is one path to problem resolution both for individual problems and those found in family relationships. Within a family member, intrapersonal conversations between self and God-construct bias selection of events to be noticed among all those happening in his or her life space and bias selection of behaviors employed in relationships with other people. These conversations can thus constrain some relationships, while facilitating others. God, although an invisible member of the family, nevertheless comes to influence powerfully family relationships.

As with human conversations, those between self and God-construct may foster suffering when the conversation is a stagnant, monological encounter, yet become a source of new ideas and creative change when transformed into a rich dialogue. As an expert in the art of dialogue, a therapist can prepare the way for new conversations to be born between self and God-construct within a client.

REFERENCE NOTES

1. Griffith, J.L. 1986. Employing the God-family relationship in therapy with religious families. *Family Process* 25:609-618.

2. Beit-Hallahmi, B. and Argyle, M. 1975. God as a father-projection: the theory and the evidence. *British Journal of Medical Psychology* 48:71-75.

3. Rizzuto, A.M. 1979. *The Birth of the Living God.* Chicago: University of Chicago Press.

4. Ginsburg, H. and Opper, S. 1979. *Piaget's Theory of Intellectual Development, Second Edition.* Englewood Cliffs, NJ: Prentice-Hall.

5. Glasefeld, E. 1988. The reluctance to change a way of thinking. *Irish Journal of Psychology* 9:83-90.

6. Rizzuto, *op. cit.*

7. Ibid.

8. Griffith, J.L., Griffith, M.E., Roth, S.A., Fischer-Bross, L.A., and Freedle, J. 1988. The God-construct and change in religious families. Workshop presented at the 46th Annual Conference of the American Association for Marriage and Family Therapy, New Orleans.

9. Griffith, J.L., Griffith, M.E., and Roth, S.A. (Submitted for publication, 1990.) The God-construct and change in religious families.

10. Griffith, Griffith, Roth, Fischer-Bross, and Freedle, *op. cit.*

11. Griffith, Griffith, and Roth, *op. cit.*
12. Varela, F.J. 1979. *Principles of Biological Autonomy.* New York: Elsevier North Holland, pp. 55-57.
13. Rizzuto, *op. cit.*
14. Ibid.
15. Ibid.
16. Ibid.
17. Ibid.
18. Griffith, *op. cit.*
19. Griffith, Griffith, Roth, Fischer-Bross, and Freedle, *op. cit.*
20. Griffith, Griffith, and Roth, *op. cit.*
21. Anderson, H. and Goolishian, H.A. 1988. Human systems as linguistic systems: preliminary and evolving ideas about the implications for clinical theory. *Family Process* 27:371-393.
22. Braten, S. 1987. Paradigms of autonomy: dialogical or monological? In *Autopoiesis in Law and Society*, G. Geubner (ed.). New York: De Gruyter.
23. Griffith, Griffith, and Roth, *op. cit.*
24. Leveton, I. 1977. *Psychodrama for the Timid Clinician.* New York: Stinger Publishing Co.
25. Varela, *op. cit.*
26. Anderson and Goolishian, *op. cit.*
27. Braten, *op. cit.*
28. Ibid.
29. Griffith, *op. cit.*
30. Griffith, Griffith, Roth, Fischer-Bross, and Freedle, *op. cit.*
31. Griffith, Griffith, and Roth, *op. cit.*
32. Leveton, *op. cit.*
33. Warner, D. *Psychodrama Training Tips, Vol. I and II.* Psychodrama Training Program, 326 Summit Ave., Hagerstown, MD 21740.
34. Griffith, *op. cit.*
35. Griffith, Griffith, Roth, Fischer-Bross, and Freedle, *op. cit.*
36. Griffith, Griffith, and Roth, *op. cit.*
37. Anderson and Goolishian, *op. cit.*
38. Penn, P. 1985. Feed forward: future question, future maps. *Family Process* 24: 299-310.
39. Tomm, K. 1988. Interventive interviewing: part III. Intending to ask lineal, circular, strategic, or reflexive questions? *Family Process* 27:1-15.
40. Varela, *op. cit.*
41. White, M. 1988. The process of questioning: a therapy of literary merit? *Dulwich Centre Newsletter* Winter 8-14.
42. Tomm, *op. cit.*
43. White, M. 1986. Negative explanation, restraint, and double description: a template for family therapy. *Family Process* 25:169-184.
44. Tomm, K. 1987. Interventive interviewing: part II. Reflexive questioning as a means to enable self-healing. *Family Process* 26:167-183.

45. Tomm, 1988, *op. cit.*

46. White, 1988, *op. cit.*

47. Fleuridas, C., Nelson, T.S., and Rosenthal, D.M. 1986. The evolution of circular question: training family therapists. *Journal of Marital and Family Therapy* 12:113-127.

48. Selvini-Palazzoli, M., Boscolo, L., Cecchin, G., and Prata, G. 1980. Hypothesizing-circularity-neutrality: three guidelines for conductor of the session. *Family Process* 19:3-12.

49. Tomm, 1988, *op. cit.*

50. Penn, *op. cit.*

51. Tomm, 1987, *op. cit.*

52. White, 1988, *op. cit.*

53. Tomm, 1987, *op. cit.*

54. Tomm, 1988, *op. cit.*

55. White, 1988, *op. cit.*

56. White, 1986, *op. cit.*

57. White, 1988, *op. cit.*

58. Leveton, *op. cit.*

59. Ibid.

60. Ibid.

Chapter Five

Spirituality and Systems Therapy: Partners in Clinical Practice

Douglas A. Anderson, PhD

AN ILLUSTRATION

A colleague shared with me the following experience of one of her friends. The friend had phoned to ask her to have lunch, sounding distraught. At lunch the friend related that her 18-year-old daughter had announced the night before that she was moving to live with her boyfriend in his apartment. The mother had been shocked and hurt by this announcement. Her husband had been enraged. He told their daughter that if she did this they would never see her again. Both parents assumed that this threat would be a deterrent since their relationship with their daughter had been fairly close. Instead, their daughter had stormed angrily out of the house and had not returned.

During the course of the next year, the mother made several attempts to convince her daughter to return home, but neither daughter nor parents would yield. As time passed, the mother felt torn between her principles and her longing to see her daughter. Her husband's position had become further entrenched, and he refused even to discuss the matter.

Sometime later the mother had a dream in which she and her husband were walking home in a terrible blizzard. The wind was blowing directly at them and they were wet and chilled and exhausted. They had several more miles to go and she knew they would not make it. She became aware that they were the only two people out in the storm. If they fell, no one would ever find them before they froze to death. She began to panic.

Just then a cottage they were passing lit up and she saw two beautiful children at the window. The children knocked on the window and beckoned for them to come in, calling out, "It's cozy and warm in here!" The mother felt a surge of relief and ran to the door. She turned the door knob, but the door did not open. The children continued to beckon as she tried to explain that the knob didn't work. The sound of the wind kept drowning out her voice. Finally, they seemed to understand. One called out, "It's a latch." The mother looked and called back, "No. It's a knob." This exchange continued for a number of times while the woman kept turning the knob and growing more irritated. She shouted at the children crossly, "Why don't you open it for me?" They looked hurt, as if they were about to cry. She insisted, "Well, why don't you open it?" The children looked puzzled and one said, "Because you have to see that it's a latch." The woman looked again. It was a knob. She grew angry, but the children just looked at her sadly. She shouted, "Latches lift up!" The children looked at each other excitedly and then back at her. "That's it," she thought, "Lift up, lift up!" She placed her hand under the knob and lifted as if it were a latch. The knob moved up and the door swung open. The children embraced her. They pulled her to the sofa by the fire, climbed into her lap and went to sleep. Their bodies and the fire warmed her. She felt incredibly happy. She looked up toward the door, which was still open. Her husband was not there. She had assumed he was right behind her. She kept staring at the door, wondering if he would appear. Suddenly she was afraid and woke up from the dream.

She awakened her husband and told him the dream. She said that she believed it to be a message from God. Her husband wept. They held each other. The next morning they telephoned their daughter and soon they met with her and reconciled.

INTRODUCTION

This experience of an actual American family resembles a number that I have come across in my vocation as a pastoral counselor. Time and again I have met families who are thoroughly stuck in a disagreement or in a family life cycle passage. Movement from either side of the dilemma seems impossible. Then something unexpected occurs that breaks the impasse and the persons involved move beyond, their relationship changed. These experiences stimulate in me a deep sense of wonder at the mystery of human change.

Like many of my colleagues I have not been content to stay with my wonder but have pursued means of making sense of this mystery. Two contemporary paradigms for understanding human experience have been of most help to me in this endeavor: the revived interest in spirituality and spiritual guidance and the growing interest in applications of systems theory to psychotherapy. While these are two quite separate and distinct modes of interpreting the human condition, taken together they help illuminate numerous experiences of human "stuckness" and human change that I meet in clinical practice.

In what follows I want to share my understanding of these two paradigms, describe how they both can help enlighten human experience, and then draw some implications for the functioning of the pastoral counselor. I will then relate a case study of pastoral counseling with another family struggling with a young adult emancipating from home, this time from the perspective of the young adult.

PARADIGM ONE: SPIRITUALITY

The first paradigm is that of spirituality or spiritual guidance. In a recent book exemplative of the revival of interest in this field, Nelson Thayer defined spirituality as ". . . the specifically human capacity to experience, be conscious of, and relate to a dimension of power and meaning transcendent to the world of sensory reality . . . and leads toward action congruent with its meaning."[1] Two parts of this definition seem important to me. First, spirituality has to do with our experience of *relating* to something beyond ourselves. Second, spirituality involves us in *behavioral responses* to that transcendent experience.

Similarly, Gerald May in his important work, *Will and Spirit*, views "spirit" as a vital energy that expresses itself in a process of *connecting*.[2] Spirit connects us with each other, with the world that is our context, and with the Mystery that transcends us and our world. May contrasts "spirit" with "will," a second vital human dimension that expresses itself in our moving toward separateness, independence, and personal autonomy, in contrast to the interdependence of spirit.

From these two human dimensions May describes two contrasting attitudes toward life, "willingness" and "willfulness." Willingness is a response of wonder and appreciation toward the cosmos, a surrendering of one's separateness, and a commitment to participate in the mystery of life. Willfulness is setting oneself apart from life in an attempt to master, control, or explain it. May concludes that since both these processes are vital to human life, something deep inside us longs for a reconciliation of the autonomous qualities of will with the unifying qualities of spirit. Because of the predisposition of will to control, however, this integration needs to be one with spirit in charge of will.

Spiritual guidance or direction is a process in which one person assists another toward that integration of will and spirit and toward connection with the Transcendent. The goal of the process is an increased willingness to say "yes" to the Mystery of life and experience of unity with the creation and its Creator. Kenneth Leech has defined the role of the spiritual guide as that of a "soul friend," who as a fellow seeker directs one's attention toward the ultimate spiritual direction, the Holy Spirit.[3] It is the Holy Spirit who draws the seeker into closer union with God. The spiritual guide teaches the seeker to listen for the Holy Spirit's voice in the events of one's own life. The result of participating in a process of spiritual guidance is an increased sensitivity to listen for God in the circumstances of one's own life and to respond to God with willingness.

When I reflected upon the experience of the family with which I began this chapter from the perspective of spiritual guidance, I realized that the Holy Spirit's voice could be heard in the wife's dream. The dream can be seen as a call to let go of willfulness, for both the parents and the daughter to "lift up" in an attitude of willingness. What enabled the family to move past their impasse was exactly such a response of "yes" to that transcendent voice, enacted by the parents contacting their daughter to seek reconciliation. The result was a deepened connection with each other and with God.

PARADIGM TWO: SYSTEMS THEORY

The second paradigm for understanding human existence that has helped me in my work is that of systems approaches to psychotherapy. Systems approaches view the person not as a separate individual but as existing in a context of relationships. Central to this context is a family organization that evolves patterns of interaction among its members. These patterns shape the behavior and feelings of the family's members and help maintain a family worldview and family organization. Therapeutic change results from altering those patterns. The therapist leads a challenge of a family's world view and organization in order to stimulate a search for new patterns. In Minuchin's words, ". . . the old order must be undermined to allow for the formation of the new."[4]

A number of systems therapists extend the view of family organization to see the family as composed of three or more generations, each generation influencing the others in a reciprocal process termed "intergenerational connectedness."[5] How each generation handles its life cycle tasks affects how each of the other generations deals with their own tasks. For example, how one's parents left home as young adults influences how their young adult children leave, and how those parents are dealing now with the challenges of the empty nest and the aging of their own parents affects the young adults in their leaving process and vice versa.

Problems in families occur most frequently at the transition points between stages of the family life cycle. For the interdependent generations to move together into a new stage, the "old order" of their patterns of relating to each other must be altered. Perhaps the most difficult transition of all is that of parents and their young adult children "letting go of each other"[6] as the young adults take up the task of forming a new family, the situation experienced by the family I described at the beginning of this chapter.

The dilemma of this family illustrates how family members most commonly get "stuck" in a life cycle transition. They begin to blame other family members for making them unhappy and to demand that they change their behavior. To enforce this demand, they may cut themselves off from the others emotionally and sometimes physically.

A systems-oriented therapist moves to interrupt this blaming and distancing behavior by encouraging the complaining family member to develop curiosity about the other family members. The therapist then coaches them to exercise this curiosity by recontacting the other members for the purpose of getting to know them. They are encouraged to view these family members as human beings with strengths and weaknesses and to appreciate them for their uniqueness. As one such therapist, James Framo, has written: "Few people ever get to know their parents as real people, few families ever share, all together as a family, the really meaningful thoughts and feelings, and few people get to that last stage with parents, that of forgiving them and telling them they are loved."[7]

I would add to Framo's words that this applies equally to parents getting to know their children as real, separate people and expressing acceptance and forgiveness of them. Such a reconnecting of generations was the experience of the family I described earlier. The image in the mother's dream in which the children embraced her by the warm fire is a wonderful symbol of this process. The reconnection this family experienced made it possible for its members to move through this most difficult life cycle passageway and to do so with deepened understanding of and appreciation for one another.

SOME COMMONALITIES AND DIFFERENCES

While I have described the two paradigms of spiritual guidance and systems therapy separately, I know that the two share some common beliefs and goals. Both emphasize the relational character of human life and the goal of restoring severed relationships. Both encourage people to translate their beliefs into actions congruent with those beliefs. Both share a cosmos-wide vision of the interdependence of all things. I find it fascinating to turn from reading a book on creation-centered spirituality by Matthew Fox, such as *A Spirituality Named Compassion*, to a book by systems scientist Kenneth Boulding, such as *The World as a Total System*, and see this common vision.[8] Fox portrays the "interconnectedness of all creatures." Boulding envisions all of reality connected in a series of levels of systems of increasing complexity, from very simple inanimate systems through highly complex social systems and all the way to an ultimate level of "transcendental systems."

Although these two paradigms have much in common, their distinctiveness needs to be kept in view. Spiritual guidance is a theological paradigm, while the systems therapies are of the behavioral sciences. These two disciplines represent two language worlds that interpret human experience from quite different core images.[9] Spiritual guidance conceives of a theistic world grounded in a personal god, a relationship with whom is the purpose of human life. The behavioral sciences hold a humanistic world view lacking that theistic end goal.

CONVERGENCE

When applied to human experience in their distinct separateness, the two paradigms are of most value to the pastoral counselor and offer mutual correction of each other's viewpoint. For example, a systems perspective can correct a tendency religious people sometimes have of over-identifying spirituality with inner experiences and feelings. Systems thinking refocuses attention upon the realities of our everyday lives as lived in the context of external relationships. This can result in a broadened understanding of spirituality such as Ernest Boyer's conception of family life as a spiritual discipline of discovering the presence of God in the midst of the trouble, suffering and routine of relational life.[10] Through concrete experiences of human conflict and caring in our intergenerational families, we find revealed the working of a Divine Love Who matures us in love as we develop as spiritual beings.[11]

Even more important is the corrective that spiritual guidance offers the systems therapies. Systems therapists have a propensity for taking active responsibility for initiating and directing change and for employing interpersonal techniques to accomplish the ends of therapy. A danger of this emphasis is the potential for the counselor to become exhausted from this over-responsibility for the change process. A greater danger is what Gerald May describes as the willful tendency of behavioral science to attempt to provide explanations, control, and mastery to human experience, a tendency that prematurely closes off the encounter of persons with unexplainable

Mystery. May states that behavioral science needs to take a secondary position to spiritual guidance, because in the healing process behavioral science can take people only as far as "... the gateway of meaning. To move through this gateway willfulness must give way to willingness and surrender. Mastery must yield to mystery."[12]

I find it interesting that a number of systems therapists join in cautioning the overemphasis on technology in their field. In workshops I have heard such well-known systems therapists as Carl Whitaker, Fred Duhl, Donald Williamson, Maurizio Andolphi, and Mony Elkaim express this concern. Michael Nichols closed his book surveying the varied schools of family therapy with these words: "Furthermore, the more we talk about techniques, the greater the danger of seeing family therapy as a purely technological enterprise .... Treating families is only an act of science and technology; it is also an act of love."[13]

THREE IMPLICATIONS FOR COUNSELING

Taking together the perspectives of spiritual guidance and systems therapy, while maintaining their distinctiveness, yields for me three basic implications for the functioning of the pastoral counselor.

The first implication is listening for God. The pastoral counselor listens attentively for the inbreaking of the grace of God in the lives of clients and in the counseling hour. In place of willful attempts to change people or to provide them with quick answers to their deepest questions, the counselor manifests "... a radical willingness to be nothing but an instrument through which God's healing and growth can happen."[14] The wisdom of the tradition of spiritual guidance teaches the pastoral counselor to remember that God is the Source of all healing and growth. Counselor and client stand together as potential channels of the grace of God for each other.[15]

In my own practice of pastoral counseling I have learned to orient myself to work in this way. Upon first awakening in the morning I use a period of prayerful meditation to focus my attention upon relying wholly upon God to provide everything I need in each hour of my work. During the counseling session itself I often visualize the presence of the Lord in our midst, extending His care and grace to each person present. As I listen to clients, I ask myself quietly — and sometimes the clients aloud — how might God be active in the events being described or in the process occurring in this room.

A second implication of using the two perspectives is that the pastoral counselor encourages clients to reconnect with family members. When encountering numerous client situations in which people describe dealing with their basic conflicts and differences by distancing from each other, the counselor advocates an opposite attitude of willingness to face the discomfort involved in contacting the members of their family and addressing painful issues. (There are, of course, the obvious exceptions to this principle of those situations in which such contact would be potentially physically dangerous or emotionally destructive for the client.)

For me the key to the process of reconnecting comes in an attitude that is central to both the spiritual and systemic traditions — appreciation. Appreciation is a stance toward other human beings that views them as unique, of great value, and full of beauty, wonder, and mystery. As a pastoral counselor I seek to model this attitude in my behavior toward my counselees so that in turn they may take this stance toward the members of their family. When I prepare counselees for making contact with members of their family of origin, I coach them to approach these persons with genuine curiosity, a desire to come to know them as individuals. I ask them to suspend judgments, tendencies to become argumentative, or wishes to change people and instead to practice listening carefully to what family members reveal of themselves. It is my belief that approaching others with an intention to appreciate them creates an optimal atmosphere for human reconnecting.

A third implication of utilizing the two paradigms is that the pastoral counselor assists clients in making meaning of their life circumstances. Humans are meaning-makers. We have a deep desire to understand the significance of being alive and of the events that compose our life stories. Both of the paradigms that I have been describing grow out of this human tendency to find purpose in our experiences.

While the pastoral counselor may draw upon both of these paradigms to assist clients in making meaning of their lives, the spiritual paradigm becomes the core resource. I noted earlier Gerald May's assertion that behavioral science can only take us to the gateway of meaning, and spirituality is needed to move through it. Charles Gerkin in his book, *The Living Human Document*, similarly posits the primacy of the theological paradigm for this task.[16] Gerkin notes that many persons suffer from distorted images of meaning that they have given to their life stories. They need in a counselor one who will help re-vision their perspective on life, "an interpreter who offers a new possibility of meaning."

In the role of interpreter, the pastoral counselor guides clients to tell their life story, clarify the structure of meaning they have given to it, and then search for new structures of meaning. As Gerkin notes, at the foundation of any structure of meaning lie critical religious questions. In clarifying and speaking to such questions pastoral counselors draw upon understandings from the Judeo-Christian tradition.

In my pastoral counseling practice, I cultivate the art of storytelling. I encourage clients to tell their life stories in concrete detail. As they do, I listen for the interpretations they are giving to their experiences. At the same time I listen for the deeper theological dimensions present. When they have finished, I respond by clarifying the issues I have heard raised and then add new stories of my own that respond to the questions raised in their accounts. The stories I share arise from my understanding of the Judeo-Christian tradition. Most often, they are also stories from my own experience of the faith in my personal and family life.

ANOTHER CASE STUDY

I want to conclude with a case study that involves all I have discussed. A few years ago a man in his late 20s, whom I shall call Joe, came to see me in a pastoral counseling center. Joe expressed concern about his six-year marriage, that he felt he and his wife, Sally, were drifting apart. Joe expressed dissatisfaction with his relational life in work and social settings as well, saying he did not feel close to anyone. In all relationships he said he had a "habit" of avoiding unpleasant subjects in conversations, especially when there was a difference between himself and others. Lately he had been consistently falling asleep at home after dinner, and he believed this was because his wife had recently surfaced some difficulties in their marriage and he wanted to avoid talking with her.

When I asked Joe about his original family, he said that he had been raised in the South by two very strict, conservative Christian parents. His parents and two siblings still lived in the South and Joe had seen them only infrequently since his marriage and move to the North. Joe's parents had raised all three of their children to suppress any expression of "negative" emotions. Joe had grown up accommodating to his parents as a "good child" but did not feel close to them nor his siblings. He had early adopted the religion of his parents' fundamentalist church, which he now had come to view as governed by black and white rules. He no longer attended church but was working out some beliefs of his own. However, he described feeling God as very distant. I noticed that Joe dressed in conservative clothing of dark, subdued colors and that he sat erect. He spoke in an even tone with little expression of emotion.

I suggested that Joe come in for the second session with his wife. He agreed, and for the next several months I saw both Joe and Sally, usually in conjoint sessions. For the sake of brevity, I will describe here only what unfolded with Joe over that time. After several months Joe and Sally mutually decided to separate. Joe wrote his parents to inform them of this decision. His parents replied with a letter addressed to Joe and Sally strongly critical of their decision.

Joe promptly telephoned his parents and for the first time in his life stood up to them. He told them he was angry at their response and that they did not understand all that he and Sally had gone through. Further, he told them that they had never known him as a person, having always treated him as a role.

In the two weeks after this phone call Joe had three remarkable dreams in vivid color. Joe saw this as most unusual as always before his dreams had been in black and white and were so uninteresting to him that he did not remember their content. When he came in with Sally for the next session, he was animated and told me the three dreams in detail.

Briefly summarized, they were as follows. In the first dream Joe saw himself in his and Sally's bedroom staring at a bright light fixture overhead that was ringed by dead flowers. Out of the light fixture flew a large spider with bat-like wings that looked like it was made out of stained glass. Joe felt unafraid of the spider. He went to where it alighted and killed it with one blow from a shoe. One of the wings flew out and landed beside Joe. He picked it up and held it in his hand, admiring it and feeling a strong sense of wonder about it.

In a second dream Joe saw himself in his bedroom in the house he had grown up in. His attention was captured by the unusual sight of a large and very beautiful impatiens plant hanging from the ceiling. Two bright-colored birds flew near it. When Joe noticed the bedroom window was closed so the birds couldn't get out, he opened the window. He then saw his mother in the room. She gently took one of the birds in her hands and carried it to the now open window, releasing it. Joe now noticed that the second bird had also gotten outside and the two birds were playing together in a tree in the yard.

In the third dream Joe saw himself at a church picnic of his childhood church. In the distance he saw three tornadoes approaching. He alerted the other people at the picnic and everyone started running, with the tornadoes pursuing them. Suddenly the tornadoes changed from being dark, ominous clouds into swirling, multi-colored lights of great beauty. One of the swirling lights went up the back of one of the men, and he was unhurt by it. At this point, Joe awakened, again feeling unafraid.

When I asked Joe what interested him about the three dreams, he replied, "All the bright colors." (I noticed that in recent weeks Joe had begun dressing in more brightly-colored clothing, considerably less conservative than when I first met him.) Joe also connected a number of the symbols in the dreams to his childhood religion, particularly the stained-glass wings and the dried-up flowers. He added that the religion of his childhood now seemed like dead flowers and he was seeking a more lively faith. Joe was also interested in the feelings in the dreams of being unafraid and full of wonderment.

I told Joe that I was interested in all these details and also in the role his mother played in the middle dream. Joe said that scene had seemed remarkable to him, but he did not understand it.

Shortly after this Joe began planning to visit his parents. I saw him alone for several sessions to prepare for his visit. Through these meetings I encouraged Joe to develop curiosity about his parents and to use the visit to get to know them. Instead of arguing with them about their religious views, I suggested he inquire about how they had come to their beliefs and how these beliefs differed from ones Joe was developing for himself. We also prepared a list of personal issues Joe wanted to discuss with them, the most important being his decision to separate from Sally and his parents' reaction to it. In our last session before Joe's trip, we role-played potential conversations with each of his parents, with Joe practicing non-defensive and appreciative responses to his parents.

Joe talked eagerly at his appointment following his return from his visit. The first words he said to me were "I had a *surprising* visit!" He had been most surprised to learn that his parents had not been the people he had remembered them to be. They had both received him very warmly, and he had numerous personal talks with them individually. He learned many things about them and was able to tell them a lot about who he had become. For Joe most surprising of all was their readiness to hear about his decision to separate and the full acceptance of him and his decision both parents conveyed to him.

One day talking alone with his mother, Joe had told her how he had feared talking to her about the separation. Mother had replied: "Joe, I'm your mother. It is my nature to love you. You can do anything you choose. You are separate from me and don't need my approval." For Joe this was his mother putting into words what he had already experienced in the visit — a separation of love from approval.

In a subsequent session I asked Joe to reflect upon this experience in relation to what he had described to me of his childhood religion. Joe discussed how he must have for a long time viewed God as Someone whose approval he needed to have but could not attain. I suggested that perhaps God was also speaking to him in the words of his mother: "It is my nature to love you." I wanted to share some of my understanding of the nature of God from my Lutheran Christian tradition and my own experience of God's loving me in my life story.

Joe then raised that the place where his understanding of the God of the Bible was most difficult at this time was the issue of divorce.

He had internalized the teaching from his childhood church that divorce was always forbidden by God. His strong feelings about this issue were making it difficult for him either to think clearly about a decision about his marriage or to discuss it fruitfully with Sally. I shared my understanding of the issue theologically, referring to mine as *one* Christian perspective, and suggested that we resume sessions with Sally present for them to talk about this issue together.

In the conjoint sessions that followed, Joe and Sally talked openly about their feelings and beliefs. I noted the results of Joe's visit to his parents in the new level of openness with which he was able to talk with Sally. The opening of channels of communication enabled Joe and Sally to come to a clear resolution of their decision about their marriage. Along the way, Joe also reported an increased level of openness in other friendships and his satisfaction that these relationships were growing to deeper levels of closeness.

I learned a lot from the two years of meeting with Joe and Sally. Most of what I have written about in this chapter stems from experiences with clients like them. As I listened to Joe I heard the inbreaking of the grace of God in his life through the marital crisis, the colorful dreams and the "surprising" visit with his parents. I learned the value of Joe gathering the courage to talk openly with his parents about the issues that mattered most to him and his coming to appreciate his parents as real people. I also learned to trust further my own openness about my experiences of God's love in sharing my faith explicitly with him.

My time with Joe and Sally closed, as it so often has for me with clients, in a deepening wonder at the mystery of human change and a growing appreciation for the grace at work in all our lives.

REFERENCE NOTES

1. Thayer, N. 1985. *Spirituality and Pastoral Care*. Philadelphia: Fortress Press, p. 55.

2. May, G. 1982. *Will and Spirit*. New York. Harper and Row, pp. 2-6.

3. Leech, K. 1980. *Soul Friend*. New York: Harper and Row, pp. 34 and 89.

4. Minuchin, S. and Fishman, H. 1981. *Family Therapy Techniques*. Cambridge, MA: Harvard University Press, p. 67.

5. Carter, E. and McGoldrick, M. (eds.). 1980. *The Family Life Cycle: A Framework for Family Therapy*. New York: Gardner Press, pp. 6-11.

6. Anderson, D. 1980. *New Approaches to Family Pastoral Care*. Philadelphia: Fortress Press, pp. 20-21.

7. Framo, J. 1981. "The integration of marital therapy with sessions with family of origin" in A. Gurman and O. Kniskern (eds.), *Handbook of Family of Therapy*. New York: Brunner/Mazel, p. 144.

8. Fox, M. 1979. *A Spirituality Named Compassion*. Minneapolis: Winston Press. And Boulding, K. 1985. *The World as a Total System*. Beverly Hills: Sage Publications.

9. Gerkin, C. 1984. *The Living Human Document*. Nashville: Abingdon Press, p. 19.

10. Boyer, E. Jr. 1984. *A Way in the World*. New York: Harper and Row.

11. Anderson, D. 1985. "Marriage as sacred mystery: Some theological reflections on the purposes of marriage." *Word and World*, 5, p. 364-69.

12. May, *op. cit.*

13. Nichols, M. 1984. *Family Therapy*. New York: Gardner Press, p. 572.

14. May, *op. cit.*, p. 295.

15. May, G. 1982. *Care of Mind/Care of Spirit*. New York: Harper and Row, p. 15.

16. Gerkin, *op. cit.*

Chapter Six

Mixing Oil and Water Religiously: Counseling Interfaith Families

Lucinda S. Duncan, MDiv

INTRODUCTION

As a figure of speech, "mixing oil and water," is an oxymoron for it juxtaposes improbable opposites into a single phrase. As a scientific experiment, mixing oil and water is something any observer could tell you is impossible. As a metaphor for religiously mixed marriages, however, "mixing oil and water" is neither a figure of speech nor a scientific experiment. It is an observable fact of life routinely experienced by couples who do not share similar religious backgrounds. Yet it is more than a fact of life. It is also a feeling that interfaith couples sometimes express about their growing sense of religious loss or inability to understand one another's motivations and responses. In this way, "mixing oil and water religiously" metaphorically taps a deeply felt fear that a sense of religious "at-homeness" or of genuine understanding and mutuality may never again be reached.

Yet in another, more domestically-oriented way, the "mixing oil and water" analogy can be applied to a situation of hope. Every Southern cook knows that by adding a variety of colorful emulsifiers to the basic ingredients of oil and water and by vigorously stirring everything together, something new is created which is thicker, more colorful, and infinitely more flavorful! While there is such a thing as over-extending a figure of speech, it does not seem inappropriate to speak of the purpose of this paper optimistically — to visualize it perhaps as a contribution of ingredients that may help to "bind" interfaith couples into new constructions of meaning based on mutual insight, if not empathy. My goal is to empower interfaith couples to appreciate the importance of each person's religious outlook and to help couples to begin to anticipate that different constructions of reality will necessarily produce gaps in communication and understanding.

Perhaps I leave this description of various "oil and water" analogies on a hopeful note because interfaith marriages are like all marriages in that they rarely begin with a bleak assessment of difficulties to be faced. When two people are in love, they envision happiness as stretching endlessly beyond the horizon. The fact that interfaith couples bring two separate ways of seeing the horizon, not to mention different ways of identifying "pitfalls," is characteristically denied or minimized. Everyone believes him or herself the potential exception to the apparent rule. Thus not only is it axiomatic that newly married couples believe in love's ability to transcend or solve difficulties, it is also precisely such faith that perpetuates the institution of marriage. Yet love alone is rarely able to bridge all interfaith differences. Even when one or both partners claim to be "uninterested" in the faith structures of their families, or when one partner agrees to attend the other's worship services and to respect the other's differences, situations arise, problems are named, and solutions are formed that express more about the pervasiveness of each partner's religious perspective than either could have anticipated.

Special help is needed, but it is rarely available. The customary solution of enrolling in a "crash course," often at the church or synagogue for a few consecutive weeks, is—while helpful—more of a practical coping activity for interfaith couples. What is needed first is a way to get a handle on the concept of faith structure and family systems and to develop a way to discuss these in personal terms that enable trust to be built, not destroyed. Common coordinates are needed to structure discussion if all involved are to be able to look for, describe, and reflect on the dynamics of their personal religious understandings.

To accomplish this, or rather to move us in this direction, an interdisciplinary approach has been adopted. This paper of necessity will be primarily philosophical in its description of interfaith marriages as the coming together not of just two people, but of two different systems of meaning. This component will discuss faith structures, boundary lines, and how the coordinates of power, affect, and meaning could help us to distinguish between three representative religious faith structures considered in this paper: Unitarian Universalism, Judaism, and Christianity.

Not only do couples need to learn how to speak and to hear what the other means, but together they would be helped by understanding some of the dynamics of multi-generational family loyalty demonstrations. This part of my discussion will draw from family systems' theory.

This approach to interfaith dialogue is based on the assumption that each person's religious heritage and accompanying set of perspectives are valid and important. It respects individuals' abilities to make sense of religion in their own way. It is fully confident that all people possess the ability to combine both intuitions and reason to reconstruct or contribute to a faith outlook that will nourish them emotionally and help them to make sense of their lives. It acknowledges that there are many variables and personal approaches to religious understanding within even the most apparently monolithic faith structures. As such, this approach stands prepared to help specific individuals in whatever religious context, whether it be church affiliated or a personal stance, to better appreciate the parameters and requirements of their and their partner's faith perspective.

Accordingly, the understanding intended for the term "interfaith" dialogue is that "faith" should be viewed in the broadest possible terms. It is my contention that faith derives as importantly from the underlying sets of cultural-linguistic understandings as it does from the more visible parameters of a particular religion. Even people who think of themselves as peripheral to religious institutions operate from a faith stance, whether they call themselves "secular humanists" or "lapsed Catholics." The process of living requires that meaning be construed by life's events and cultural context. Sartre's observation that all people are "stalkers of meaning" is true, but what people ultimately grab a hold of is determined by the cultural-linguistic lens they use to see what is there.

This approach will focus on the religious faith structures of Judaism, Christianity, and Unitarian Universalism, but it is not limited to theistic conceptions of ultimate power. Humanism and other non-theistic faith structures are equally respected.

APPROACHING FAITH STRUCTURES: BOUNDARIES AND COORDINATES

The term "faith structure" refers to the structural characteristics of a *religious* world view.[1] Broadly speaking, a faith structure is a cultural-linguistic context for perceiving and responding to life experience. It relates to faith because, although every person must make meaning out of life, its meaning-making has been named and organized by the religious dimension. It is a structure because it locates and names the nature of God (or ultimate authority), accounts for and defines human nature, and lays out *patterns* of individual and societal relationships.

In many ways it resembles Thomas Kuhn's classic definition of a "paradigm" as "an entire constellation of beliefs, values, techniques, and so on shared by the members of a given community."[2] Yet Kuhn's paradigms are expressive of a meaning-making structure that is explicitly *scientific* in orientation and results. Both faith structures and scientific paradigms direct our attention to the multi-generational patterning which characterize every person's family of origin. Both structures understand that it is the emotional and rational milieu into which people are born and first begin to sort through meaning, which determines deeply ingrained patterns of thought and observation. If this is true to a greater or lesser degree, then each person is born into a cultural linguistic faith structure, which is then reinterpreted, rejected, or reinforced by critical meaning-making experiences occurring throughout their growing-up years.[3]

What emerges from these critical years is an imprint of our own distinctive theology, which stands in dynamic relationship to our family's practices and beliefs. Our theology is how we attempt to express the religious world view which determines how we experience everyday life. It expresses what we see and what we fail to notice,[4] how we conceptualize, the grammar and vocabulary of our language, and how we arrive at our personal sense of appropriate responsibility and role.

While theological perspective springs from and is confirmed by ordinary experience, the activity of theological construction begins with the reflective assessment of what we are doing or believing and why. Much theological expression is unpretentious. We all seek to make meaning of life's experiences, to interpret how and why good and bad things occur, to place ourselves in relationship to knowledge and power. Theological construction is the activity of interpreting our own or of comparing others' religious world views. It is the ability to reflect on the structure of meaning itself—to see it as the scaffolding that surrounds and determines our personal perspectives. It is to understand ourselves as having the critical and reflective skills to assess which scaffolding best helps us to live according to our personal understandings.

Burton employs a structural approach (grounded in the work of Kantor and Lehr) to the explanation of religious world views.[5] He calls them "faith structures" and demonstrates that each faith structure contains a story that explains, a style that expresses, and a structure that manages. He names and explains three distinctive styles of pastoral response that reflect each faith structure: the traditional, the negotiating, and the individualistic responses. Burton's concern was to help ministers understand the extent to which they perceive and react to problems according to how each faith structure operates. His psychological, process-oriented description of different decision making models draws attention to the interfaces between the minister's manner of resolving issues and the congregation's faith stance prescription for the response to problems. Does the congregation's faith structure lead them to expect solutions to be handed down from minister to the people, for example? Does it expect a collaborative partnership between the minister and the congregation? Or does the congregation's structure locate both the responsibility and the authority for solving problems with the people?

Burton's *minister*-oriented faith structure model suggested to me the educational benefit of comparing and contrasting the essential configurations of three distinctive *religions'* faith structures: the Jewish, the Christian, and the Unitarian Universalist. Rather than employing Burton's descriptive categories of ministerial relationship to power, however, I will use the coordinates of *power, affect,* and *meaning* to pull forth each faith structure's distinctive character. As what is emphasized in each faith structure becomes clear, the visualization of "boundaries" (allowing or preventing passage into each particular faith structure) will complete the picture. It is important to keep in mind that the focus on each faith structure's dominant coordinate is not in any way meant to be reductive. Each faith structure contains and relies upon all three coordinates. The purpose of focusing on the dominant coordinate of each is to provide a structural reference and an accessible vocabulary to enable thoughtful assessment of similarities and differences.

When I speak of the *power* coordinate, I am looking at how the faith structure assigns ultimate authority—to whom or what does the ultimate source of power belong? Note that I refer to ultimate authority as that power which renews when all else fails. Theistically, this power may be understood as God with uncounted variations. Humanistically, this power is believed to reside in and to be created by human beings, again with multiples of variations. While political power often parallels in an attempt to replicate the understanding of where ultimate authority is found, political power is not what is meant in this discussion.

The *affect* coordinate refers to all the ways in which a faith structures the expression of feelings and behaviors related to nurturing connection. It is the corporeal side of religious experience; the "doing/being" of the covenant. It includes the verbal, but goes far beyond the rational-cognitive. The affective components of a faith structure are all those things that make up the process of doing. They include feeling, seeing, speaking, hearing, singing, chanting, moving, touching, smelling, behaving, and visualizing. Through the affective an intuitive sense of intimate primary relationship is established.

The *meaning* coordinate isolates the central truth of a particular faith structure. All faith structures include multiple layers of meaning, each of which is interpreted in a divergent spectrum of ways. This can be confusing, or even appear to provide the basis for judging some as "true believers" and others as "heretics." This happens in every religion, for the existence of a faith structure cannot preclude broad variations of culture, origin, and circumstance from affecting the expression of meaning. Within Christianity, for example, there are so many variations of interpretation and emphasis that one might be tempted to exclude one or more denominations from qualifying as "real Christians." Yet meaning, in the context of this paper, is intended to pinpoint that which is the unifying linchpin for the faith structure as a whole. It is the central understanding, no matter how variously it is interpreted. As such, it is meaning that protects the continuity of affect.

Gordon D. Kaufman, Harvard Divinity School professor of theology, makes the case that the essential coordinate of each faith structure is the way in which it locates, speaks about, and responds to God.[6] Yet "God," as understood in this way, becomes a three-letter concept or image that represents the location of ultimate power. As such it does not have to be the traditionally conceived "wholly other" notion of God; it can just as legitimately apply to that which emanates from and is expressed by human creativity.

If the power coordinate is seen as a religious term, it assumes a transcendent quality that places people in holy relationship with that which extends beyond human capacities. If the power coordinate is seen humanistically, then the notion of that which renews when all else fails can be the human spirit in cooperation with or in defiance of denial of a God-concept.

For our purposes the most important aspect of the power coordinate is not whether or not it is theistic, but how it operates to shape understandings of human nature and the world. It never operates independently of the entire faith structure. Because "God is the idea of that on which all else depends," argues Kaufman in his book, *An Essay on Theological Method*, it cannot stand alone.[7] "God is not an isolated term in the language . . . rather . . . *the key term* in a complex of meanings which is intended to grasp all experience and reality."[8]

In the context of an interfaith marriage, say between a Christian and a Jew, both partners subconsciously pull their essential understandings of what life is like and what religious devotion means from this foundational power coordinate. They may see it as an understanding of God; they may see it as a questioning or refutation of God; they may see it as a celebration of the human spirit. The power coordinate approach is not intended to deny the power and authority of God in a particular faith structure, nor is it designed to belittle or to relativize that which is known as God or ultimate power. It is intended to suggest, however, that the structure of *all* understanding, and not just of liturgical practices, reflects the life-ordering patterns that flow logically and emotionally from humanity's deepest sense of where and how ultimate power resides.

The religious tendency to equate "God" with "ultimate power" is particularly difficult for interfaith couples where one or both of them thinks of themselves as "atheist" or "agnostic" in their faith orientation. What this structural approach to religious paradigms suggests is that even our uncertainties are conditioned by the faith structure's posited certainties—even our self-definition is bounded by the prescription for communal or liturgical behaviors.

The situation is not so clearly reactive when it comes to the location and understandings of humanism. Unlike atheist rejections and agnostic musings, humanism is defined by what it is for, not what it is against. Humanists' pragmatism leads to a reluctance to postulate a premise about God as the power coordinate. They cannot prove that God exists, although they know that science and religion ask the same foundational questions about origin. Because they cannot find a transcendent power, they choose to see reality through human lenses.

Humanists' positive assessment of the marvelous capacity of human reason and creative expression may not close out the possibility of a transcendent power. Some believe in the possibility that a Grand Unification Theory will ultimately be understood as true. This leads some humanists to define themselves as "humanists *first.*" I suspect this is not so much a difference of naming ultimate power as it is the difference between the religious and the scientific approaches to meaning-making. What matters for interfaith family counselors is that we realize that the location and naming of the source of ultimate power may be given different parameters by interfaith couples, but that every faith structure contains a power coordinate.

The importance of the power coordinate does not diminish the coordinates of affect and meaning, however. All three aspects are present in every person and each religion's faith structures. What distinguishes one person's faith stance from another or one religion's configuration from another's is the way in which one of the coordinates is emphasized over the other two. Seeing how the three coordinates are viewed and stressed enables us to construct faith structure models of Judaism, Christianity, and Unitarian Universalism which look quite different. At the risk of over-simplification and for the purpose of creating a clarity of contrast to use in work with interfaith couples, I will argue that each of the three religious perspectives is shaped by a dominant coordinate. The dominance of affect distinguishes Judaism, the dominance of meaning distinguishes Christianity, and the dominance of concern for power distinguishes Unitarian Universalism.

JUDAISM AS AFFECT

Jews understand themselves as a people bound in covenantal relationship to God. The coordinate of affect refers to the corporate aspect of the Jewish faith structure. It refers to the understanding that it is not so much the individual that matters, but the entire people throughout history. Peoplehood ties Jews to history and creates for them a world-wide, present sense of themselves. The notion of Jewishness as conferring "peoplehood" can be rejected by individuals, but that does not mean it does not exist.

Martin Buber describes in his book, *Two Types of Faith*, the sense of corporate Jewish trust that is created by the sense of peoplehood.[9] If one believes in the reality of peoplehood, then one accepts that right actions confirm relatedness. Buber suggests that the real difference between Jewish and Christian faith structures lies not in the quality or quantity of their respective leaps of faith, but in their peculiar understandings of what faith is and how it relates them to God. Buber draws a clear distinction between a Christian perception of faith as individual truth, and Jewish perception of faith as corporate demonstration of trust. He says:

> There are two, and in the end only two, types of faith. There are many contents of faith, but we only know faith itself in two basic forms. Both can be known from the simple data of our life: the one from the fact that *I trust someone*, without being able to offer sufficient reasons for my trust in him; the other from the fact that, likewise, without being able to give sufficient reason, *I acknowledge a thing to be true*. In both cases

my not being able to give a sufficient reason is not a matter of defectiveness in my ability to think, but of a real peculiarity in my relationship to the one whom I trust or that which I acknowledge to be true.[10]

Buber's distinction between trust and truth helps to make the connection between the affective coordinate as distinguishing for Judaism and the meaning coordinate as distinguishing for Christianity. It makes intelligible the Jewish affirmation that to be Jewish is not to be an individual, but one of a whole people. With the realization that the affective result of trust requires that Jews *do* something with their beliefs, it becomes clear that the daily, weekly, and yearly observances of Jewish ritual are an affective expression of their understanding of their on-going and historical relationship with God. Jewish mystic and philosopher Abraham Heschel expresses this exact point in a reflection titled "Something Asked." He writes, "The beginning of faith is not a feeling for the mystery of living or a sense of awe, wonder, and amazement. The root of religion is the question of what to do with the feeling for the mystery of living, what to do with awe, wonder, and amazement. Religion begins with a consciousness that something is asked of us."[11] To understand this means to realize that Jewish people are not just "observing religious customs"; they are *collectively participating* in the trust that arises from the requirement that they act as a people throughout history.

This is not merely a philosophical difference. It is even felt to be true by individuals new to Judaism. A 34-year-old woman was explaining to me the process of her gradual conversion to Judaism from Unitarian Universalism. She was explicit about the impact of the affective component of participating in Judaism. For her, it felt like an enormous relief. She said, "When I was a Unitarian Universalist, all my beliefs went first to my head to be reasoned through, and then to my actions to express what I already understood as true. In Judaism it's just the reverse! We act out our Judaism in all sorts of little ways; we do special things daily, weekly, and during holidays. It's this process of doing my faith that then seems to create my gradual understanding of what it means to *be* Jewish."

By understanding that the coordinate of affect is primary in Judaism and that it springs from the corporate sense of Jewish *people-hood*, one can visualize Judaism's boundaries as drawn around the practices of *an entire people*. This affectively demonstrated identity is protected and promoted by the meaning coordinate's strict rules, which govern who is or is not considered a Jew. These rules apply to cultural and blood heritage as well as to affective practices of liturgical involvement. Yet it is important for interfaith Jewish and Christian couples to realize that while Judaism is a religion, it is first and foremost a people. To be Jewish is to have a corporate history. Even if a person of Jewish heritage does not understand or practice the religious tenets, the awareness of being linked with a specific religious history is unavoidable. Many contemporary Jews, raised in a secular world, speak with surprise about their growing awareness that their cultural membership in the peoplehood of Judaism will eventually require them either to re-think their religious obligations or to live with a sense of having defaulted on their people. Oftentimes their denial of this corporate reality is highest at the threshold of an interfaith marriage.

This dimension of secular Jewish identity is particularly important. When this long-denied identity is triggered by other life-cycle developments or critical life-marking transitions (birth of a child, death of a parent), sometimes what was originally "just" a cultural awareness becomes a full-blown religious identity as well. My work with interfaith couples confirms the confusion that such a transformation could create, especially for the non-Jewish partner who thought his or her spouse was "not religious." But it is surprising to the "non-religious" Jew as well. One man who had never regarded himself as "Jewish" told me he could hardly believe his adamant insistence that his 11-year-old son, raised in a non-practicing interfaith household, prepare to be bar mitzvahed. "I just don't get it," he said. "When I was 22, I wasn't Jewish. So now that I'm 42, what is this? I'm Jewish again, all of a sudden!" Indeed, one of the trickiest aspects of "Oil and Water" marriages is anticipating and understanding as normal the mid-life desire to renew cultural identity patterns, often through return to the religion practiced by one's family of origin or through life-marking ceremonies desired for one's children.

CHRISTIANITY AS MEANING

In dramatic contrast to Judaism, Christianity's faith structure emphasizes individual truth (or meaning) over corporate behavior (or affect). In its most general dimension, Christianity is a religion that understands God's truth as revealed through Jesus Christ. The Christian emphasis on truth as received by individuals and its reliance upon the central truth of a single individual (Jesus) give its faith structure a different configuration.

There are, of course, a surprising number of variations within the "meaning coordinate" of Christian truth. Between Catholic and Protestant, as well as within Catholic and Protestant groupings, there are many different ways of understanding and expressing the central meaning of Jesus Christ. The nature of the power coordinate varies, for example. Practicing Catholics stress the hierarchical nature of revealed truth, placing the authority to interpret with the church officials. Liberal Christians, on the other hand, interpret Jesus' commandment that we love our neighbors as ourselves as a radical freedom given to Christian individuals to create ways in which to live ethically and compassionately within the truth of Jesus' intentions.[12] Some Christian denominations hold creedal content as the requirement for membership. Others, like the Episcopalians, recite creedal affirmations during worship services but regard them primarily as statements "of the heart." Failure to believe or recite a particular creed does not preclude membership in the Episcopal Church.

What is central to Christianity's identification as predominantly meaning-oriented is the unifying presence of Jesus. However defined and interpreted, belief in the primacy of Jesus is central to Christian self-definition. Furthermore, while Christianity tells of the spread of Christian truth, it is not — like Judaism — the story of a people. Its emphasis on individual truth — both the truth of the believing individual and the truth of the defining identity of one person to the faith structure — does not result in the same purpose underneath affective behaviors and responses as Judaism. While Christianity is the cultural-linguistic faith structure for much of the Western world, if an adult wishes to enter into *practicing* membership, an acknowledgment of Christianity's truth by the entering member is necessary. The exception to this boundary confession, however, is found in the Christian practice of infant baptism. Baptism has a specific doctrinal meaning for adults; yet the fact that it has occurred triggers an affective response which can have great power and meaning years later for many of its recipients. One Lutheran adult, who had returned to full involvement following a period of disillusionment and questioning, explained, "It was in realizing that I was baptized as an infant that I was later able to affirm that I had received the grace of God." To be fair to the meaning-oriented Christian faith structures, one might point out that the Christian Church liturgy affectively *relates* specific meanings associated with one individual, Jesus Christ, to each individual practitioner of the faith.

This means that one would necessarily visualize different boundary configurations for Christianity. Unlike the closely bound, rigorously defended Jewish boundary around its "peoplehood," the line around Christianity is looser. Some Christian communities require creedal affirmation for individual membership, others do not. Yet all who would seek Christian membership must assent to the meaning coordinate, however posed, based on the central truth of Jesus Christ.

UNITARIAN UNIVERSALISM AS POWER

Unitarian Universalists sometimes argue over whether they are more like Christianity or more like Judaism. While their liberal religious outlook developed within and grew from Jewish and Christian traditions, a Unitarian Universalist model of the location of ultimate authority (the power coordinate) would look quite different from a Jewish or a Christian construction.

Actually, Unitarian Universalist traditions began separately. Unitarians trace their history to all those Greek and Christian questioners of the Bible's explicit justification of a "triune" God. The fact that these questioners[13] were condemned during life or after death as "heretics" makes their contributions to the intellectual history of religious thought no less valued to Unitarians. Yet "Unitarians" as a named religion were not fully organized in the United States until the early years of the nineteenth century when increasingly vitriolic

arguments between the unitarian and the trinitarian factions of the
Puritan church led to a formal split in 1827. Trinitarian Congregationalists pulled away from Unitarian congregations all over New
England, leaving picturesque "First Parish" church buildings to the
majority faction in each locale. Unitarians' reliance upon reason in
religious issues attracted and held a highly educated membership,
which was noteworthy during much of the nineteenth century for
the number of distinguished leaders it contributed to every sphere of
society.

Universalists began four decades earlier in the United States in
the 1780s. Their belief that God's love guaranteed universal salvation provided an appealing alternative to the dourly fatalistic Cal-
vinist brand of Christianity prevalent at the time. Because Universalists were largely made up of rural, working class people, the
theological optimism they shared with the Unitarians for most of the
nineteenth and half of the twentieth centuries was secondary to their
deeply ingrained class distrust of the manipulative dimension of
Unitarian power and money. Finally, after repeated failed efforts to
come together, the two denominations were able to merge in 1961,
largely because the Universalist Church of America could no longer
financially support its member congregations. Together the two religions became the somewhat mutually wary "U.U.A." or Unitarian Universalist Association of congregations. After a long period
of adjustment to one another financially and theologically, they
hammered out a joint theological statement of "Purposes and Principles," which was adopted after extended debate in their annual
General Assemblies of 1984 and 1985.

The merger created a history still in the making, one might say.
One of the most confusing aspects of being a Unitarian Universalist
today is reaching agreement about the theology underlying the
"power" coordinate. They are still in disagreement as to where
ultimate power and authority should be located and how it should be
named. A historical perspective of this issue helps to understand the
present difficulties. Beginning in the late eighteenth century with
Universalism and in the mid-nineteenth century with Unitarianism,
the hitherto strictly theistic constructions of God began to give way
to constructions that emphasized humanity's inner divinity.

Universalists' early popularity had stemmed from the fact that their notion of God's power was based on love, not judgment. It was an energizing, attractive alternative to the terrifying God handed down from the Calvinists and Puritans. "God is Love," preached the Universalists. They were utterly convinced that the nature of this love was so reliable that every person could be guaranteed salvation. The understanding of God's nature changed the role of human beings. In stark contrast to pre-Reformation Roman Catholicism, Universalists did not have to work to ensure their place in heaven. Instead they chose to set a moral example on earth. Their certainty of God's love of all people became more than a theological justification of personal salvation; it became the morally charged reason underlying their involvement in *political* causes opposing all forms of social injustice. Their fervent belief in God's endorsement of their actions as moral human beings paved the way for two later assumptions about both Universalists and Unitarians: religious liberalism is always the same as political liberalism and religious liberalism is merely a cover for "secular humanism" because of the emphasis on human agency.

In a similar way Unitarian belief in reason and progress also led to a developing humanistic emphasis by linking humanity with God in an optimistic, cosmically directed "onward and upward" progression. Since God was Reason, human ability to reason was demonstration of the divinity that lay within. Like the Universalists, the Unitarian confidence in human reason paved the way for the later reconstruction of the location of ultimate power as quite possibly emanating from human beings alone.

The impact of these optimistic assessments of the importance of individual moral and reasonable effort led the two denominations over nearly 100 years to finally agree to merge in 1961. The merger did not exclude theistic power and constructions from the theological spans represented by the new Association of Unitarian and Universalist churches — such theistic interpretations were still subject to debate and disagreement — but it did enable the humanistic constructions of each religion to be interpreted as mutually shared, common ground. Thus, both theologically and structurally, the distinguishing characteristic of the merged Unitarian Universalist outlook has become their strong affirmation of worth and dignity of every human being. Consequently, if one were to draw boundary parameters for Unitarian Universalists, the sketch would yield a collection of small circles around each individual, yet the *proximity* of the circles would indicate their individuals' collective willingness to "stand in community." Unlike Judaism's elaborate and systemic boundary protection of its "peoplehood" or Christianity's boundary protection of its Jesus-centered truth, Unitarian Universalists' boundaries are closely drawn around and in protection of the sanctity of each *individual*.

This theological orientation explicitly leaves the location of God's presence or ultimate authority with individual decision makers. This individual orientation also changes the nature of religious community, for where power is shared, authority becomes horizontal.

It would be easy to conclude from this description of the power coordinate that Unitarian Universalists are not Christian. That hasty assumption has caused as many Christians to inform Unitarian Universalists of their non-Christian status as it has caused reactive Unitarian Universalists to disavow all "restrictive" (i.e., Christian) labels. The fact is that the question of meaning, although centrally significant to mainline Christians, is not as important to understanding the structure of a Unitarian Universalist faith structure as is the question of the location of ultimate power. The reality that as few Unitarian Universalists as Christian apologists understand this structural distinction results in many futile debates, hard feelings, and significant misunderstandings both within and between the two faith communities. The fact that each religion is using its own primary coordinate as the rule against which the other religion's "faithfulness" is judged proves again that effective interfaith dialogue could be assisted by structural insight in combination with comparative doctrinal discussion.

THE IMPACT OF FAMILY

The Family As a Meaning-Making System

To this point we have identified two ways of identifying meaning-systems: cultural-linguistic "paradigms" and religiously expressive "faith structures." Both provide overall contexts out of which specific patterns of meaning are shaped. Yet there is a third such meaning-system that is of crucial importance when working with couples of different religious persuasions: the family.

When working with couples who have brought different faith structures into their marriage, it is extremely helpful to understand the dynamics and the impact of loyalty as it is expressed and expected by families. Often a couple will down-play the influence of their parents' opinions about an interfaith marriage, claiming that their parents "don't understand" or that they as consenting adults "can make their own choices." This, of course, is always true, yet there are aspects of family loyalty that are not anticipated, and that characteristically pop up at both developmental life cycles and at "fork-in-the-road" life-altering decisions.

When working with conflicting faith structures within an interfaith marriage, what we know about family systems theory becomes particularly useful. Family systems theory envisions family as a relationship continuing over several generations. The model is helpful as a guide to re-visualizing relational patterns in light of the immutable and often hidden dynamics that play off one another in self-regulating and balancing ways. Indeed, the theory itself models scientific thinking in its reliance upon the observable fact that systemic balance abhors imbalance.

As adapted into a multi-generational family structure, the idea pictures an on-going family identity in equilibrium, which has as its fulcrum accepted notions of a controlling world view. This perspective is expected to guide family members' life decisions in observable ways. It can be explicitly religious, as in "All the Kennedys are Catholic," or it can establish a world view in which the religious affiliation is not a dominant coordinate. This understanding also means, however, that whenever any one member of the family "betrays" this understanding of identity by changing his or her identity role in some significant way, the system as a whole feels "out of balance."

Family systems theory moves our focus from the content of any particular faith structure to what happens when any member of the family tries to effect a personal religious change. Change is frequently felt to be threatening. If the change is between structurally different religions, such as a shift from Judaism into Unitarian Universalism, the threat is perceived as even greater. In reality, a shift from one branch of Judaism to another or from one type of Catholicism to another might effect just as big a difference, but denominational boundaries are usually thought of as "safe." "Oh well," it could be rationalized, "At least she's still Lutheran."

By focusing on the family as an emotional identity system that abhors change and seeks on-going balance, one should be aware of the change in emphasis that is occurring. Some family systems theorists deliberately down-play the problems of meaning that can occur between two faith structures in order to emphasize the occurrence of psychologically-motivated responses. The meaning of each religious framework is no longer the primary issue. Indeed, for some family systems therapists, like Rabbi Edwin Friedman, the issue of couple's religious differences is only a "front" for deeper motivations being played out. Friedman writes that "When it comes to intense moments in an emotional system, [religious] issues are often red herrings, displacement issues which disintegrate when the emotional processes that produce them are nullified."[14] He goes even further to declare that issues of religious difference are universally proposed as a kind of cultural camouflage for the deeper and unresolved emotional issues blocking family process. From Friedman's point of view, any therapist focusing on the meaning coordinates of religious differences is actually colluding with the couple to deny that anything else might be going on in their relationship!

Not only does Friedman's argument not coincide with the experience of many interfaith couples struggling with how to accommodate one another's religious perspectives while raising a family, it is simply too one-sided to be uncritically adopted. While it is often true that couples can subconsciously collude to produce a "safe issue" to fight about (which stays away from the real reason fueling their hostility), Friedman's perspective of religion as a universal "red herring" essentially overlooks the communication difficulties created by differing faith structures.

Furthermore, if ministers were to adopt Friedman's view that religious differences are merely "red herring" that mask deeper issues, then the only regulative principle available to make meaning of life would be that offered by the psychologist-as-God! It would seem that if therapists can honor the construction of multi-generational world views, then surely we ought to be able at least to acknowledge the existence and power of multiple-generational religious constructs! The point is to honor the existence of a paradigmatic world view, to look below surface disagreements for deeper issues, and to realize that understanding may not be accomplished by merely "explaining" where the problems lie.

I would suggest, by way of analysis of Friedman's views, that his suggestion that religion is a "red herring," used by couples as a cover for deeper emotional issues, illustrates vividly that Friedman has not recognized the way in which each partner's faith structure may have caused them to apply the wrong lens in judgment of the other. Just as Christians may be quick to tell Unitarian Universalists that they are "not Christian" because they do not comply to the meaning coordinate rule, Friedman is quick to tell all couples that because religious differences are insoluble, there must be deeper psychological issues at work, thus negating the legitimacy of those differences. From a systemic perspective religion simply cannot be reduced to a symptom. Religion may be related to deeper issues, as we shall see below, or it may not. Faith should always be considered as its own issue *in relation to* others.

The point of this paper is that *more help* with these issues, not less, is needed if interfaith couples are to begin to understand the ways in which their differing faith structures may be impeding one another's ability to hear or understand what the other means and why.

Let us suppose, however, that religious differences begin to occur before all this perspective about faith structures can be explained. (Usually several varieties of problems have to occur before an interfaith couple is willing to admit they need help!) In my experience, levels of religious differences exist and can be anticipated. It is important to assess which level of help is being requested by a couple. A simple question by a Jewish-Christian couple regarding the location of their wedding ceremony may not be answered best by an extended analysis of faith structures! Yet knowing that religious places and symbols always pack *collective* identity memories can help interfaith counseling anticipate differences at a practical, solution-seeking level. Awareness of the extended history of Jewish persecution by Christians and a brief explanation of the horrible impact of the Christian crusades, inquisition, pogroms, and holocaust on Jewish consciousness might help the non-Jewish partner to appreciate negative feelings many Jews still carry about Christian churches. The affective impact of collective memory lives on and most predictably reoccurs at life transitional ceremonies. Therefore, by focusing on each partner's sense of their own (and their family's) emotional response to religious symbols and locations, a sensitive counselor can help an interfaith couple to reframe practical solutions that are more appropriate to the requisites of their *combined* faith structures.

The Family As a Loyalty-Enforcing System

In terms of meaning-making, family systems theory points out that whenever a family member moves away from the faith structure of the family, counter reactions by various family members even two generations later can be observed. Thus, a look at how family members collude to maintain a perceived corporate identity, perhaps understood as common religious beliefs, will help all who work with interfaith couples. Part of any counselor's work with interfaith couples should be to explore the family system to reveal any potential emotional dynamic that affects on-going sentiments of indebtedness.

It is essential to understand that although families are *propagated* by lineage, they are *protected* by loyalty. Ivan Boszormenyi-Nagy and Geraldine Sparks[15] offer significant insight on this matter. By characterizing families as "loyalty scales," the motivation for on-going action and reaction is established. No matter what else seems important, they say, in reality "commitment, devotion, and loyalty are the most important ingredients of family relationships."[16] Of these three, it is *loyalty* that demonstrates the unendable sense of existential indebtedness that a family member has for both the extended family system and the individuals within it. According to Boszormenyi-Nagy and Sparks, "Loyalty commitments are like invisible but strong fibers which hold together complex pieces of relationship 'behaviors' in families as well as in larger society . . . . To be a loyal member of the group, one has to internalize the spirit of its expectations and have a set of specific attitudes to comply with the internalized injunctions . . . . "[17]

Of course, the existence of such an intergenerational loyalty ethic also creates an understanding that consequences should be felt by those who are understood to be "disloyal." The guilt felt by change-oriented individuals may actually be a family-balance mechanism that is consciously or unconsciously applied as a way of pressuring the errant individual back into "the fold." Nearly every interfaith family has at least a couple of "guilt stories" to share. It is easiest to recognize when it is laid on them in the form of blatant or subtle accusations.

I have found, when working with interfaith couples that reading the following outrageous "letter" helps them to share their own experiences about guilt more freely, perhaps even with a measure of humorous relief! The letter was allegedly sent by a Jewish mother to her grown son immediately after hearing of his intention to marry a Christian woman:

> Dear Herbie,
>
> Well, if you want to commit suicide, I guess there is nothing I can do. But I can't tell you how much this 'shiksa' business is hurting your father and me. I don't know if you realize that this will hurt us financially. We will probably have to leave town and I will certainly have to give up my job teaching Hebrew. . . .
>
> Your father is sick over this—you know he hasn't been well. All I can say is that if he dies, I will hold you responsible.
>
> Mary says that she loves you, but have you told her that we Jews think of Jesus as an illegitimate son? Love, Mother.[18]

The usefulness of the letter lies in its less-than-subtle incorporation of three familiar types of blaming behavior. First, for example, both Herbie and his fiance were blamed for "marrying out." (She was called "Shiksa," a derisive label used by Eastern European Jews and their descendants to point at the non-Jewish woman who tempts Jewish men away from religion and family.) This form of blaming is not peculiar to Jewish families. In one form or another the myth of the religious outsider is told in every religious tradition as a way of encouraging the conversion or compliance needed to maintain consistent family balance.

Second, the letter suggests in very simple form that what Murray Bowen has termed "triangulation" could be underway. This term describes the effect of unconscious behavior that occurs when "any two [people] in a [family] system begin to become uncomfortable with one another. At that point they will 'triangle,' or focus in on a third person or issue as a way of stabilizing their relationship with one another."[19] Without knowing the details of the relationship between Herbie's parents, it is possible to speculate that the intensity of the blaming aimed at Herbie's actions has as much or more to do with reinforcing the parents' own relationship with one another and as Jews as it does with the stated effects of the couple's decision to marry.

Working with interfaith couples on emotional triangles can be both helpful and frustrating. It is helpful for couples to see that emotional triangles are frequently multi-generational and often form in reaction to the implicit expectations, wishes, or fantasies of a person who is no longer alive. Perhaps Herbie's mother was really reacting to her own sense that her long-dead father would be disappointed in her if Herbie married a Gentile. While the scenario may seem unsubstantiated, it is often suggested that the "child" in each of us sometimes attempts to re-balance family "loyalty scales" with parents or grandparents by behaviors addressed to children or grandchildren!

The frustrating part of this increased understanding about family dynamics is realizing that emotional triangles resist logical confrontation. If Herbie were to accuse his mother of deliberately implying that his marriage would hasten his father's death, the result would probably be an even greater show of righteous anger. Ironically, the harder that Herbie tries to make either his mother or his father see things from his point of view, the more likely it is that he will wind up carrying the stress of them both. It is most helpful for couples in interfaith marriages to realize that it is far more effective to assess what makes them feel vulnerable to blaming attacks than to try to focus on and "figure out" reactive relatives' toxic behaviors.

The third kind of blaming behavior may be harder to spot, yet perhaps easier to feel. Receiving such a letter, or telling oneself that such thoughts are being experienced by others in your family can cause blame to turn inward. From my conversations with interfaith couples and their parents, I would say that such inner blame is probably fairly common and that it occurs as frequently with parents as with individual partners in interfaith marriage. There is a nagging feeling that "because of this marriage, I am being disloyal." Because the consequences of feeling or of being perceived as being disloyal can be severe and are emotionally distressing for all concerned, the issue of disloyalty needs to be acknowledged and explored if it is ever to be worked out.

Parents are likely to experience a sense of rejection, and most certainly loss, when their son or daughter unexpectedly marries across religious lines. Nagging questions like "What did we do wrong?" cross many parents' minds. They turn the blame inward on themselves. The loss of a grown child into marriage is always a poignant moment; but if family life cycle issues also intersect with the marriage, the emotional reaction is bound to be stronger. One set of mainline Christian parents told me of the hurt they felt when their youngest son married a Jewish woman and both young people decided to join a Unitarian Universalist church. Facing the "empty nest" was hard enough for these parents, but facing the empty church nest compounded the pain.

It is helpful for interfaith couples to talk freely with one another, to learn from each other that there are a variety of ways of addressing the pain felt by both sets of parents. It is probably accurate to say that most parents do not want to "over-react," yet they may not know how to deal with the inexplicable feelings of loss that may occur, especially at holidays and on special occasions. One woman in her mid-thirties who had completed training for the Unitarian Universalist ministry but had not been ordained, told me of her parents' reactions to her gradual decision to convert to her husband's Judaism. "It wasn't easy for them, I know," she explained. "They had been active Unitarian Universalists and were really thrilled that I had decided to enter the ministry. It was like a culmination of their dreams. But when I shared with them how enriching I felt the Jewish tradition to be and how at home I felt in it, they understood that for me this was a good decision."

When asked if either she or they had experienced ambivalence or sadness about this change, she exclaimed, "Oh, I think we've all felt ambivalence! That's part of the move from one religion into another. As for sadness, I've felt it for my parents but not so much for myself. It was so hard to see their dismay when they came into our home one mid-December, right after I had decided we would not celebrate Christmas. It was as if they all of a sudden realized that they would never see a Christmas tree in my house again! They were really mourning for *their* loss, but it was hard for *me* to take. I realized later that I wasn't the one feeling sad; *they* were." The young woman was sensitive enough to help her parents by asking if they would like to invite their grandchildren to their own home for an exchange of presents around their Christmas tree.

Individuals are just as likely to experience an inner sense of disloyalty as parents. They, too, show a propensity for emotionally tallying their *own* actions as disloyal, even if those actions would be reasonably explained. The inner sense of disloyalty gets tucked away and is sometimes forgotten, but it resurfaces at odd intervals in nearly every interfaith marriage. Unless the sense of disloyalty is spotted and released, it acts like a submerged air bubble that must eventually hit the surface of awareness. When it dislodges years later, it is characteristically during periods of heightened emotion.

One young Jewish woman explained that the guilt she felt at even trying to understand her husband's Catholicism felt like "a time bomb" in her psyche. She had been especially close to her Jewish grandfather, adoring his company as a little girl, sharing specifically Jewish experiences like childhood Seders, and becoming aware that her adult trip to Malz and Dachau had been emotionally associated with him. For her the time bomb exploded on a "tear-filled Easter morning. I was sitting in that Catholic Mass, and the whole time I was thinking, 'My God, what would my grandfather think if he saw me here right now?' I think about him a lot. I feel that if I turned away from Judaism I would be doing something horrible to him."[20]

So much emotion comes loose at life cycle transitional services that these events require special care and approach for interfaith couples. Submerged loyalty issues, for example to the memory of a beloved grandparent, can release longings for the comfort of a religious tradition that one or both interfaith partners never expected to want or need again. Because transitional life and death occasions have a special intensity of meaning, the intensity of religious feeling is frequently equally intense and can be very upsetting.

I have learned how easy it is to be critical of or angry at family members who do not understand why one would decide to leave their religion. We would all like to believe that the people we know and love would understand our need to lead our own lives, just as the young Unitarian Universalist woman's parents were able to do. But the dichotomy between the rational aspect of understanding and the emotional aspects of family systems and religious feeling perpetuates a type of blaming that is hard to overcome. Labeling Herbie's fiance a "shiksa" is one example of such behavior; telling the grandchildren on weekend visits that they are "really Catholic" is another.

Life Cycles in Religious Identification

Life cycle issues occur in everyone regardless of religious identification. They are developmental in that different levels of maturation create unique perspectives, issues, and problems. Erik Erikson's eight life stages[21] are predicated on the need for human beings to process different issues sequentially and developmentally throughout the life span. Whatever occurs then, according to Erikson's perspective, will be processed according to the life cycle issues of each person's meaning-making frame, resulting in differing interpretations of the same action. For example, a 20-year-old son's decision to leave home will most certainly be understood in different ways by the autonomy-seeking young adult and his caregiving, mid-life parents! If this same son's decision involved leaving both the home and the religion of his parents, the emotional impact of the decision would be significantly compounded.

Life cycle issues can also be situational. Predictable life cycle events, such as marriage, the birth of children, or the death of a parent, can evoke complicated sets of feelings for individuals and forces within families. Unanticipated events, such as marital separation, the death of a child, or loss of employment, precipitate the same unsettling sense of fluidity with more pain. "Non-events," or things that happen more slowly but are not recognized as "life-marking" occasions, such as independence, failing health, or aging, also generate feelings of uncertainty and transitional worry, yet are harder to respond to definitively.

The importance of life cycle issues, whether developmental or situational, is that they create a sense of uneasiness in the individual, couple, or extended family unit. Deeply ingrained expectations of what life should be like can become vulnerable to new scrutiny whenever a life cycle interval or issue is reached. There is no avoiding the sensation that change is underway. Not only do the situations act as "thresholds" between old and new ways of seeing, understanding, or doing things, but occasionally the entire meaning system is felt to be "on the line."

The relationship between life cycle resolution and religious identification lies in understanding both the cultural and the personal impact of a faith structure. People grow up with expectations for how life will be, for what is a threshold event, and for how such events should be managed. These expectations, both named and assumed, are shaped to a large extent by the family and culture's operative faith structure. A religion's validity is often measured or confirmed by its ability to recognize and respond to specific life cycle stages or events both pastorally and liturgically. If there has been a continuity of faith structure outlook throughout the family's multiple generations which is supported by the larger faith structure of the culture, then the family's expectation of what is needed will be in fact a description of the religious community's response.

Yet because the life cycle maturational or situational events are life-altering in some significant way, there is always the risk that people will be disappointed. The very nature of threshold circumstances means that personal vulnerability is at its highest. Even behind the most defensive of personal fronts, the privately central concern is, "Will things work out here as expected or will something different happen?" Much is at stake in terms of on-going religious identification. If predictable expectations are matched by the anticipated and desired response, then the individual or family's sense of "being" that religion will be both justified and compounded. If expectations either are not discerned nor responded to, then the degree of one's identification with a particular faith structure can also become problematic. In addition, religious care-givers who fail to provide expected responses to deeply felt emotional expectations are sure to be severely criticized. The point to remember is that most people *want* their faith structure to help them through life cycle situations. When it does not, normal transitional confusion is compounded by a sense of uncertainty about the religious perspective itself.

Life cycle events can also trigger emotional reactions in family members' religious understandings. Remember the 42-year-old father who believed he had long ago left Judaism until his 11-year-old son approached the traditional age for a bar mitzvah ceremony? The life cycle stage of his *son* triggered feelings and desires that had been buried so long that the father had assumed they were gone. His sense of total surprise was genuine, but perhaps the situation he found himself in was not such a surprise after all.

Robert Kegan, an educational psychologist at Harvard University's Graduate School of Education, describes a notion of "embeddedness."[22] Kegan's fascination with the cognitive-structural learning sequence developed by Swiss educational theorist, Jean Piaget, led him to try to determine *how* pre-school children see themselves in relation to their worlds, and to contrast that view with the perspective of five- to seven-year-olds. What he discovered was that the younger set of children displayed a characteristic "embeddedness" in their belief systems. Says Kegan:

> An "error" in the child's ability to perceive an object is not something he or she is likely to catch or correct, because according to the terms of the child's present adaptive balance . . . no error is being made. The deep structure . . . is that the child is subject to his perceptions in this organization of the physical world. He cannot separate himself from them; he cannot take them as an object of his attention. He is embedded in them. They define the very structure of his attention. For the pre-operational [that is, pre-rational] child, it is never just one's perceptions that change; rather the world itself, as a consequence, changes.[23]

While Kegan's observation of embeddedness was made in order to clarify the profound cognitive shift that occurs somewhere between the ages of five and seven when children develop the ability to differentiate between themselves as people and the perceptions they hold of the world, I relate Kegan's understanding of embeddedness to the possible reality of an on-going religious orientation. As Kegan describes human development, growth has a primarily *cognitive* impetus. Embeddedness leads one to project onto the world one's personal constitution of reality.[24] Growth, therefore, "always involves a process of differentiation, of emergence from embeddedness, thus creating out of the former subject a new object to be taken [as the new constitution of reality]."[25] Kegan comments that although Piaget called this growth a process of "decentration," or the loss of an old center of meaning, he preferred to label it as a movement toward "recentration," or the re-establishment of a new center of meaning. When this occurs, the former center of reality is now seen as an earlier understanding of the way things used to be; it becomes, in other words, separated from the individual's on-going constitution of self-identity.

The impact of the notion and nature of embeddedness is central to our consideration of changing religious identities. One wonders if Piaget's labeling the process in terms of *loss* that is felt is in the long run more accurately reflective of how the change is deeply understood. One might also question, for example, the contemporary educators' focus on the *cognitive* shift as that which is most essential for measurement. Of course, both aspects of the movements towards re-constituting a new center of reality have important ramifications for our understanding of changing religious identities. As I see it, embeddedness is largely emotional with cognitive justification. While Kegan works on the impetus for and consequence of cognitive shifts throughout life, I remain intrigued by the possibility that remnants of the original sense of embeddedness are never relinquished. Could this emotional grounding be the intuitive level at which one's faith structure is originally felt to be real? Could this "pre-operational" — pre-rational — state of human development be one which is not so much replaced as *layered over*? Studies of the evolutionary development of the human brain[26] have found that the earliest type of brain stems contained the emotional basis for understanding the world and that "higher" forms of cognitive ability extended, rather than replaced, that stem, giving human beings multiple forms of intelligence. Could it be that to work effectively with couples from different religious backgrounds more attention should be given to the on-going emotional presence of a "pre-operational" religious intuition, which is creating expectations of the self, the world, and of how life "should be?"

This is not an argument against cognitive thinking about religious frameworks. Certainly a significant part of maturation is involved in gaining both the experience and the perspective to re-think earlier conceptions about life. It would seem that most people undergo changes in their thinking about and understanding of religious ideas as they mature. Some expect to change, and a few explicitly state that the process of the search for meaning is more important to them than the meaning itself. Yet all of these positions point us to cognitive shifts in religious understandings. What has been less well-understood, however, as the changing adult religious viewpoint is assessed, is the influence that the *original* faith structure may continue to have on an individual throughout his or her life. Even if you are sure you have "changed religions," the images and understandings from your original faith structure may well be carried along inside you and may in fact continue to influence your opinions about your "new" faith structure.

A 40-year-old woman who grew up with liberal religion learned, when her grandfather spoke Yiddish on his deathbed, that part of her religious heritage had been Jewish. A capable theologian, she now observes that the Unitarian Universalist could be strengthened by creating a stronger sense of community with an identifiable theology.[27] Could some aspect of her earliest intuition of her family's Jewish-Unitarian Universalist faith structure be justifying her yearning for a theologically identifiable community? While this might be beyond verification, it suggests the possibility of an essential continuation of one's original faith structure as a deeply buried, pre-rational foundation upon which life cycle development and issues are continually re-grooved.

Attending to the possibility of a deeply intuitive faith structure as an on-going feature in our implicit reactions to religious issues may help to explain the mystery people feel at an apparently unprompted, mid-life return to the religious faith structure of one's youth. Sharon Parks of the Weston School of Theology has noted[28] that interfaith marriages most often occur when young adults are in their early

20s. At this age, she notes, their life cycle stage is often at its most profound point of cognitive difference from the perspective with which they were raised. Parks explains that this is normal; indeed it is part of a young adult's work at growing up to become someone quite different from his or her parents. Thus, marriage to someone from a different religious background during this stage can feel right for both young adults. Less anticipated is the possibility that as each partner matures and recycles through issues which bear on faith structure perspectives, they may suddenly "decide to return" to the religion of their childhood as part of a normal, mid-life cycle. One woman in her mid-40s was caught totally by surprise when her husband, whom she had always thought "was Congregational," decided after 19 years to travel some distance every week to attend high Episcopal church services. She found it odd that when the boys they had raised in the Congregational Sunday School left for college, her husband simply left the church. When this theory of mid-life religious return was explained to her, she reflected, "I'd always known that David's grandfather had been the rector at that Episcopal church when David was a little boy, but it never occurred to me that David *understood himself* as Episcopalian." Embeddedness not only shapes expectations, but even children's life cycle endings and beginnings can cause old religious identifications to resurface with new validity.

SPECIFIC DYNAMICS
OF INTERFAITH CONSULTATIONS

Decision Making

Interfaith couples are not "odd ducks." The problem that bothers them is deciding on whose pond to swim in: yours, mine, or ours? Some of the anxiety feeding this dilemma comes from the underlying perception that to be "truly married," couples must agree on all the *big* issues, in order to allow the "little differences" in preference or approach to be tolerable. While many religions with strong boundary orientations or well-defined membership requirements endorse this approach to marital consensus, it does little to guide conscientious adults with the solution to "Who decides?" or what the other partner should do if the "solution" is emotionally or doctrinally incompatible.

It is not surprising that many couples postpone making any decision until their first big life-transition. For some couples, depending on the issues involved, this occasion is forced by the design and location of their wedding ceremony. For others, it occurs with the anticipation of the baptism or bris of their first child, with the decision of where to enroll the children for religious education, or with the sudden death of a family member and the need to account for religious expectations at a moment of genuine crisis.

The issue of whose place of worship to attend is so difficult for many couples that they frequently postpone the issue in a variety of ways. Some decide to relinquish all expectation of involvement with any religious community and decide to use their free time on weekends in other, mutually enjoyable ways. Others manage by the consensus of silence to attend their own religious services until children are born, at which point the partner with the "stronger faith" is tapped to raise the children in his or her faith tradition. Many couples tell me with pride and hope that they are "raising their children as 'nothing'," figuring that their children will then "be able to decide for themselves when they're older."

I suggest that an interfaith religious goal should be for the recognition or creation of commonalities, while simultaneously embracing differences as enriching, not enraging. This is a delicate balance and always difficult, yet more realistic of how people naturally make sense of their world and its meanings. Of course, each couple and each partner within the couple present different issues that must be considered when trying to decide whose tradition to honor. But whether one is assisting interfaith couples with premarital, couples, or family issues, participants need informed assistance about options, combination of options, and consequences of different patterns.

Where children are involved, I encourage each partner to openly share memories and meanings from their religious heritage and to discuss openly with each other and clergy how to approach life-marking religious transitional services when children are involved. The issue really is not how many or what combination of differences children can absorb. The issue is whether or not the parents know what they believe religiously and have found a means for nurture and relatedness to meaning that enriches their life separately or together.[29] My experience as an educator, counselor, and parent confirms that children naturally mix and match ideas and traditions from whatever source. Therefore, to assume that children will become "confused" simply because their experiences are not wholly Jewish or wholly Christian reflects a doctrinal rather than a developmental point of view.

Styles of Spiritual Expression

Interfaith couples who have decided to deal with, not dodge, the issue of "Whose tradition—yours, mine, or ours?" need lots of help and lots of credit for any decision they make. No decision will be entirely right. If they decide "yours" or "mine," at least they will have the comfort of being pilgrims: They will know the goal and at least one of them will see the path. If they decide "ours," then no matter which church they enter, they are courageous pioneers and should be lauded as such.

I do not believe that interfaith couples must necessarily decide to attend the same church, although if they do and can do so with commitment, they will find that the "ours" they create has many family advantages. One understands one's partner or growing children better when comparative reactions and responses to commonly shared religious experiences can be discussed later at home. Self-knowledge and reflective awareness of one's own family traditions also comes into sharper focus when one's own reactions are compared with those of others in your family unit. Yet people can attend different churches and still share the same religious values. Or they may attend the same church and have different styles of spiritual expression. Finding the right blend of religious perspective and spiritual style can take some experimenting. For example, my husband was born and raised a Unitarian (not a Unitarian Universalist). I was raised liberal Congregationalist but became at age 17 a Unitarian Universalist. During 22 years of shared Unitarian Universalist membership, we had more disagreements about what constituted "worship" than we do now that my husband attends Quaker meeting. His worship at Quaker meetings brings forth an affective spirituality which much more nearly matches my own affective/cognitive balance of (nearly Universalist) spirituality. Although we now worship in different denominations and value different liturgical structures, what we believe and how we make sense of God and the world is more similar than ever before.

THE JOB AHEAD:
GATHERINGS, GRIEF WORK, POSSIBILITIES

The job for family counselors, ministers, religious educators, and congregations is to encourage each partner in an interfaith marriage to express what they are experiencing as religious feelings, memories, and expectations. With that to build on, we must look for many opportunities to explore and share our different impressions and questions. I offer groups (both brief and extended) with titles such as "Growing up Jewish [Catholic . . . etc.] in Literature and Real Life" or "Two December Holidays in One Home?"

Sometimes I suspect when I hear of parental concern over their offspring's religious identity that what is really occurring is a sense of loss over their *own* religious heritage. When one relates Elisabeth Kubler-Ross' stages of death and dying[30] to the feelings being expressed by interfaith couples, you hear their words in an entirely new way. Loss is what many of them are feeling. Grief work is what many of them are doing. It is hard to remember, after spending many years feeling comfortably "at home" in one's own faith structure, that when anyone begins to recreate meaning—either by adapting liturgies, language, or meanings from the past or starting out "fresh" with new symbols, new vocabulary, and new understandings—they feel very tentative about what it is they believe or do not believe. The intuitive precedes the ability to articulate meaning! So many aspects of worship and spirituality become re-opened to consideration; so many questions and words from the past are re-asked, re-examined. In many ways, the whole notion of what a faith structure even represents becomes open to new emotional and cognitive meanings.

When a new religious construct is being pieced together day by day, experience by experience, it takes a long time to feel that you have the security of a newly encompassing faith structure. More work is needed on whether this perception of "newness" is equally affected by the emotional and cognitive levels of human understanding. Yet one's anticipation of what will make it "right" will be different for different faith structures. Judaism requires time in which to live the behaviors to make them one's own. Christianity requires an integrated Christology. Unitarian Universalism requires that religious ideas make personal sense and flow into the expression of ethical action. Building a new framework is both an imaginative leap of faith and an enormous risk. It is a following of glimmerings, feelings, and senses, most of which imply conceptual frameworks yet are born without words. It is an acknowledgment that letting go of the certainty and the fullness of what once encompassed you is a legitimate and deeply felt loss. Because of the uncertainty of such profound periods of transition, the use of power, affect, and meaning as stabilizing comparative coordinates could be both reassuring and helpful to interfaith couples.

Nevertheless, to begin anew is to set aside, not to totally forget. As I have listened to people in interfaith marriages, I most often hear a sense of loss pointing to a need for grief work. Yet I also feel, along with their tentativeness, a sense of excitement and of tremulous possibility. New understanding is within reach, new identity and patterns of response are already beginning.

REFERENCE NOTES

1. The term "faith structures" comes from Laurel Arthur Burton (1988) in *Pastoral Paradigms: Christian Ministry in a Pluralistic Culture*. Washington, DC: Alban Institute.

2. Thomas Kuhn. 1962. *The Structure of Scientific Revolution*. Chicago: University of Chicago Press.

3. Sharon Parks. 1986. *The Critical Years and the Young Adult Search for a Faith to Live By*. San Francisco: Harper & Row.

4. Maria Harris. 1989. *Fashion Me a People: Curriculum in the Church*. Louisville: Westminster John Knox.

5. Burton, *op. cit.*

6. Gordon D. Kaufman. 1975. *An Essay on Theological Method*. Missoula: Scholars Press.

7. Ibid., p. 13.

8. Ibid., p. 15, emphasis added.

9. Martin Buber. 1951. *Two Types of Faith*. New York: Macmillan.

10. Ibid., p. 7, emphasis added.

11. Abraham Heschel. 1983. "Something Asked," in *I Asked for Wonder: A Spiritual Anthology*, ed. Samuel H. Dresner. New York: Crossroad Publishing Co., p. 38.

12. G.D. Kaufman, unpublished article. "Doing Theology from a Liberal Christian Point of View."

13. Religious "heretics" such as second century Greek philosopher, Origen; third century unitarian priest, Arias; thirteenth century priest and university professor, Jon Huss; and fourteenth century Spanish doctor, Michael Servetus.

14. Edwin Friedman. 1982. "The Myth of Shiksa," in *Ethnicity and Family Therapy*, ed. M. McGoldrick. New York: Guilford Press, p. 514.

15. Ivan Boszormenyi-Nagy and Geraldine Sparks. 1973. *Invisible Loyalties: Reciprocity in Intergenerational Family Therapy*. Hagerstown: Brunner-Mazel.

16. Ibid., p. 5.

17. Ibid., pp. 39, 37.

18. E. Friedman, *op. cit.*, p. 499.

19. E. Friedman. 1985. *Generation to Generation: Family Process in Church and Synagogue*. New York: Guilford Press, pp. 35-36.

20. Paul Cowan, *op. cit.*, p. 58.

21. Erik Erikson. 1963. "The Eight Ages of Man," in *Childhood and Society*, 2d ed. New York: W.W. Norton, chap. 7.

22. Robert Kegan. 1982. *The Evolving Self: Problem and Process in Human Development*. Cambridge: Harvard University Press.

23. Ibid., pp. 28-29.

24. Ibid., p. 31.

25. Ibid.

26. See brain studies written by Howard Gardner in particular.

27. The Reverend Judith E. Meyer. "The Personhood of All Believers," in *UU Advance*, Paper no. 59, 1988, pp. 7-8.

28. Sharon Parks, *op. cit.*

29. Lee F. Gruzen. 1987. *Raising Your Jewish/Christian Child*. New York: Dodd, Mead & Co., p. 157.

30. Elisabeth Kubler-Ross. 1969. *On Death and Dying*. New York: Macmillan, pp. 38-112.

Chapter Seven

Family Therapy with the Faithful: Christians As Clients

Anne F. Grizzle, MS

> Family structures . . . are manifestations of the value of the cultural group to which the family belongs. The therapies employed also reflect cultural values . . . . Cultural values, which shape the relationships between family and therapist, which influence their respective perceptions of self and others, and which affect their manner of communication, occupy space in the core of therapy.
>
> *Ethnicity and Family Therapy*

One of the values that is central to many clients is their religious faith. Although the importance of understanding the impact of religious beliefs in clients' lives has been addressed in the general therapy literature, very little has been written within the field of family therapy. Yet without understanding their clients' faith and how it impacts on their relationships, family therapists are operating with a vital value system and possibly even member of the family, God, left at home and ignored. This chapter offers a general model for assessment as well as more specific therapeutic tangles and resources for working with clients with strong faith.

Why is a client's religious faith so vital an area for understanding by the systemic therapist? For a client with a strong faith or for one who comes from a family of origin where faith is critical, this faith system provides the value system for setting norms in family relationships, it determines many of the family's activities, and it offers the glasses from which the family views the rest of the world. For clients whose faith is in a living and personal God, as it is in the Jewish and Christian faiths, having faith also involves an actual relationship with God as well as with other members of the faith community. For family therapists, this means another layer of relationships that can offer helplessly complicated triangulation or wonderful resources for new relationships. To ignore their faith or even to pass it off as minor is to close one's eyes to a vital therapeutic factor. In fact, many strongly religious clients are hesitant or even fearful to see secular therapists out of concern that their faith will not be appreciated and perhaps even scorned or analyzed as pathological.

Just as ethnic values are extremely diverse, so too are religious values. The beliefs of strongly committed Christians will be used in this paper to illustrate the process of understanding and incorporating religious faith into family therapy treatment. There are great differences among Christian denominations, both Protestant and Catholic, that need to be understood. However, there are certain core similarities, especially among those who are highly committed in their Christian faith, that can serve as a useful basis for developing basic principles for understanding. This core aspect involves belief in a living personal God who created humans for relationship with God. God became tangibly present and offers forgiveness of sins through faith and following of Jesus Christ. The Bible is accepted as the Word of God and as a guidebook for learning spiritual truths and gleaning directions for right relationships. The church is the body of Christ's believers who are called together to worship, to love one another, and to minister in the world. The author's work with over 100 clients with strong Christian faith will be used to illustrate the theoretical principles. Although the details of faith will be specific to Christians, many of the ideas discussed will apply to other faiths, particularly those that involve a personal faith relationship with God and/or the faith community.

ASSESSMENT MODELS FOR NATURAL AND SPIRITUAL RELATIONSHIPS

Just as in an alcoholic system where it is important to assess carefully the place of alcohol within the whole family system, for clients with strong faith the faith relationship should be carefully mapped within the whole family system. Particularly when faith involves belief in a personal relationship with God, this relationship needs to be carefully assessed as part of the family system.

Several models from family therapy can be helpful in understanding some of the relational dynamics that may occur between natural and spiritual relationships. The essence involves understanding the potential reactions, repetitions, conflicts, and resources where more than one or two sets of parental figures or family groups are involved. One model is that of foster care or adoption, particularly where the natural and adoptive families have contact. Frequently, reactions to natural parents may be played out in relations with foster parents. Or foster parents become the Santa Claus to make up for all parental misdoings. Here it is vital that the relationships between families are clarified and conflicts, or confusions worked through. Another model is that of a three generational family, where the older grandparent is part of the family along with the parents. Roles can become confused and competitive, or they can be clear and complementary.

For the purposes of assessment, two possible adaptations of the genogram for use with families of strong faith might be:

1. Presenting God as a triangle (representing the Trinity for Christian clients) or star of David (for Jewish clients) above the overall genogram, with lines of strength or weakness or cut off connection drawn to various family members (ideally in a different color). Particular denominational affiliations or aspects of faith could be written on the connecting lines:

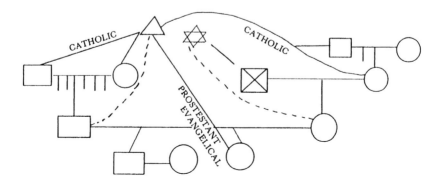

2. Depicting faith through a surrounding circle (preferably in a different color) for each member of the family. Lack of strong faith would be indicated by no circle. A bold circle would indicate strong faith, a dotted line weak faith, a jagged line conflictual faith, and a slashed line cut off faith.

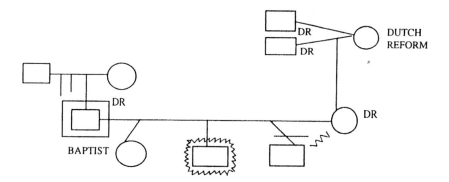

Along with depiction on the genogram, a spiritual history should be taken for clients with strong faith (or past faith) to determine the spiritual pilgrimage and relationship to other events and members of the family. These events should be included in a family timeline.

For further assessment or where the relationships are hard to clarify, the family therapy technique of sculpting can be used, with God being included in the cast of characters.

BIBLICAL RELATIONSHIP PRINCIPLES

For the purposes of family therapy, the impact of faith on family norms and relationship principles is extremely important to be understood. A 1989 Ackerman Institute training conference described an approach of "changing belief systems" of clients. They stressed the importance of recognizing and addressing basic belief systems that held dysfunctional behavior in place. While it is not generally appropriate to challenge the basic faith beliefs of clients, it can be extremely helpful to point out in their own faith language how they may have followed one extreme principle to the exclusion of another within their own faith framework. Knowing these principles can help the practitioner address these belief systems in a faith supportive manner.

While the Bible is not written as a family therapy text, nevertheless it is full of stories of relationships and guidelines for living in relationship. For the purposes of family therapy, these have been distilled by the author into several basic relationship principles.* Many of these combine two seemingly opposite values in what results in a necessary balance. Relationships become imbalanced when they move to one extreme without the other. Many of these principles correspond with family therapy principles; however, understanding their biblical source and language can be helpful in utilizing them with faithful families. These are useful to the practitioner for understanding the normal expectations of a Christian client's belief system. However, they are also useful in assessing and explaining to clients in terms of their own belief system some of the imbalances that have developed that may be related to the symptom they are presenting for help. Often clients may have taken one aspect of belief to an extreme without recognizing the other balancing principle. By pointing this out within their faith framework, they may be able to modify their patterns without feeling their basic beliefs have been challenged.

Freely Chosen Love

Christians believe that God's model for relationship is one of freely given love. The whole reason for sin is based on people having been created with the free will to choose to obey and love God or not. The importance of this free will must be extremely great to be worth the terrible pain of sin, both personally and societally. Robot relationships are not God's intention, but rather relationships based on independent, freely chosen love. In the Hebrew Testament, God's people are often admonished in the right ways and then encouraged to choose life and not death. In the Christian Testament (Galatians 4), Christians are reminded that they are not slaves, born of the bondwoman, but instead are children, heirs of the free

---

*All Bible references are from *The Holy Bible, New International Version*, International Bible Society, 1984.

woman. Jesus calls his followers to be servants of the Lord and other people, but as a choice — not a legal requirement. In the parable of the prodigal son, the son is given the right to choose to leave the father and is still received with great love and forgiveness when he returns after squandering his life. Although he offers to be a servant, the father will not hear of it but rather desires a continuing free son relationship.

Individuality Within Unity

One of the most difficult concepts within Christianity is the Trinity, a belief in one God yet in three persons. Jesus and the Father are one according to Scripture, yet Jesus has a particular role distinctive from the Father, and Jesus talks with the Father from a separate point of view (e.g., "take this cup from me; yet not my will but yours"). In St. Paul's letter to the Romans, he states, "We have many members in one body and all the members do not have the same function, so we who are many, are one body in Christ, and individually members one of another." The principle of seeking unity must be balanced with the principle of encouraging individuality. While the harmony of the body as a whole must always be sought, the expression of the uniqueness of each person must never be lost. Problems develop when individuals become separate and self serving or when their individuality becomes stifled by conformity.

Authority with Understanding

Relationships within countries, jobs, and families are portrayed as having clear authority structures to maintain order in a sinful society. Within the church, elders are given authority to teach and discipline as needed, and members are instructed to respect and honor their authority. Within the family, husbands are given authority over wives according to some Christian beliefs, although both are to submit to God. Parents are given responsibility over children, to love and discipline them, and children are instructed to honor their mother and father. When these authority structures and boundaries are not honored, many Christians believe problems and even chaos can develop.

Yet authority has definite limits. First, God is the final and eternal authority for all. Everyone submits to God and has authority only under God. Second, with authority comes greater responsibility and culpability, as well as the necessity of caring concern for those under them. The requirements for elders in the church are great, including specifically temperance, gentleness, uncontentiousness, and good management (I Tim. 3). Within the family, parents are instructed not to provoke their children to anger, and not to abuse their authority or be insensitive to their children. Finally, before the Fall and in eternity, there is a picture of no earthly leaders, masters, bosses, husbands, or parents who have authority over others. So our present order is due more to the presence of sin than the ultimate intention of God to have people having authority over other people.

Leaving/Cleaving Cycle

Within the process of individual and family life development, Scripture outlines a leaving and cleaving cycle. This principle is first given in Genesis 2 when God, after creating man and woman, declares, "Therefore shall a man leave his mother and father and cleave to his wife and the two shall become one flesh." When Scripture speaks of marriage, it begins with the necessity of leaving that which has been most close and binding — mother and father. As long as a person is still primarily attached to parents, that person cannot truly cleave to a marriage partner. Without this leaving, a new marriage cannot be made well. Within the marriage children are often born, and parents are called on to nurture their children with secure cleaving love. Fairly soon, however, they must begin allowing their children to mature by teaching them to become competent themselves. By adolescence, the primary task turns once again to leaving — freeing a child to become the adult, which is the final parenting goal. Spiritually, adults are called to leave father and mother and follow Christ. Repeatedly as men and women decide to follow Jesus, they leave their father or boat or home or riches to follow Jesus. Although they are never to stop honoring parents (Mark 7:10), they are called to leave them as primary attachments. Jesus proclaims at one point that His mother and father and brother and sister are not his natural family. His family consists of those who do His will (Mark 3:33). So individuals are called to move into chosen adulthood and to build new relationships within a faith family.

Love Combined with Discipline

Growth, both naturally and spiritually, is portrayed as occurring through receiving both love and discipline. The heavenly parent God offers great and unfailing love, but also disciplines the children (Heb. 12). Followers are encouraged to become mature rather than remain childish. In a parallel way, parents are instructed to bring up their children in the nurture and discipline of the Lord (Ephesians 6). Parents need to provide a solid foundation of loving acceptance and care. To that they need to add discipline, or teaching toward maturity.

Go Directly to Resolve Conflicts

The model for dealing with conflicts in Christian Scripture begins with going directly to the person involved. Matthew 18:15-16 says, "If your brother sins, go and reprove him in private; if he listens to you, you have won your brother." Gossip and talking to others before the person offending is to be avoided. Even going to God without working things out with the person in conflict is addressed, "If therefore you are presenting your offering at the altar, and there remember that your brother has something against you, leave your offering there before the altar, and go your way, first be reconciled to your brother, and then come and present your offering" (Matthew 5:23-24). So the Bible gives clear admonitions to go directly, avoiding the pitfalls of triangulation that therapists know all too well.

Speak the Truth in Love

Ephesians 4:5-6 counsels, "Speak the truth in love. Be angry, yet do not sin." This principle balances being honest and direct in speaking—telling the truth, acknowledging anger—with speaking in love. Most people in their dealing with conflict tend toward one end or the other of this spectrum, from passive to aggressive. Those who are passive tend to bury their feelings and thoughts, push them down or let them fester until they come out in hurtful ways like depression or headaches or caustic comments. Those who are aggressive say just how they see things, but often at the expense of others' feelings, by being blunt, sarcastic, or blaming. The goal is the middle ground of assertiveness.

TYPICAL TANGLES OF NATURAL AND SPIRITUAL RELATIONSHIPS

In the ideal construction of natural and spiritual relationship, loving natural family relationships would lead to a growing personal relationship with God, which in turn would encourage more loving relationships with others. Unfortunately, relationships often go astray and instead of complementing one another, they complicate one other. In order to aid assessment and treatment, the most common tangles encountered in the author's work with faithful families have been categorized, with description and clinical goals.

Faith of Our Fathers (and Mothers)

Children learn about the world from their parents. They adopt many of their beliefs and are introduced to people they know. Usually during adolescence and adulthood, they begin to reexamine what they have been taught and decide for themselves what they believe and plan to follow. With relationships, they may no longer keep them up, they may remain in touch as a friend of our parents or they may move to actually developing their own adult relationship with them.

God is one of those relationships that parents introduce to their children (or keep them from meeting). Their faith is an important part of their belief system that children learn. Sometimes the normal adolescent examining and adult developing of personal beliefs and relationship with God does not progress. Children's beliefs and relationship with God may remain stuck as a replication of their parents into adulthood, never developing the vibrancy of a personal faith and relationship of their own.

In one example, Sue sought counseling due to conflicts between her faith and actions. In the discussion, it became clear that her faith was stuck in the exact system of her mother, with much rigidity in relationships and little appreciation for the talents of women. Although she affirmed this outwardly, she found herself doing things entirely opposite of these beliefs. She needed to step out of the faith mold of the family to develop her own personal faith relationship that would integrate fully into her life as an adult. When she was asked about her praying to God for herself and thinking through her faith personally, she reacted with surprise that she could actually do that rather than just accept completely the rigid "faith of her mother." Once she allowed herself to question her faith and personalize it in finding her own church, trying new methods of prayer, and using her singing talents in a youth group, her faith became much more vibrant. She was then able to relate and behave in ways that were congruent with her faith.

The difficulties may, for some people, be stuck in isolated areas, rather than a whole relationship. Jim came for help from depression. His faith in fact was a tremendous resource to him. However, his controlling and harsh father's constant childhood messages of God being ready to judge and condemn him if he did not follow what his father said stayed with him on a deeper level. Until he confronted this directly, reasoned, prayed, and experienced his new faith directly in relationship to his pervasive guilt, he was not fully freed.

One variation of this tangle is no faith of our fathers. Parents may be strongly committed atheists or simply without spiritual interest. Children adopt this attitude as well. As they grow, they may keep this stance without exploration, being stuck rather than considering the possibility of their own spiritual pilgrimage. Whether parents have strong faith or no faith, it becomes one's own only with individual exploration and wrestling.

A second variation comes not from adopting the faith of one's family but of a boyfriend or girlfriend. Often people adopt the faith of the person they are dating. In some cases, this is the beginning of an active personal spiritual pilgrimage. In other cases, it is a stale adoption of a faith that never becomes their own. This becomes particularly apparent when the relationship breaks up and the faith is given up as well. If the faith is genuine, it in fact may be matured by the separation.

The goal when "faith of our fathers" has continued without becoming personal is for the individual to work at developing his or her own personal beliefs and faith relationship. This involves examining parental beliefs and patterns, questioning and praying for oneself, and moving to a relationship of faith that becomes one's own pilgrimage. The starting point is usually one's own family, particularly when the family faith is strong. But everyone must walk on his or her own pilgrimage from that starting point to arrive at a living faith.

God in the Image of Dad or Mom

Children learn about relationships — attitudes, interactions, roles, and rules — from their first family of origin. Even if their family is spiritually inactive or cut off, they are still the relationship models. These patterns of interaction are brought into our relationships with others outside the family and into a relationship with God. The most classic example is when an individual with a harsh father views God as a judgmental heavenly father and has difficulty experiencing the love of God.

Susan came for counseling due to depression. She came from a family that was emotionally distant. They saw each other with some regularity but they avoided talking about personal issues and had never supported each other emotionally in times of difficulty. Susan naturally approached relationships cautiously, holding back intimate sharing and keeping an intellectual overtone. She had become a committed Christian while in college and followed basic prescriptions for faith. However, her relationship with God took on the same impersonal, distant quality as relationships in her family. She once asked, "Does God ever show His love in personal ways you can really experience?" She seemed to be asking, "Is God's love really any different from my family's? Can I expect to be genuinely comforted?" Through the vulnerability and trust of the therapeutic relationship, she began opening up more emotionally. She was encouraged to reach out to build friendships, speak and inquire more personally in her conversations, and develop neglected extended family relationships as well. As her natural relationships began to be more intimate, she began as well to be able to pray more personally and allow her faith to become a resource for a fuller emotional life.

Another young woman sought help due to terrible anxiety over a growing romantic relationship. Whenever she became close to her boyfriend, she would have dreams or flashes of God being angry and wanting her to give it up. In exploring her relationship patterns, it was clear how overinvolved she was as the only child in a family where her mother had come to depend almost entirely on her rather than her father. Several times in the past when she had been preparing for a trip, she had experienced the same anxieties. She had felt called to overseas mission work for a number of years, but had never been able to move very far in the practical steps toward that goal. Despite the fact that her boyfriend was a committed Christian, she felt she must choose God or him. Ultimately, it became clear that she had lived in a family where the rule was that only one close relationship was possible. Her parents had not stayed close to one another while loving her. They had never had more than one child to share their attention. She had never been able to break from her mother to actually pursue missions. And now she feared that she could not marry her boyfriend and remain committed to God. The goal became learning to have multiple relationships within a healthy natural and spiritual family. Only then could she move ahead positively — to lessen involvement with her mother, increase it with her Dad, and grow with both God and her boyfriend. The goal when God is built in the image of family (which happens to some degree for almost everyone) is to recognize the duplicating patterns and work toward allowing God to be God rather than the image of God protected by the family.

A variation of this tangle is the church fellowship family repeating within its relationships the same flaws as the families of origin. The characteristics of natural family become so ingrained that often people carry them into their faith families. So a family who has a hard time allowing their children independence also are in a church with a domineering parental pastor. Rather than freeing a family from its weaknesses, the faith family simply reinforces them.

One young man, Tom, came from such an overinvolved devoted

family and needed to learn emotionally and spiritually to make decisions for himself and become more mature. However, he joined a church that operates much like his family and looked to the leadership to tell him what to do about all kinds of even personal decisions. The church is led by a pastor who also is from an overinvolved family and who has taken on the same role his father played, of protecting and instructing rather than coaching toward maturity. So the church attracts people like Tom, and the people and pastor repeat the weaknesses of their own families. Often, this leads eventually to great difficulty for the church, since it is functioning like an unhealthy family, which develops symptoms in one way or another.

The challenge is to allow the faith family to be a source for change and healing rather than repetition of natural family flaws.

Faith to Avoid Facing Flaws

God's promises of help and health are great in the Bible. Many verses of Scripture speak of God lifting people up and making things new. Another calls believers to think on the good and lovely. Another says to be anxious for nothing. These words can be words of comfort and new life; or they can be words for denial. Many people prefer to avoid problems rather than to deal with them. The pain of admitting difficulties and the work in wrestling with change can be tremendous. This natural tendency toward avoidance can be either magnified or conquered with faith. If faith is used to increase avoidance, it becomes a trap.

This trap works in several ways. The first way is when people use the promise of God's healing to bypass any participatory work themselves. So the woman who is overweight repeats the promise of God to help without first acknowledging her failure and working to change the patterns that contribute to the problem. Or the man whose marriage is distant due to his lack of emotional involvement simply says that God will work things out since they believe. To them to need counseling is to admit that God cannot heal alone or that one's faith alone is not sufficient. The human element and God's human process is bypassed. Inner pain for the person or outer pain for those in the family results.

A second way this trap works is when Christians feel that they must model perfect behavior rather than realize they are sinners in the process of redemption. This makes acknowledgement of failure the same as lack of faith. So a Christian, particularly one of many years or one in a leadership position, feels his or her life cannot fall short or God will be caught short. So the common flaws of temper or inconsideration are not acknowledged. Or in a more serious vein, the alcoholic or sex addict or even workaholic hides the addiction to avoid discredit.

One man, Jack, was emotionally neglectful and at times physically abusive to his wife. However, by maintaining Christian activities and verbally acknowledging Christian beliefs, he put on the appearance of a righteous person to outsiders. His wife alternately tried to be faithfully understanding but then became overwhelmed with anger and unable to tolerate the situation. Both had hoped for many years that the problems would disappear with sufficient faith. Instead they simply built up and became compounded and produced years of wounds that later were almost unreconcilable.

To move past this trap, a deeper understanding of human sin and the freedom of God's forgiving love is needed. A more complex understanding of God's ways of healing and people's responsibility in acknowledging failures and participating in change is vital. Otherwise pain continues under the mask of faith that eventually results in stale disillusionment or tragic emotional crisis.

Trouble at Home Means Trouble with God

A crisis in one relationship often spills over into other relationships. This happens between natural relationships and spiritual relationships in at least two ways.

Everyone at times blames bad things that happen on others, whether or not they are responsible. When the boss misjudges a person at work, a worker will come home and blow up at the kids. When a mistake is made, a convenient scapegoat is often found. Often when bad things happen — illness, conflict, accidents — people blame God. After all, if God is really in control, God must have caused this or at least allowed it to happen. So God becomes the scapegoat or person to blame in trouble. People get angry, they blame, they wrestle, or they may just leave God out.

For example, one young couple found that when the husband developed a serious form of cancer he was able to maintain his faith and optimistic outlook on life. His wife however, the more realistically minded of the two, had great difficulty. And the hardest part turned out to be not only her fear of losing her husband but her already present loss of her faith relationship because of her anger toward God. As a by-product, she also lost many fellowship relationships because her church friends could not empathize with her and support her through the anger.

Another spillover from trouble at home to trouble with God happens when people find themselves with feelings, behavior, or relationships that they feel are contradictory to God's ways. In natural families, if people do something they think their parents will not like, sometimes they just do not tell them or do not go home, to avoid an unpleasant discussion. They take the easy road out, ducking away rather than wrestling with differences. People often treat God, as heavenly parent, in the same way. When there is some sort of relationship problem, they often blame, hide, or leave God rather than confront God and let the conflict mature their faith relationship. So they lose on both natural and spiritual relationship fronts.

One example of this occurred in a young woman who had married and become a committed Christian while still an alcoholic. As the conflicts mounted, she eventually was able to give up her drinking but found that the relationship remained an extremely destructive one caught in the alcoholic patterns which she was not able to change alone. After an heroic attempt at salvaging the marriage due entirely to her belief in the sanctity of marriage, she came to the conclusion that the relationship was simply unworkable and destructive. Her natural conclusion, supported in part by Christian friends, was that she was therefore doomed to lose not only her marriage but also her God. Although there is clearly no biblical condoning of divorce, she was encouraged to continue wrestling with her God who forgives and knows human shortcomings all too well. The hope was that she could find God a resource in her time of trouble rather than a condemning judge to whom she could no longer turn in her moments of despair and that she might work to build a new life. As the saying goes, two wrongs do not make a right. So too, two divorces, from a marriage and from God, did not make things right.

The goal in these tangles is to try to separate the natural and spiritual relationships. This does not mean to keep them totally apart, but rather to wrestle through each one more directly. If a person tends to avoid conflicts in natural relationships, they will likely do so in their faith relationship as well. But when conflicts are present, avoidance leads to isolation when the need is for tough dialogue. So the woman who was angry at God needed to work through the anger with her husband and also with God rather than simply blame and leave. The woman approaching divorce was encouraged to wrestle with God rather than automatically assuming God had rejected her, and to work through a faith that understands faults and failings and gives hope for growth in the future. Of course, this wrestling is harder to do sometimes with God than people, since the relationship is less physically tangible. But God can certainly be more understanding. And the practical steps of open prayer, journaling, and spiritual counsel help in making the process practical.

Married to the Ministry

A believer, who is convinced not only of God's presence but of God's call on his or her life, is like a person in love. The relationship can become all consuming, even to the exclusion of other relationships. While God certainly calls His people to make God the first love, clearly one mark of a mature faith relationship is its helping believers to love other people around them as well. Of course, it's easy to focus on the hungry, the poor, and the spiritually needy while failing to see the neighbor at home. A very typical tangle, and a struggle for almost every minister, is balancing the demands of ministry outside the home with the needs for time and attention of natural family at home. Several successful ministers sought counsel due to home conflicts that had at their root a lack of time and attention to the marriage resulting from the minister's devotion to his work. A wife who has always appeared faithful and devoted may be simmering inside or depressed, since it would not be acceptable to display outward conflicts or consider separation. They become martyrs, sacrificed for the ministry. However, such an imbalance eventually leads to symptoms, if not in the marriage then in the children. Without a home in order, which includes time, attention, and care to the daily emotional and physical needs of family, the toll will at one point or another reach the ministry itself.

The marriage-to-ministry tangle is not limited to people in full time ministry. It happens as well when a woman or man becomes committed in her or his faith and turns all her or his time and attention to church ministry. Meetings four nights a week and calls that interrupt family times weigh heavily on family life. A call to ministry should have as a required safety factor regular assessment and attention to balancing ministry with marriage and family, or other relationships.

Another version of this typical tangle is what may be called "Ireland at home." Ireland is bitterly divided by Protestants and Catholics; it is one country in near civil war, with the conflicts passed down one generation to another. And although the conflict is labeled by religion, it in fact goes much deeper and beyond religious differences. So it is in many families. What begins with a religious difference can permeate all aspects of family. Or once one member makes a change in religion, it serves as a lightning rod to express other simmering conflicts. Family members can become wedded to their faith in a way that creates emotional divorce at home.

This division within families usually occurs when religion is quite important. If religion does not matter, differences do not matter. But when faith is strong, even small differences can become major areas of conflict. In one marriage, a husband from English background and a wife from a German background met with their Christian faith as a meeting ground. Later in their marriage he took a more charismatic bent in his faith while she remained more private in her expression. This caused a tremendous distance and conflict. Without a common ground for resolution and unity in their faith, their lives suddenly seemed completely alien to one another. In another marriage, a Hindu man and Christian woman married with their romance and care for each other bonding them. After some time, the differences in religion began to grow, especially as the wife began looking to church friends for the support she now found missing at home.

What causes the greatest ongoing problem in these situations is the breakdown in communication. Terrorism and rumor must be replaced with honest discussion and sharing if the house is to continue running without being emotionally or physically torn apart. Common grounds and respect must be sought for diligently recognizing that faith differences should not be the basis for a lack of love and growing alienation within the family.

Co-Dependence in the Name of Helping

With an emerging literature bringing greater understanding about codependence, Christians will have to learn to differentiate a call to service of others from bondage to patterns of addiction. A person who has learned from his/her family a pattern of supporting the dependence or addiction of another family member will find certain Scriptures that feed this pattern. Calls for service need to come from a freedom in serving a higher power rather than a bondage to codependent patterns of self-preservation.

The line between selfishness and selffulness is a critical one. A tangle can develop in a person who finds in his/her faith a self deprecation that does not allow respect and the full development of self in the image of God. Giving then becomes destructive to self as well as to the one who is made dependent. Instead, giving one's life should lead to finding it.

People prone to service due to a lack of self-esteem or due to finding self in being better than others need growth in the area of learning to love themselves, seeing themselves as children of a loving God, able to respect and see that others are respectful of them in that way. Out of that self full growth will come a service from joy and freedom in areas of calling rather than dependence.

SPIRITUAL FAMILY RESOURCES

While the presence of a strong faith brings with it the many typical tangles and conflicts discussed above, it also brings the possibility of tremendous resources. Practitioners need to be alert to these possibilities.

Parent of Origin Healing of Natural Wounds

When clients come to a counselor for healing of family hurts, they often find help in the guidance of new patterns as well as healing through the relationship of caring itself. This same sort of healing guidance and relationship can happen when people come to faith in a personal God. Many people who have had harsh parents or lack of caring find in their faith relationship with their heavenly parent a source of acceptance and encouragement. In the Scriptures and devotional books, they find the guidance and principles for living that were lacking in their own natural families.

This parent of origin healing can be facilitated by careful counsel and prayer with ministers or counselors experienced in understanding the spiritual and emotional interactions. Guiding a client toward meditative prayer and reading as well as journaling and retreat experiences can be helpful, with follow up to understand both positive and confusing experiences within an ongoing faith pilgrimage.

Hope Through a New Spiritual Family

While the faith relationship proves to be a source of healing, the tangible relationships of the fellowship community can supplement that in a vital way. Although there can be pitfalls when the faith family simply replays old, dysfunctional patterns from the natural family, there is also the potential for having a new loving family to provide models for new relationship patterns. Despite their failings, the fellowship community is united in their faith and have a common grounds for developing caring relationships with the Bible as a guidebook. This group of people can provide the real people to make faith come alive in terms of changed relationship patterns. Particularly for those whose wider support network is small, the fellowship family can become a vital relationship resource.

One woman came from an alcoholic family in which she was physically abused by her older brothers and lived with fear and distrust of each member of the family. She found after she became a Christian and joined a faith family that it provided a safe context for beginning to make herself vulnerable to others to be loved and to try to love more directly. Granted not all were perfect members, and there were conflicts that had to be worked through. But compared to her own unpredictable, abusive home, this offered a realistic family with common understandings and mutual desire to build each other up.

Even when people play out old destructive patterns, the Christian body offers a context for lovingly confronting and challenging one another as everyone is trying to move from old relationship patterns to biblical relationship patterns. This happens more effectively when a small group of believers are committed in some tangible way in sharing in one another's lives. Often the real healing comes in one or two relationships of love that are so different from early relationships, much as a therapist-client relationship provides healing through the relationship.

This faith family can be a resource for healing that offers a wonderful entre into new relationship patterns. And once learned in a caring community, changes can be brought back into the natural family relationships as well.

Faith Forces Facing Issues

Although faith can be used to continue denial of problems, it just as often becomes a motivating force for change. People whose lives have run chaotically or in destructive patterns, often are forced to become accountable when they come to faith. They suddenly have more purpose in living, are offered hope for change, and have supporters to help them in that. Stories of confronting alcoholism, affairs, gambling, drugs, and various forms of selfish behavior once a person converts to Christianity are numerous. Reconciliation with family and people who have been wronged is part of the expected course of growth.

Several couples who might have otherwise taken the easier road of separation and divorce sought counsel and worked extremely hard to build a better relationship primarily due to the command and resource of their strong faith. Eventually, they ended up experiencing reconciliation and deepened marriages. One minister came for counseling realizing he had to mend relationship scars and patterns if he was to be an effective pastor. His hard work and change in perspective on relationships ended up benefiting not only himself but the many parishioners who came to him for guidance.

Resource in Trouble

Many clients come with a wealth of painful personal experiences and dysfunctional patterns developed over long years. In fact many people are drawn to faith precisely because of their pain and the hope that the gospel offers for new life. Their coming to faith does not instantly make these problems disappear (much to their dismay at times!). However, it does offer a resource in the midst of working to heal and change them. For clients who have this resource to draw upon, therapists would do well to encourage their tapping into it as fully as possible, to offer hope in dark hours, support from fellowship in the process of change, and one more resource to speed the change process. Neglecting this resource is no more acceptable for a responsible therapist than ignoring extended family, environmental supports, or ethnic factors. Coordination with pastors can avoid the systemic conflicts that can arise between therapist and pastor and put everyone on the same side for change.

THERAPEUTIC GOALS FOR THE FAITHFUL

People start learning about loving from their natural family, picking up both strengths and weaknesses in their patterns of loving. They bring these, in the typical tangles discussed, to a faith relationship or lack of relationship with God. In untangling them, the goal is to develop a relationship with God that is not molded by family weaknesses but rather is a distinctive relationship and is available as a resource. In developing a relationship of love with God, and with the church to the degree that it can be free of the worst of the typical tangles itself, people can experience inner healing and learn new patterns of open relationships. As this healing comes and the relationship deepens, it in turn becomes a resource for approaching old family and friend relationships with new openness and love. People then become free to pass on the caring to their neighbors in much broader ways as well.

This overall model for growth for the faithful is best summed up and explained to clients by the biblical great command, "This is the first and great command. You shall love the Lord your God with all your heart, and with all your soul, and with all your mind. The second is like unto it, you shall love your neighbor as yourself.'' A direct and right relationship of faith with God, that is personal, flexible and growing over time must be encouraged. Distinct but complementary are the natural family and friend relationships of caring, honesty, and growth that must flow from that.

Several practical goals can be useful in the process of aiming for this larger goal of direct and growing, complementary relationships.

Detriangle God

When God is caught in the natural tangles of family relationships, the goal is to detriangle Him. This happens through recognizing the traps, working to understand through reading and prayer what God Himself is like, and directly confronting conflicts with family members.

Periodic stepping back to check out unhealthy tangling of relationships and plan ways to unknot those tangles is needed. Sometimes old patterns keep recurring. Other times, new tangles develop.

Growth can then be pursued in an ongoing way by attending to each relationship individually. Clients can be encouraged to find specific ways to develop to nurture each relationship—family, friends, and God. That means time alone with honest dialogue, open ways of handling conflict, treasured times together.

Connect the Relationships Positively

Attention also needs to be paid to noticing and developing positive intertwining of relationships in complementary ways. For example, restoring time alone with God might include time for reflection about how to increase the care in each of the other relationships. Or one might covenant with a family member or friend to hold him or her accountable and be a support in plans for developing the faith relationship.

Negative tangles can be turned into positive intertwining. For example, a husband might notice that whenever he is angry with his spouse he withdraws and withholds love, often seeking out God instead. He might change this negative avoiding to a needed time out with the Lord for restoring right attitudes and prayerfully planning ways to directly reconcile with his mate.

Envision Wholeness

When relationships are tangled and self-esteem is low, hope is needed. One way to develop hope is to envision restoration, wholeness, and right relationships. There is a Scripture that says, "Without a vision the people perish." That can be true in therapy and personal growth as well.

Giving hope through beginning to imagine positive change can be done using a variety of techniques. Sculpting can be used not only to assess tangles but to envision right relationships. Those who pray can seek a vision of growth and right relationships for which they can aim. Sometimes a simple image or theme can unite the therapy toward a goal.

For example, the woman from the highly enmeshed family who had difficulty conceiving of two simultaneous relationships needed to be offered a practical picture of how she could continue to be a caring daughter while married and still have a growing faith relationship. For her, this meant being able to tell her boyfriend she needed 30 minutes of quiet prayer time in the morning alone. It meant talking to her mother perhaps even on a daily basis but not giving up all her plans when her father did not want to be around to help her mother. Another timid woman who had always held things in and been afraid to speak up — to her husband or God — needed to be offered a picture of her speaking her feelings and ideas freely, with a number of close and supportive friends, as well as eventually her husband and God.

CONCLUSIONS

Whether a therapist holds similar or widely differing beliefs from his/her client, an appreciation of the faith system of the client is critical for therapeutic growth. Without it, the therapist is proceeding as if a dominant grandmother in the family were unmentioned or a family secret never acknowledged. In those cases, much work can be done with little progress. Until the full picture is viewed, with all systems included, the work is stifled and change rarely takes place in a way that can be sustained. Change must be addressed within the client's belief system and incorporating his or her full beliefs and relationships, including God, even if the therapist does not believe in that God.

Particularly when the therapist feels that a client's belief system is contributing to the difficulties, it is vital to understand that faith. Positive relational principles and language from within that faith must be found to share the therapist's change message. Only by offering change in a faith congruent way will the client hear and process the hope offered by the therapist.

For family therapists, the faithful offer yet another layer of relationship complexity. Yet once understood and appreciated themselves, they are clients who should fully appreciate the heart of the family therapy perspective that individuals must be understood in the context of relationship. For the heart of the Biblical message as well is that people are created for relationships—with their God, their family, and others.

REFERENCES

Gibson, W. C. Psychotherapists, Psychotherapy, and Religious Beliefs: A Review of the Literature. Paper presented for research in clinical psychology class, Adelphi University, 1986.

Griffith, J. L. 1986. Employing the God-Family Relationship in Therapy with Religious Families. *Family Process*, 25: 609-618.

Lovinger, R. J. 1984. *Working with Religious Issues in Therapy.* New York: Jason Aronson, Inc.

McGoldrick, M., Pearce, J.K., and Giordano, J., eds. 1982. *Ethnicity and Family Therapy.* New York: Guilford Press.

Miller, C. Religious Issues in Family Systems Therapy. Paper presented at Center for Family Learning Conference on Issues in Family Therapy, March 1980.

Spero, M. H. 1985. The Reality and the Image of God in Psychotherapy. *American Journal of Psychotherapy*, 39:1, 75-85.

Spilka, B., Hodd, R. W., Jr., and Gorsuch, R. L. 1985. *The Psychology of Religion.* Englewood Cliffs, NJ: Prentice-Hall, Inc.

RESEARCH

Chapter Eight

Assessing the Role of Religion in Family Functioning

Melvyn C. Raider, PhD

The systemically oriented family therapist is confronted with a formidable task in developing a conceptual framework for assessing the role of religion in family functioning. The task requires explicating prescriptions for family living derived from the religions of families coming into treatment, then integrating the behavioral and structural outcomes of these prescriptions with theory and research on the nature of religious commitment within the context of family systems theory. The forthcoming assessment model is a beginning attempt to develop such a framework. However, a caveat is in order. Although illustrations of the ways in which religion influences family structure and process will be provided in the course of presenting the assessment model, these illustrations must be regarded as examples rather than generalizations. It is beyond the scope of this article to provided a systematic survey of diversity among western religions. For such a survey to be comprehensive it would need to incorporate the wide diversity among Protestant denominations as well as for the large number of sub-groups among Baptists and Pentecostals. It would need to consider the differences among Catholics, such as Roman Catholic, Greek Orthodox, and Russian Orthodox, as well as the various divisions among Judaism such as Orthodox, Conservative, and Reform (Lovinger, 1984).

CONCEPTUAL FRAMEWORKS

There are several theoretical frameworks which serve as conceptual frameworks for development of the model to assess the role of religion in family functioning. These are family systems theory as proposed by Rae Sedgwick (1981), Larry Constantine's (1986) extension of David Kantor and William Lehr's (1975) typology of family structure and process, James Anthony's (1986) extension of Allport's (1967) means extrinsic and intrinsic orientation to religiosity, and this author's research on religious commitment and family style. These are briefly summarized below.

FAMILY SYSTEMS THEORY

Sedgwick conceptualizes the family system as having six components. The family system

1. is made up of sub-systems that are interdependent and mutually interactive;
2. has boundaries or constraints that surround the system and serve to filter and translate the flow into and out of the system;
3. exists within a larger network of systems;
4. possesses openness or permeability of boundaries that allow for exchange between the system and other systems;
5. reveals proximity of sub-systems within the system and proximity of system to larger networks of systems;
6. has patterns of organization which strongly influence function. (Sedgwick, 1981, p. 12)

David Kantor and William Lehr attempted to provide a description of family process in which general systems theory was combined with an empirical study of family life. Kantor and Lehr proposed that the family system is composed of three sub-subsystems that interact with each other as well as the outside world. The purpose of the interaction is to attain goals of affect, meaning, and power through the way in which they regulate the media of space, time, and energy (Kantor & Lehr, 1975, p. 23).

Larry Constantine extended Kantor and Lehr's work and proposed a Quadruplex Model of Family Paradigms. Three of the four paradigms incorporated into Constantine's model are taken directly from David Kantor and William Lehr's (1975) empirically based typology of the forms families use to shape their processes. Kantor and Lehr identified three basic types: closed, open, and random. The fourth paradigm called the synchronous form was identified by Constantine.

According to Constantine, "The synchronous paradigm is a model of families whose members remain uninvolved and disconnected from each other yet somehow maintain relatively unvarying or even rigid patterns of behavior. In the synchronous paradigm, calm agreement and harmonious unity of action are valued above all" (Constantine, 1985, p. 515).

Kantor and Lehr indicated that the primary goal of the closed-type family is stability in all family processes. Durability, fidelity, and sincerity are the closed-family type's ideals in the affect dimension. Family loyalties are valued above those to friends. Affection is composed with emphasis on enduring sense of belonging. In the power domain authority and discipline predominate, rules are extensive and clear; obedience does not mean submission but apprenticeship to something bigger than self. In the meaning domain the closed-type family strives to maintain a stable identity; belief and values afford family members a great deal of certainty about the world; judgments and decision are made from a frame of reference of a traditional ideological system (Kantor & Lehr, 1975, pp. 145-149).

The primary goal of the open-type family is to create a family environment that is adaptive to the needs of both individual and family. According to Kantor and Lehr, responsiveness, authenticity, and the legitimacy of flexibility in expressing honest feelings are the affect goals of the open-type family. Emotions are more overtly expressed than in the closed-type family. Nurturance and intimacy, which enable the family to adapt, are sought. In the power domain, complete family member participation in decision-making encourages and assures that all members are heard. Persuasion rather than coercion is the open-type family's mandate. Opposition is accepted and worked through as the family seeks resolution of its problems. In the meaning domain the open-type family values authenticity. Relevance, affinity, and tolerance are its goals. Its reasoning process progresses from a rational frame of reference. Argument and debate are viewed as the mechanisms to reduce conflicting evidence so that as complete a view of reality as possible will be obtained (Kantor & Lehr, 1975, pp. 145-149).

The primary goal of the random-type family is exploration. Unlike the closed family, the random-type family accepts non-universal answers. According to Kantor and Lehr, exploratory nurturance and intimacy are the random-type family's goals in the affect domain. Emotions are variable and may reflect intensity at both ends of the emotional spectrum. Emphasis on spontaneity, novelty, and humor prevail. In the power domain, individual choice is the norm. Rules are relaxed and relationships are informal. Interchangeability, free choice, and challenge rather than unity are the ideals. In the meaning domain all points of view are possible. Ambiguity is permitted and even encouraged for representing the perplexity and diversity of life. Creativity is valued and encouraged (Kantor & Lehr, 1975, pp. 145-149).

RELIGIOUS COMMITMENT

Religious commitment is viewed as a construct that has four dimensions. These dimensions are intrinsic, extrinsic, quest, and orthodoxy. These dimensions derive from the writings of Allport, Anthony, and Batson/Gordon. Allport (1961) proposed a theory of personality in which religious commitment was viewed as the major integrating factor in the mature personality. Allport proposed that religious commitment could be described by two orientations: extrinsic and intrinsic. Persons with an extrinsic orientation are disposed to use religion for their own ends. The term is borrowed by axiology, to designate an interest that is held because it serves another, more ultimate interest. Extrinsic values are always instrumental and utilitarian. Persons with this orientation may find religion useful in a variety of ways—to provide security and solace, sociability and distraction, status and self-justification. If there is a creed, it is lightly held or else selectively shaped to fit more primary needs.

Also, according to Allport and Ross (1967), persons with an intrinsic orientation find their primary motive in religion. Other needs, strong as they may be, are regarded as of less ultimate significance, and they are, so far as possible, brought into harmony with the religious beliefs and prescriptions. If there is a creed, set of religious values, or religious prescriptions for living, the individual endeavors to internalize it and follow it fully. It is in this sense that he *lives* his religion.

Based upon re-examination of Allport's earlier writing on immature and mature religion, Anthony (1986) proposed a quest orientation to religion. The quest orientation may be defined as the degree of open-ended, critical struggle with existential questions. Quest orientation involves facing complex issues while resisting superficial, apparently clear cut, pat answers. An individual who approaches religion from a quest perspective recognizes that he or she does not know and probably never will discover ultimate answers to existential questions.

Added to the three dimensions of religious commitment described above, this author added a fourth dimension, which is orthodoxy. C. D. Batson (1983, 1986) views orthodoxy as an important attribute of religious commitment. Batson's position was based upon the earlier research of Glock and Stark (1965). According to Batson, orthodoxy is the extent to which an individual believes in traditional religious doctrines. It is an indicator of adherence to the literal, exact, and formal beliefs, doctrines, prescriptions, rules, and/or creed of one's religion.

RELIGIOUS COMMITMENT AND FAMILY STYLE

Based on the conceptual frameworks described above, this author carried out a two-year research project to describe the relationship between religious commitment and family style. It was hypothesized that there was a direct relationship between religious commitment that was authoritative and/or exact and a closed-family style. Similarly, it was hypothesized that there was a direct relationship between religious commitment that was collaborative and/or dialogical and an open-family style. The study involved conceptually defining and operationalizing religious commitment and family styles, assembling a sample large enough to include sufficient variability to facilitate statistical analysis, and describing findings (Article under review: *Journal of Marital & Family Therapy*).

No statistically significant relationship was found between religious commitment which was collaborative and an open-family style. However, the hypothesis that there was a direct relationship between religious commitment that was authoritative and/or exact and a closed-family style was partially accepted.

It can be asserted that for religious families, beliefs and values which in turn define the family's boundaries tend to be fixed, whereas family structure and processes, such as emotional climate, norms, problem solving, decision making, and communication, tend to be more flexible and therefore amenable to change. This assertion derives from the author's research. It was demonstrated that respondents with higher mean scores in orthodoxy were associated with a closed paradigm or image of their families. Respondents with lower mean scores in orthodoxy were associated with an open paradigm or image of their families. This relationship was statistically significant at the .05 level. No statistically significant relationship was found between orthodoxy and regime. To an extent, this finding supports practice wisdom that religious families tend to be fixed in their beliefs and values and are less open to guidance and information from sources outside of the church, synagogue, temple, or family system. However, findings suggest that this generalization is valid only for the respondent perceptions of their family's paradigm, which is composed of shared beliefs and values. It does not hold for respondents perceptions of their family's regime. Regime is comprised of the patten of behaviors the family uses as it interacts with one another, as well as the family's structure, which is comprised of the ways in which the family organized itself and establishes rules to regulate family interaction.

Similar to the relationship of orthodoxy to a closed paradigm is the relationship of an end orientation to religion and a closed paradigm. Respondents with higher mean scores in end orientation were associated with a closed paradigm or image of their families. Respondents with lower mean scores in end orientation were associated with a random paradigm of their families. This relationship was significant at the .05 level. Although this finding is not exactly similar to the one discussed above, it is parallel since end orientation, like orthodoxy, is a measure of religious commitment in which the individual internalizes and lives his/her religion. Further, both the open and random paradigm reflect responsiveness to information and communication from outside the family system. Both paradigms or images are flexible and amenable to change. In fact, the random paradigm may be viewed to some extent a more extreme form of the open paradigm.

The parallel nature of the relationship of both orthodoxy and end orientation to a closed paradigm are particularly useful to family therapists for assessing how a family uses its religion. Orthodoxy may be assessed rather quickly both in terms of interview and observed behaviors, whereas end orientation is more difficult to assess requiring extensive interviewing or completion of lengthy instruments. This suggests that assessing orthodoxy may be an easier and more convenient approach for assessing how religious commitment relates to family style.

Recognizing that for religious families it may be easier to intervene and possibly change family process and structure than it is to change family values, beliefs, and boundaries, it is useful to examine each component of the assessment model in detail.

THE ASSESSMENT MODEL

I. Family Structure

A family system is made up of sub-systems that are interdependent and interactive. The sub-systems are individuals who interact with each other and thereby establish relationships. The basis for the relationship may be utilitarian, such as economic, legal, physical, and/or socio-emotional (Sedgwick, 1981). Perhaps the most obvious influence of religion on family functioning is the area of family structure. In fact, sociologist Cal Zimmerman has suggested that all the major world religions have very rigid and almost identical family systems in common (Zimmerman, 1974). These family systems standardized the family unit — relations between husband and wife and relations between parents and children — and in so doing provided the main unit out of which societies could be built. "In other words, the most sacred or divine aspect of society is considered to be the family system and being religious is tantamount to being a good husband, a good wife, or a good parent . . . . " Judaism, Christianity, Confucianism, Hinduism, Zoroastrianism, and Islam all explicitly join family life and religion (Zimmerman, 1974).

Religions have specified rules and norms concerning marriage, divorce, contraception, abortion, premarital sexuality, fidelity, cohabitation, procreation, and sex roles. The Orthodox Jewish religion structures family relationships on the basis of writings in the Torah, Talmud, and Mishnah. These sources establish the husband as head of the family unit and owner of its property. It also defines family membership as having three criteria: blood relationship, legal ties (marriage), or geographical proximity. Benjamin Schlesinger cites four values from the Talmud that structure Jewish families. The first is purity in the family, which emphasizes chastity prior to marriage, absolute fidelity within marriage, and encourages procreation to perpetuate the Jewish people. Companionship between husband and wife is also a value adhered to to encourage mutual physical and emotional well-being. The second value is effective child rearing, which specifies parenting roles with regard to the physical, social, educational, and religious needs of children. The third value requires that children accept the authority of mother and father and seek to provide parents with a status of dignity throughout their lives. The fourth value is family compatibility, which seeks to maintain family cohesiveness. It involves (1) coordinating the fulfillment of individual potentialities and aspirations; (2) a strong feeling of identity with others in the close and extended family groups; (3) a pooling of resources for the benefit of all; and, (4) a sense of family pride (Schlesinger, 1974, pp. 29-30).

Roman Catholic guidelines formulated to structure family living were formalized in 1933 in the encyclical *Casti Connubii* and remain largely affirmed in the most recent document (1983) on marriage and family titled *Educational Guidance in Human Love*. William D'Antonio has suggested that traditional teaching with regard to family life were reaffirmed in *Casti Connubii*. These traditional teachings were (1) procreation and rearing of children is the prime purpose of marriage; (2) conjugal love is an important purpose of marriage; (3) family size may be limited for licit reasons; (4) periodic abstinence is the only licit means of birth control for married couples; (5) total abstinence from any sexual activity is the rule for the unmarried and masturbation is a serious sin; (6) marriage is a sacrament, indissoluble except through annulment; and (7) a woman's proper place is in the home (D'Antonio, 1985, p. 396).

In 1983 the Vatican released a document titled *Educational Guidance in Human Love,* which was meant to provide a framework for sex education. The document essentially reaffirmed traditional teachings as did *Casti Connubii*, but it also offered a positive orientation to human sexuality within the context of marriage (D'Antonio, 1985).

Patrick McNamara has attempted to provide an overview of conservative Protestant Pastoral literature as it relates to family structure. Significant presuppositions are these: (1) The family is the most significant factor in living. (2) Primary love relationships in the home must be that of husband and wife. This is to create an atmosphere in which children will learn the importance of a loving home, where values are communicated and laws are respected — effective parenting provides firm discipline of children in combination with manifestations of love. (3) The husband is viewed as the head of the family with submission of wife to husband. Decisions are not, however, to be made without hearing and evaluating the wife's views. Also, respect for the wife is viewed as essential to maintaining a love relationship. The husband is to be unselfish, gracious, trusting, sincere, polite, generous, humble, kind, and patient. Problems between husband and wife are to be resolved by mutual decision. (4) Love of others as well as self can flourish only in service to others (McNamara, 1985, pp. 454-456).

Questions to assist in assessment of the ways in which religion influences family structure follow:

1. To what extent does the family's religion specify rules and norms concerning marriage, divorce, contraception, abortion, premarital sexuality, fidelity, cohabitation, and procreation?
2. To what extent does the family's religion specify sex roles?
3. To what extent does the family's religion specify children's roles?

4. To what extent does the family's religion specify parenting roles, values, and practices?
5. To what extent does the family's religion specify relationships with extended family members?
6. To what extent does the family's religion value family life?
7. To what extent does the family's religion define family membership?
8. To what extent does the family's religion emphasize subordination of individual needs and benefits to family group needs and benefits?

II. Family Processes

Family systems evolve processes that, taken together, determine the pattern by which the family organizes communication and interaction among family sub-systems. Family processes regulate how the family processes information, makes decisions, resolves conflict, facilitates individuation, provides socio-emotional support, accommodates stress, and responds to change. Family processes or system linkages are emotional bonding, decision making, information processing, conflict resolution, and communication.

Emotional bonding is the amount of depth of feeling and breadth of attachment among family members. Positive emotional bonding is loving and caring and provides a sense of connectedness that brings the family together. Helen Harris Perlman describes this quality as "a human being's feeling or sense of emotional bonding with another. It leaps into being like an electric current or it emerges and develops cautiously when emotion is aroused by and invested in someone or something and that something and that someone connects back responsively" (Perlman, 1979, p. 15).

The relationship allows family "to feel secure and thus to go forward to risk new learning and new experiences. It combines a warm acceptance of each person in his/her specialness and his/her present being. . . ." (Perlman, 1979, p. 30). Emotional bonding also influences the quality of the sexual relationship between husband and wife.

Information processing refers to the patterns of information utilization. Effective information processing combines the use of both information within the family as well as information from community sources such as neighbors, physician, school teacher, and pastor. Beavers (1985) suggests that effective information processing is based on a framework where knowledge is viewed as limited and finite and that the family never possesses unchallengeable truth.

Decision making is the process of choosing among alternatives so that the process results in a choice that is consistent with the family members age, experience, resources, and ability. Effective decision making is a process that seeks a balance between rigidity and diffuseness. Effective decision making involves systemic openness whereas ineffective decision making is characterized by family rules and myths that deny uncertainty.

Conflict resolution is a process of managing differences. Effective conflict resolution accepts that harmony is not necessarily always healthy and in which differences are tolerated as each individual in the family changes and grows. Disagreements are handled openly rather than smoothed over or ignored.

Communication is a process in which words, actions, and gestures are used by each family member to share information and express his or her opinions, feelings, and personal desires. Effective communication involves skills in verbal expression, active listening, and negotiation or solutions to problems. Positive communication also involves the ability of each family member to define his/her own wishes and needs clearly.

Implications of this author's research findings on the relationship between religious commitment and family style are potentially very important for family therapists. They suggest that therapists who are respectful of the family's image of themselves as orthodox in their religious beliefs may potentially engage religious families and may help the family to change its structure and/or process. Further, by acknowledging and supporting the family's religious values and beliefs, the family's own religion may be creatively utilized as a framework to help them alter dysfunctional family structure rules and interactional patterns.

Questions to assist in assessment of the ways in which religion influences family processes follow:

1. What is the religious orthodoxy of each member of the family? Are the orientations of each family member similar? Which family member's religious orthodoxy predominates in the family?
2. Which dimensions of family process (emotional bonding, decision making, information processing, conflict resolution, communication, adaptation, regulation, and identity) may be characterized as open, closed, random, or synchronous? To what extent does the family's orthodoxy influence the characterization of family processes?
3. To what extent does the family's religion emphasize emotional closeness, nurturance, and intimacy among family members?
4. To what extent does the family's religion offer guidelines for family problem solving and decision making?
5. To what extent does the family's religion influence the family's openness to information from the environment?
6. To what extent does the family's religion influence the family's time orientation (i.e., past, present, and future)?
7. To what extent does the family's religion influence each other (i.e., persuasion, logic, and coercion)?
8. To what extent does the family's religion influence the family's capacity to tolerate diversity and different points of view?

III. Boundaries

The family system is separated from other systems by boundaries. These boundaries serve to sort out, accept, or reject information that comes into or flows out of the family system. "Boundaries that surround the family are social (norms, expectations, myths), physical (space, territory, housing), emotional (feelings), historical (legacy, belief, expectation), and individual (ability, need, desire)" (Sedgwick, 1981, p. 13). The family is also bounded by its beliefs, morals, and values. These beliefs are the basis for the formal and informal rules and norms that the family establishes to guide its members in the ways they behave toward each other, as well as other people and groups that comprise other systems in the environment. Boundaries evolve as a function of family history, social contact with others, and religious values.

Family morals and values and religious morals and values often become intertwined. Hines and Boyd-Franklin suggest that among many Black Baptist families, values are directly or indirectly derived from religious doctrine (McGoldrick, 1982, p. 96). Similarly, among Fundamental Protestants, Christian religious values serve as the major frame of reference for determining family values and ethical positions. For example, love is viewed as possessing qualities of devotion, loyalty, and social responsibility. Future orientation is more valued than present time or past orientation. Self-reliance and/ or reliance on the church is preferred over public and social services.

Family norms, rules, and expectations also may reflect religious teachings and doctrines. Irish Catholic families often reflect a profound sense of guilt and suffering. McGoldrick indicates some Irish Catholics find virtue and sanctity in silent suffering or in offering up their pain to God in imitation of Christ (McGoldrick, 1982, p. 319). This norm, based upon the concept of original sin, derives from the belief that people are bad and will suffer deservedly for their sins. Jewish families also perceive suffering to be a shared value. Originating from religious persecution, suffering is assumed to be a basic part of life; and by virtue of the burden of oppression, Jewish families reassure themselves that they are God's chosen people. Suffering binds families together and helps establish boundaries of the Jewish community as well. In addition to suffering as a value, religion is the basis for family norms and expectations for Jewish families. Herz and Rosen indicate that some of these are the centrality of the family in life and intellectual achievement. The priority of family living for Jewish families is derived from the first commandment in the Torah (Bible), which is "you shall be fruitful and multiply." Marriage, raising children, and establishing a family has been at the core of Jewish tradition. The belief in the importance of family as a sacred institution stems from the idea that it is a violation of God's law not to marry.

Jewish families value education as a central ethos, perhaps also as important as the family itself. The importance of education and intellectual achievement evolved from the study of the Torah and other religious writings. As an outgrowth of the Jewish family's valuing of intellectual achievement, Jewish families often expect that a college education is virtually mandatory (Herz and Rozen, 1982).

Religion is also a powerful determinant of the nature of boundaries between families and others in their environment. According to McGoldrick, Fundamental Christian families may establish boundaries between themselves and outsiders by projecting fear and hostilities on outsiders in the form of scapegoating. Jewish families have historically established boundaries between themselves and non-Jews by actively discouraging intermarriage. Intermarriage was perceived to be a threat to the survival of the Jewish people and a violation of a major family value as derived from traditional religious documents.

Similarly, Hans Mol concluded that based on his survey of census data in Australia, denominational adherence has a significant effect on whom one marries in Australia. This suggests strong family boundaries exist resulting in a high within-denominational marriage rate and a low mixed denominational marriage rate for over 70 years.

Questions to assist in assessment of the way in which religion influences family boundaries follow:

1. To what extent does the family's religion influence family rules, norms, and expectations which determine how family members behave?
2. To what extent does the family's religion influence the ways in which the family relates to friends, neighbors, and people of different beliefs, religions, and races?
3. To what extent does the family's religion influence family morals, values, and ethical positions?
4. To what extent does the family's religion specify the role of the family in the religious community of congregation?
5. To what extent does the family's religion influence the ways in which the family makes use of community resources such as educational, health, mental health, and social service institutions?
6. To what extent does the family's religion influence the family's choice of residence locality?
7. To what extent does the family's religion influence the degree

of permeability of the family's boundaries with the neighborhood, community, and outside environment?

IV. Family System Equilibrium or Integration

Religion is an important mechanism for providing the family with a means whereby it integrates its identify as a family unit. This integration of identity provides the family with a mechanism for preserving itself as a unit over time. From a systems perspective, religion enables the family to establish its equilibrium. Equilibrium refers to a state of balance among system components or sub-systems. Equilibrium is achieved when members of the family are comfortable and secure with the nature of the interaction among sub-system components and the type and quality of exchanges with the larger network of systems. Stability occurs when there is a commitment to a set of shared expectations. When such commitment exists, energies of family members become available for other things since family relationships are sufficiently stable.

Hans Mol speaks to this integration of identity or establishment of an equilibrium from a sociological perspective, which he identifies as "sacralization." As he would have it:

> There seems to be at least four mechanisms of this sacralizing process. Together or separately they seem to protect crucial sources of identity and meaning from the onslaught of change and differentiation. The first of these dimensions one may describe as objectification: The projection of order into a beyond where it is less vulnerable to contradictions, exceptions, and contingencies — in other words, a rarified realm where major outlines of order can be maintained in the face of temporal, but all-absorbing dislocations of that order. The second mechanism might be called commitment: the emotional anchorage in the various proliferating foci of identity. The third one is ritual: The repetitive actions, articulations, and movements which prevent the object of sacralizations to be lost from sight. The fourth one is myth: the integration of various strains in a coherent, shorthand, symbolic account. We may assume that sacralization takes place when certain foci of identity (be it the

self, the group, society, or whatever) are structurally important. (Mol, 1974, p. 94)

Zimmerman also has identified this sacralization role of religion in family life. He pointed out religion standardized the mores and made sacred the rules of the highest order concerning the relations between family members (Zimmerman, 1974). Most basically religions have integrated other worldly love with familial based upon marital, parental, and sibling emotional bonds (Thomas and Henry, 1985).

It is possible that the most important mechanism of sacralization that religion has institutionalized in family life is the ritual. From an anthropological perspective, rituals both preserve as well as transform families. Rituals function to preserve by "perpetuating myths, reinforcing and rigidifying beliefs, and suppressing information which could produce change. In bringing about change they may introduce new ways of ordering and conceptualizing reality" (Hartman and Laird, 1983, p. 106). Religious priorities carried out both at home or in places of worship provide all the necessary characteristics of a ritual. According to Sally Moore and Barbara Myerhoff (1977), these characteristics are repetition, acting, special behavior or stylization, order or organization, evocative presentational style, and social meaning.

On the basis of this writer's practice experience with families, it may be observed that quest religiously oriented families are most often associated with few or underutilized rituals whereas intrinsically religiously end-oriented families are often associated with a pattern of rituals that have meaning and value. Extrinsically religiously means-oriented families are often associated with rituals that are devoid of meaning.

1. To what extent does the family's religion emphasize prescribed family rituals that are characterized by repetition, acting, stylization, and order?
2. To what extent does the family's religion emphasize tradition, stability, and order?
3. To what extent is religious devotion and worship integrated into family life?

4. To what extent does the family's religion shape the family's identity?
5. To what extent does the family's religion provide the family with a sense of history or legacy?

REFERENCES

Abrahamson, Mark, and William P. Anderson. 1984. "People's Commitments to Institutions," *Social Psychology Quarterly* 47, No. 4: 371-81.

Allport, G.W., 1961. *The Individual and His Religion*. New York: MacMillan.

Allport, G.W., and J.M. Ross. 1967. "Personal Religious Orientation and Prejudice," *Journal of Personality and Social Psychology* 5(4): 432-443.

Anthony, James. 1986. Religiosity and Mental Health, Unpublished Doctoral Dissertation, The Fielding Institute.

Bahr, Howard M., and Bruce A. Chadwick. 1985. "Religion and Family in Middletown, USA," *Journal of Marriage and the Family* 47 (May): 407-14.

Batson, C.D., and L. Raynor-Price. "Religious Orientation and Complexity of Thought about Existential Concerns," Unpublished Manuscript, University of Kansas.

Batson, C.D., and P. Schoenrade. 1986. "Brother Love or Self-Concern?: Behavioral Consequences of Religion," in L.B. Brown and M. Argyle Eds., *Current Topics in Psychology of Religion*. New York: Pergamon.

Beavers, W.R. 1985. *Successful Marriage*. New York: W.W. Norton.

Bergin, Allen E. 1980. "Psychotherapy and Religious Values," *Journal of Consulting and Clinical Psychology* 48, No. 1: 95-105.

Brutz, Judith L., and Bron B. Ingoldsby. 1984. "Conflict Resolution in Quaker Families," *Journal of Marriage and the Family* 46 (Feb.): 21-26.

Constantine, Larry L. 1986. *Family Paradigms: The Practice of Theory in Family Therapy*. New York: Guilford Press.

D'Antonio, William V. 1985. "The American Catholic Family: Signs of Cohesion and Polarization," *Journal of Marriage and the Family* 47 (May): 395-405.

Demerath, N.J. 1965. *Social Class in American Protestantism*. Chicago: Rand McNally.

Framo, J.L. 1976. "Family of Origin as a Therapeutic Resource for Adults in Marital and Family therapy: You Can and Should Go Home Again," *Family Process*, 15, June.

Gaw, Albert. 1982. *Cross Cultural Psychiatry*, Boston: John Wright.

Green, James. 1982. *Cultural Awareness in the Human Services*. NJ: Prentice-Hall.

Glock, C.Y., and R. Stark. 1965. *Religion and Society in Tension*. Chicago: Rand McNally.

Hartman, A., and J. Laird. 1983. *Family Centered Social Work Practice*. New York: The Free Press.

Herz, F.M., and E.S. Rosen. 1982. "Jewish Families," in Monica McGoldrick, *Ethnicity and Family Therapy*. New York: The Guilford Press.

Hoffman-Graff, Mary Ann. 1977. "Interviewer Use of Positive and Negative Self-Disclosure and Interviewer-Subject Sex Pairing," *Journal of Counseling Psychology* 24, 184-190.

Kantor, David, and William Lehr, 1975. *Toward a Theory of Family Process.* San Francisco: Jossey-Bass, Inc.

King, M.B., and R.A. Hunt. 1975. "Measuring the Religious Variable: National Replication," *Journal for the Scientific Study of Religion* 14: 13-22.

Lenski, G.E. 1953. "Social Correlates of Religious Interest," *American Sociological Review* 18: 533-44.

Lovinger, Robert J. 1984. *Working with Religious Issues in Therapy*. New York: Jason Aronson, Inc.

Lum, Doman. 1986. *Social Work Practice with People of Color*. Monterey, CA: Brooks/Cole.

McCarthy, Patricia, and Nancy Betz. 1978. "Differential Effects of Self-Disclosing Versus Self-Involving Counselor Statements," *Journal of Counseling Psychology* 25, 479-482.

McGoldrick, Monica, and John Pearce, Joseph Giordano. 1982. *Ethnicity and Family Therapy*. New York: The Guilford Press.

McNamara, Patrick H. 1985. "The New Christian Right's View of the Family and Its Social Science Critics: A Study in Differing Presuppositions," *Journal of Marriage and the Family* 47 (May): 449-458.

Mol, Hans. 1974. "The Sacralization of the Family with Special Reference to Australia," *Journal of Comparative Family Studies* 5, No. 2: 98-108.

Moore, S., and B. Myerhoff. 1977. *Secular Ritual*. Amsterdam: Van Gorcum.

Nilsson, David, and Donald Strassberg, Jill Bannon. 1979. "Perceptions of Counselor Self-Disclosure: An Analogy Study," *Journal of Counseling Psychology*, 26, 399-404.

Perlman, H. 1979. *Relationship*. Chicago: University of Chicago Press.

Ragan, C., and H.N. Malony, B. Beit-Hallahmi. 1979. "Psychologists and Religion: Professional Factors and Personal Belief," *Review of Religious Research*, 21, 208-217.

Rveneni, Jri. 1979. *Networking Families in Crisis*. New York: Human Sciences Press.

Schlesinger, Benjamin. 1974. "The Jewish Family and Religion," *Journal of Comparative Family Studies* 5, No. 2: 27-36.

Sedgwick, Rae. 1981. *Family Mental Health*. St. Louis: C.V. Mosby Co.

Speck, R.V., and C. Atteneave. 1973. *Family Networks*. New York: Vantage Books.

Thomas, Darwin, and Gwendolyn D. Henry. 1985. "The Religion and Family Connection: Increasing Dialogue in the Social Sciences," *Journal of Marriage and the Family* 47 (May): 369-379.

Thorton, Arland. 1985. "Reciprocal Influences of Family and Religion in a

Changing World," *Journal of Marriage and the Family* 47 (May): 381-394.

Warner, R.S. 1979. "Theoretical Barriers to the Understanding of Evangelical Christianity," *Sociological Analysis* 40, No. 1: 1-9.

Whitaker, C., and D. Keith. 1981. "Symbolic-Experimental Family Therapy" in *Handbook of Family Therapy*, Gurman, D., and Kniskern, D., Eds. New York: Brunner-Mazel.

Zimmerman, Carl E. 1974. "Family Influence Upon Religion," *Journal of Comparative Family Studies* Vol. 5, No. 2: 1-16.

Chapter Nine

Religion in Family Therapy Journals: A Review and Analysis

Eugene W. Kelly, Jr., PhD

INTRODUCTION

Religious values are closely associated with family values. And religion is important to most Americans. In the 1986 Gallup poll (Gallup, 1987) 55% said that religion is very important in their lives; 31% said it was fairly important. Seventy-one percent reported belonging to a church or synagogue, and 42% attended a religious service in a typical week. These percentages were not significantly different from the previous six years. This extraordinarily broad, and in many instances, deeply personal investment in religious values has a potentially significant bearing on family therapy, especially with religiously oriented clients.

Although deep differences persist regarding the positive and/or negative effects of religion on mental health (Bergin, 1980; Ellis, 1980; Walls, 1980), there can be little doubt that religious values influence the ideas, feelings, and choices of many persons in the realm of marriage and family life and intimate interpersonal relations. Bergin (1980), a religious believer, and Ellis (1980), an atheist, both hold that values are an inevitable and pervasive part of psychotherapy. Bernal and Ysern (1986) have argued cogently that contemporary family therapy is significantly influenced by ideology, that is, a set of values, beliefs, and ideals that inform people of their social reality. Zuk (1978) has emphasized the importance of formulas to deal with religious and ethnic difference in families.

Despite religion's potentially major influence in family and interpersonal dynamics, religious factors, as reflected in the relevant literature, appear greatly underrepresented in psychotherapy in general (Bergin, 1980, 1983) and family therapy in particular (Lantz, 1979; Pattison, 1982; Zuk, 1978). This study was undertaken to examine this apparent discrepancy and the manner in which religion is treated in family therapy journal literature.

Specifically, the purposes of this study were threefold: first, to determine quantitatively the extent to which religion occurs in articles of journals specifically devoted to family therapy; second, to analyze qualitatively how religion is perceived and handled in family therapy as represented in the same literature; and third, to provide recommendations for practice and research based on the findings of this review and analysis.

Family therapy journals alone were chosen for this study because it was reasoned that the body of literature in these journals would be most representative of mainline thinking and practice in the field of family therapy. Other types of journals, although certainly including occasional pieces on family therapy, were excluded in order to retain a focus specifically on the field of family therapy as distinguished from other forms of therapy, for example group therapy. A single focus on family therapy journals also made the study manageable within the resources available for the study. A more extended review is projected for future studies.

METHOD

The first step toward identifying the mainline journals in family therapy was a review of all journal titles in *Ulrich's International Periodicals Directory* (1987) under the categories of psychology, psychiatry, social service and welfare, and sociology (neither "family" nor "family therapy" are listed as separate categories). This search yielded an initial list of 36 journals that appeared to be devoted exclusively or primarily to family therapy. This list was further reduced to a list of 12 journals by eliminating journals that are focused on family issues or group work generally and not on family therapy, publications that are more in the form of newsletters than journals, publications with a religious emphasis, and journals not published in English. The study used this final 12-journal list, which consists of the following titles: *American Journal of Family Therapy, Australian Journal of Family Therapy, Child and Family Behavior Therapy, Contemporary Family Therapy* (formerly *International Journal of Family Therapy*), *Family Process, Family Therapy, Family Therapy Networker, International Journal of Family Psychiatry, Journal of Family Therapy, Journal of Marital and Family Therapy* (formerly *Journal of Marriage and Family Counseling*), *Journal of Psychotherapy and the Family,* and *Journal of Sex and Marital Therapy.*

With only a few exceptions, consisting of several issues that could not be located, all article titles in all volumes of all 12 journals were surveyed, for a total of approximately 3,615 articles. This total is given as an approximation because certain pieces (e.g., editorials, author responses) were sometimes included and sometimes excluded, depending on the nature of the piece. In any case, over 3,600 articles were surveyed. When an article title suggested, even slightly, that religion might be included, the article was scanned for any mention of religion.

EXTENT OF RELIGION IN FAMILY THERAPY JOURNALS

Of the approximately 3,615 articles surveyed, 94, or 2.6%, dealt with or included some reference to religion. This number by itself, however, is only minimally enlightening. Many articles mentioned religion only in a passing or insignificant manner. Others included it as a subcategory or secondary aspect of a larger factor, for example as one of several cultural factors. Still others contained references to religion only in its pathological or deficient expressions.

To obtain a better picture of the extent to which religion occurs in family therapy journal literature, the 94 articles were arranged in six categories along two dimensions (2 × 3 matrix): the extent to which religion was treated (major or slight component of article), and the predominant valuation of religion in the article (positive, negative, neutral). Religion was judged to be a major component when it was the leading theme of an article or occurred as a significant subtheme with an important bearing on the substance of an article. Religion was considered to have been treated in a positive light when it was presented, at least in part, as a legitimate element of effective living and therapy. In those articles in which religion appeared entirely or predominantly as a source of pathology or as detrimental or unrelatable to effective therapy, a negative classification was used. In those articles in which no value was placed on religion, the neutral category was used. The results of this classification are presented in Table 1.

Religion occurs as a major component of 43 articles, or 1.3% of all 3,615 articles. Of these, only 27 articles, or .7%, deal with religion in a major and positive way. Even when those articles which refer to religion in a slight and positive manner are included, religion occurs in a positive light in only 41 articles, or 1.1%.

RELIGION AS THEME OR SUBTHEME

As an additional way of viewing how religion was treated in the 95 identified articles, they were divided into 10 subject categories according to the primary topical focus of each article. The 10 categories are: religion and clergy/pastoral counselors vis-à-vis secular counselor as primary or co-primary themes (8 articles), values (6),

TABLE 1. Extent and Valuation of Religion in Family Therapy Journal Articles

	Extent		
Valuation	Major	Slight	Total
Positive	27	14	41
Negative	11	10	21
Neutral	5	27	32
Total	43	51	94

Note: The values represent the number of articles in each category.

culture (16), death and mourning (9), philosophy/aesthetics (6), fundamentalism/cults (5), marriage encounter/enrichment and premarital counseling (13), measurement/computers (11), sex (4), miscellaneous (16). Because these broad topics are not mutually exclusive and two or more often occur together in one article (e.g., sexual values, death rituals in different cultures), the categorization used here is not hard and fast. However, it is a reasonable portrayal of this literature and helpful for analyzing its contents.

Religion As Primary Theme

Nine articles were judged to have religion or therapist-clergy relations as their primary or co-primary focus; all approached religion in a predominantly positive way. Pattison's (1982) work in particular offers a compact but comprehensive guide for effectively managing religious issues in family therapy. Among specific suggestions for the positive use of religion in family therapy, Griffith (1986) describes methods for therapeutically employing family members' personal relationship with God, Lantz (1979) discusses therapeutic strategies for counseling Protestant evangelical families based on an understanding of the religious beliefs and practices of these families, and Midelfort (1962) describes how positive therapeutic change can be reinforced by therapist-clergy collaboration that facilitates a return to responsible Christian living (see also Yost, 1986). An excerpt about the prodigal son from an encyclical letter of John Paul II, with a favorable introduction by Gerald Zuk, provides a deeply religious perspective on forgiveness in the family (John Paul II, 1981). Mutual understanding and methods of collaboration among secular therapists, pastoral counselors, and clergy are the theme of other articles (Boverman & Adams, 1964; Sander, 1970; Kaslow & Gingrich, 1977).

Values Theme

Somewhat surprisingly, five of the six articles in the "values" category had only slight to negligible references to religion (Abroms, 1978; Cortroneo & Krasner, 1977; Pittman, 1985; Trotzer, 1981; Wendorf & Wendorf, 1985). Coles' (1987) discussion of religious beliefs and practices of a family under stress presents religion in a significant and positive light.

Cultural Theme

Religion appears in a predominantly neutral to negative aspect in the 15 articles whose major theme was cultural factors in family life and therapy. For example, Catholicism is associated with authoritarianism and moral rigidity in Irish Americans (McGoldrick & Pearce, 1981) and Slovak Americans (Stein, 1973, 1978) and with heavy drinking among Puerto Rican and Mexican Americans (Panitz, McConchie, Sauber, & Fonseca, 1983) and Irish Americans (Ablon, 1980). Religion is presented as an integral part of Malaysian (Kinzie, Sushama, & Lee, 1972), Hindu (Narain, 1964), Turkish (Gardner, 1970), and Kenyan (Wilson, 1982) cultures and as important to understanding family dynamics in these cultures. But in none of these articles is religion explored beyond its cultural manifestations or examined as a potential source of benefit in family living and therapy. Religion further appears as a complication in interethnic marriages (McGoldrick & Preto, 1984), as a probable cause of the raising of women's status and the consequent dissolution of the nuclear family in an Aborigine society (Huffer, 1973), as a source of conflict with modern values for Jewish Orthodox (Juni, 1980) and Islamic families (El-Islam, 1983), and as a factor in social patterning and, when pushed with missionary zeal, in undermining indigenous culture (Lau, 1984). Religion is described as more prominent and influential in some cultures, e.g., Irish and Black American, than others, e.g., Jewish American (McGoldrick & Rohrbaugh, 1987). Jewish American families are described as generally high on secular values, which are related to success in family therapy and a high rate of health care seeking (Zuk, 1978).

These culturally oriented articles portray religion only in its specifically cultural manifestations. Religion is treated as a set of beliefs, practices, and rituals that tend to persist as a pervasive cultural influence on family behavior. Perhaps it is the nature of such cultural investigations that the creative and life-enhancing faith experiences and beliefs underlying the cultural manifestations and distortions of religion are rarely explored. The wellsprings of religious faith do not appear here; only cultural superstructures. It is certainly important to know and use these superstructures in family therapy. However, a concentration on the cultural aspects of religion to the neglect of religious wellsprings obscures the potentially positive influence of religion for effective family functioning and family therapy.

Death and Mourning Theme

Religion appears in a mixed light in nine articles on death and mourning. Religion is described as a significant, and in some respects, helpful part of the mourning process for Irish, Black, and Puerto Rican Americans (McGoldrick, Hines, Lee, & Preto, 1986). A positive connection between death and religious faith is powerfully illustrated in a compelling biographical piece about an AIDS victim who, with the support of his religiously oriented family, recovers a mature religious faith as he approaches his death (Bradley, 1988). However, in only one article are religious (Judeo-Christian) values and rituals clearly described and presented as potentially valuable adjuncts to therapy with families in the grieving process (Bowlby-West, 1983). In contrast, Gelcer (1983) maintains that families in mourning are increasingly without the support of religious customs, and, therefore, therapeutic procedures based on mental health principles and practices are becoming more important in the mourning process. In other articles, religion is mentioned in passing as sometimes helpful to families at the time of a child's death (Easson, 1980), as often a source of fright to children in their understanding of death (Glicken, 1978), and as offering a sense of the sacred at the time of death, although this sacredness tends to be undermined by hospital procedures and the insensitivity of some clergy (Bertman, 1980). In two biographical pieces, a suicide victim states in a final letter that he dies praying to God (Anonymous, 1982), and a therapist-author, describing his relationship with his deceased father, notes briefly his comfort in a religious practice (Taggart, 1980).

With only three exceptions (Bradley, 1988; Bowlby-West, 1983; McGoldrick et al., 1986), these eight articles present religion as a relatively insignificant factor in either understanding or helping in death and mourning experiences. Yet religion in all forms speaks powerfully to the meaning and experience of death and mourning. Mature religious faith and practice engage persons and communities in an effort to understand, confront, and eventually accept death in a positive way. Despite these profound links between religion and death and mourning, family therapy journal literature generally gives only minor attention to the therapeutic possibilities of religion in treating death and mourning experiences.

Philosophical and Aesthetical Themes

Six philosophically/aesthetically oriented articles, with just one exception (Jordan, 1985), contain only slight or definitely subordinated references to religion. Jordan describes favorably how the Chinese spiritual tradition of Taoism helps to elucidate the use of paradoxical intentions in family therapy. In an article on systems theory, religion occurs in a case illustration and is treated in a therapeutically respectful manner (Elkaim, 1985). In two articles dealing primarily with aesthetics and family therapy, religion or spirituality is touched on lightly (Allman, 1982; Keeney & Sprenkle, 1982). An article on existentialism (Feldman, 1980) and another on epistemology (Liddle, 1982) allude in passing to religious or spiritual categories. Except for an elucidation of Taoism in relation to family therapy, references to religion in this set of articles are clearly subordinate and largely inconsequential to other themes which the authors are developing.

Fundamentalism and Cults

Religion appears in some of its more distorted, unattractive, and uncommon expressions in five articles dealing with fundamentalism, cults, and spiritualism. Whipple (1987), describing how certain tenets and attitudes of Christian fundamentalism tend to impede family therapy, especially in the treatment of wife abuse, offers a number of therapeutic strategies for working effectively with, rather than against, clients' fundamentalist beliefs. On the other hand, the beliefs and practices of Puerto Rican spiritualism, a mixture of folk religion and healing, are characterized as largely congenial to family therapy for alcoholism (Singer, 1984). Two articles (Schwartz &

Kaslow, 1979; Schwartz & Zemel, 1980) describe cults as pseudo-religions that use emotionally and mentally coercive techniques to alienate vulnerable youth from their families. It is suggested, however, that involvement in cults points to legitimate unmet spiritual needs and that ministers might be helpful in the treatment of ex-cult members. Another article (Frederickson, 1983), examining demonic possession and exorcism as a process of family projective identification, offers a picture of religious belief in an especially curious form. Although these articles present religion in unusual and generally unappealing aspects, several of them also offer a number of approaches for the positive use of religious beliefs and aspirations in family therapy.

Marriage Encounter and Marriage Enrichment

Most of the articles on marriage encounter, marriage enrichment, and premarital counseling underscore the religious origin and content of many of these programs. Becnel and Levy (1983) emphasize the positive influence of religion in the marriage encounter program and suggest, on the basis of their data, that the program may enhance "finding meaning in life." Although several articles present evidence for the effectiveness of marriage encounter and marriage enrichment (Giblin, Sprenkle, & Sheehan, 1985; Lester & Doherty, 1983; Milholland & Avery, 1982), the religious component of the marriage encounter program in particular receives criticism. De-Young (1979) faults the program for not properly informing participants about its significant religious component. In a series of four articles (Doherty, Lester, & Leigh, 1986; Doherty, McCabe, & Ryder, 1978; Doherty & Walker, 1982; Lester & Doherty, 1983), Doherty and his colleagues offer evidence of casualties of marriage encounter and criticize the program's secrecy, coercive methods, and emotional intensity. These deficiencies appear related in large part to the religious and nonprofessional elements of the program. On the other hand, Mace and Mace (1986), pioneers in marriage enrichment, cite the positive importance of marriage encounter in the marriage enrichment movement, and explicitly note that Doherty's studies fail to carry conviction. Indeed, Doherty's summary of all marriage encounter studies to that time (Lester & Doherty, 1983) presents overwhelmingly positive results. DeYoung (1979) also, despite his criticisms, states that he and his wife thought that the encounter program helped their marriage. The significance of religion and religious groups for marriage encounter and marriage is clear in other articles (Dinkmeyer & Carlson, 1986; Diskin, 1986), but appears only as secondary to other themes. Two articles on premarital counseling (Bader, Microys, Sinclair, Willett, & Conway, 1980; Schumm & Denton, 1979) note the heavy involvement of churches in premarital counseling and the prevalence and legitimacy of pastoral premarital counseling.

The entire group of articles on marriage encounter, marriage enrichment, and premarital counseling shows the pronounced concern and role of religion and religious institutions in family life. Evidence for the success of marriage encounter and marriage enrichment is fairly impressive. Nevertheless, the serious criticisms expressed by several authors, especially about marriage encounter, appear closely tied to the program's religious element and suggest significant reservations by some professional family therapists regarding religion's role in marriage enrichment programs.

Instruments and Methods of Measurement

In 11 articles on instruments for measuring various family characteristics, religion or some aspect of religion is included as an instrument item or subscale. A religious or moral-religious emphasis is discussed as an important subscale in studies by Moos and Moos (1976) and Bloom (1985) using the Family Environment Scale (FES). In several reviews of family measures (Bagarozzi, 1985; Beach & Arias, 1983; Forman & Hagan, 1983, 1984; Stephen & Markman, 1983) and in two articles on the use of computers in family therapy (Lehtinen & Smith, 1985; Olson, 1985), items about religion appear in several instruments but are not discussed. In a study comparing the Card Sort Procedure (CSP) and the FES, Oliveri and Reiss (1984) suggest, but do not confirm, that the moral-religious emphasis of the FES might indicate rigidity and dependence and therefore be inversely related to flexibility and openness as measured by the CSP. Overall, this subset of the journal literature indicates that religion has a definite but modest place in several prominent family measures.

Sexual Theme

Religion in relation to sex is discussed in four articles. McConnell's (1977) historical presentation of the sexual value system describes religiously based morality (at least in the West) as having had a significantly negative impact on sexual attitudes and behaviors. In two articles in which Jewish religious values occur as a co-primary theme with sex, the degree of religious observance is shown to be significantly related to sexual attitudes and behaviors (Notzer, Levran, Mashiach, & Soffer, 1984) and the sex therapy process (Ostrov, 1978). In a case study presentation, the sexual attitudes typical of Buddhism are contrasted with the stringency of sexual taboos in Christendom and described as influential in the formation of an unusual sexual paraphilia (Dewaraja & Money, 1986). This small group of articles points to the importance of religious beliefs in sexual development and practice and in the treatment of sexual issues. Although religious Jewish observance is treated impartially, Western religious morality in general is viewed as a negative influence on sex. There is certainly no indication or discussion in these articles of a potentially positive relationship between mature religious faith and fulfilling sexual behavior.

Miscellaneous Themes

In the miscellaneous category of articles, religion is discussed as a strongly positive force in the treatment of alcoholics and drug addicts (Berenson, 1987; Coleman, Kaplan, & Downing, 1986). In three closely related articles about integrative psychotherapy, Friedman (1980, 1981, 1982) lists and emphasizes the spiritual-religious dimension as a major category for understanding and treating families. In Luthman's (1978) discussion of the internal emotional structure as the preeminent source of personal creativity, religious doctrine is presented as a self-alienating external structure, parts of which, however, can be positively integrated into the self insofar as these fit the individual's own internal life structure. In several other articles, some aspect of religion appears only tangentially as part of a survey of family therapists (Rait, 1987), as an example for encouraging a difficult family decision (Schiff & Belson, 1988), as a problematic family dynamic in a case illustration of "future mapping" (Penn, 1985), as a largely nominal rather than practice-oriented descriptor of parents in a study on shared parenting (Irving, Benjamin, & Trocme, 1984), as a limiting factor in the early ethnographic studies of family rituals (Wolin & Bennett, 1984), as a source of myths shielding families from guilt and painful conflict (Stierlin, 1973), and as a cultural element in the training of family therapists for rural settings (Piercy, Hovestadt, Fenell, Franklin, & McKeon, 1982). In his discussion of treating single parent families, Weltner (1982) notes that church congregations have a great, but rarely tapped, potential for meeting many needs of single parents.

RELIGION IN FAMILY THERAPY PRACTICE AND RESEARCH

Clearly, religion receives limited treatment in family therapy journal literature. This literature does, nevertheless, offer some information and insights which are useful for assessing the role of religion in family therapy. These may be summarized as follows.

Religion As Strength and Deficit

There is in the family therapy journal literature evidence that a religious orientation or philosophy in the family may contribute to healthy family functioning. Moos and Moos (1976), on the basis of a cluster analytical study with the Family Environment Scale (FES), identified a "Moral-Religious Emphasis" as one of six major family clusters. They additionally found that none of the clinic or disturbed families in their 100 family study were included in the moral-religious cluster. Bloom (1985), in a series of four empirical studies, identified "Religious Emphasis" as one of 15 dimensions of family functioning. This religious emphasis dimension was one of three personal growth or value dimensions—all of which significantly differentiated intact from disrupted families and suggested characteristics of well-functioning families. Coleman et al. (1986), in two studies of drug addict families, found that addicts, compared with normal and psychiatric outpatients, are less invested in religion and that addict families generally do not share a healthy philosophy or religious belief system. These findings are consistent with Schumm's (1985) summary of family strength studies suggesting that religious orientation has a pervasive and positive influence on family strengths; Coles' (1987) description of the power of prayer and religious belief in the face of great family difficulty; Berenson's (1987) thesis that a spiritual reality is integral to the success of Alcoholics Anonymous; Bradley's (1988) description of how a genuine religious faith brought peace to a young man whose life was destroyed by AIDS; and Schwartz and Kaslow's (1979) suggestion that involvement with cultic pseudo-religions may signify a family's failure to meet the needs of a genuine spiritual quest.

On the other hand, family therapy journal literature illustrates that religion is also expressed in uncritical, narrow, rigid, distorted, pathological, and destructive forms that negatively impact on families. In these forms, religious beliefs and practices may contribute to or be associated with the oppression and abuse of women (Whipple, 1987), fear of death in children (Glicken, 1978), dysfunctional sexual attitudes and behaviors (McConnell, 1977), unprofessional practices (DeYoung, 1979; Doherty et al., 1986), the development of cults (Schwartz & Kaslow, 1979), pathological and bizarre behavior (Frederickson, 1983; Schatzman, 1971), decision-impeding guilt (Cotroneo & Krasner, 1977), authoritarianism and moralism (McGoldrick & Pearce, 1981; Stein, 1973, 1978), and self-alienation (Luthman, 1978).

Family therapy research and practice can benefit by clearly distinguishing between religious faith that enhances personal and family life and distorted forms of religiosity that impede personal and social development. A discussion of the elements of this distinction is beyond the scope of this paper. The point emphasized here is that there are forms of religious faith, development, and practice rooted in life-enhancing experiences and beliefs, and, on the other hand, there are myriad cultural, institutional, and personal expressions of religion that restrict and distort the root, life-enhancing reality of religion. An understanding of these different meanings of religion is basic to constructively integrating religion into family therapy research and practice and to avoiding an indiscriminate classification of all religion either according to its restricted expressions or its essentially positive aspects.

Religion in the Practice of Family Therapy

On the basis of family therapy journal literature, the management of religion in family therapy may be discussed in three broad categories.

First, regardless of her or his own beliefs, the family therapist is encouraged to adopt an open-minded sensitivity toward clients' religious background, beliefs, and practices. Fundamental to this sensitivity is the therapist's self-awareness of her or his own beliefs and attitudes about religion and how these may affect, both consciously and transferentially, responses to explicit and implicit religious facets of families in therapy (Pattison, 1982). Self-awareness and openness about religion attune therapists to the possible therapeutic value of a family's religious beliefs, to potential therapeutic obstacles rooted in religious beliefs or in misunderstandings about religion between the therapist and family, and to self-defeating expressions of religion in contrast to religion's life-enhancing dimensions.

Second, a variety of approaches are available to family therapists for the effective therapeutic use of a family's religious beliefs and practices. For example, in the early phase of therapy, a therapist may ask a family about its religious affiliation or life belief system with a view toward having the family claim from their heritage elements that would promote healing (Midelfort, 1962; Yost, 1986). A family's religious orientation, even when elements of it contribute to family problems (Whipple, 1987), may contain beliefs, symbols, resources, and language that the therapist can, and even should, use to effect change (Lantz, 1979). A family's relationship to God, as distinct from any specific belief about God (Griffith, 1986), or a family coalition with the supernatural (Pattison, 1982) can be a crucial and beneficial determinant of family behavior. The therapist can use such spiritual relationships to identify family strengths (Coles, 1987) and effect significant therapeutic change in the family. In the case of drug addiction (Coleman et al., 1986), alcoholism (Berenson, 1987), and personally disruptive sexual behavior (Notzer et al. 1984), a turn toward genuine religious observance or a spiritual perspective may be part of a solution.

Religious rituals (Bowlby-West, 1983) and religious beliefs (Bradley, 1988; Easson, 1980; McGoldrick et al., 1986) related to death and dying may be used to help a religiously oriented family with the grieving process. The therapist may also find a family's belief in the power of prayer to be a strong and positive force in times of crisis (Coles, 1987), and its belief in God's mercy to be a stimulus to therapeutic forgiveness (John Paul II, 1981).

For families with church or synagogue ties, therapists may find value in consulting with clergy for sharing relevant information and coordinating clergy support and interventions adjunctive to therapy (Boverman & Adams, 1964; Kaslow & Gingrich, 1977; Lantz, 1979; Pattison, 1982; Schwartz & Kaslow, 1979; Whipple, 1987). Churches and synagogues may offer opportunities for support to families on an on-going basis or in times of crisis (Weltner, 1982). Therapists can also look to religious institutions for extensive offerings of marriage encounter and marriage enrichment programs as a possible complement to marriage counseling, especially with religiously open clients living in moderately troubled marriages (Becnel & Levy, 1983; DeYoung, 1979; Doherty et al., 1986; Mace & Mace, 1986; Milholland & Avery, 1982).

Third, the family therapist can expect to be confronted occasionally with religious attitudes, beliefs, and practices that contribute to a variety of family problems (Frederickson, 1983; Glicken, 1978; Huffer, 1973; Pattison, 1982; Schwartz & Kaslow, 1979; Whipple, 1987), including sexual problems (McConnell, 1977), and alcoholism (Ablon, 1980; Panitz et al., 1983) and hinder therapy (Cotroneo & Krasner, 1977; Elkaim, 1985; Juni, 1980; Penn, 1985; Whipple, 1987). Even in these cases, the most appropriate therapeutic approach is usually to begin empathetically with the client's beliefs as a point of entry into the realm of life-enhancing religious beliefs (see, for example, Elkaim, 1985; Penn, 1985; Whipple, 1987). The therapist can then use the latter to broaden or shift the client's religious or life perspective in a more therapeutically positive direction (Griffith, 1986; Lantz, 1979; Whipple, 1987).

Pattison (1982) describes how even typically positive religious processes in the family may become disadvantageous. For example, sacralization (Pattison, 1982), a process by which the patterning of family structure and function is guided by a religious orientation, can provide cohesion and coping strategies but also may result in a nonadaptive rigidity (see, for example, El-Islam, 1983; Juni, 1980; Stein, 1973, 1978). Similarly, family coalitions with the supernatural (Pattison, 1982) can provide values and commitments that strengthen the family but also may shift responsibility outside the family (see, for example, McGoldrick & Pearce, 1981). When these processes become damaging to the family, the therapist should not simply dismiss the religious element but rather help the family to explore differences between beneficial and detrimental expressions of religious belief.

Religion in Family Therapy Research

From a measurement perspective, family therapy researchers who regard religion as a potentially significant element in family functioning may select from several religiously sensitive instruments. Religiously oriented items and subscales are included on several measurement instruments (Bagarozzi, 1985; Bloom, 1985; Beach & Arias, 1983; Lehtinen & Smith, 1985; Moos & Moos, 1976; Olson, 1985; Stein & Kleiman, 1984). On the other hand a number of other similar instruments have no items related to religion (Forman & Hagan, 1983, 1984).

In terms of research content, this review of family therapy journal literature indicates that family therapy research generally slights religion. However, it also suggests the potential for a wide variety of studies on religion in family functioning and family therapy. Since this present review was limited to family therapy journals, a logical next step in research would be a study that includes relevant studies from all appropriate literature categories, not just family therapy journals.

In addition, this present review suggests several lines of potentially fruitful research. For example, because a religious orientation appears to be a source of strength for some families while certain religious beliefs and practices appear detrimental, it would be valuable to know more about the characteristics of the former in contrast to the latter. Process research could lead to a better understanding of how the therapist can move a religiously oriented client from detrimental to beneficial religious expressions. Research into the religious beliefs, practices, and attitudes of family therapists would help to clarify the typical stance of the family therapist toward religion in therapeutic practice and what effect this stance might have on therapy.

CONCLUSION

Religion is a significant factor in the structure and functioning of many families. For some, perhaps many, it is a source of family strength. For others, it is expressed in debilitating ways. In any case, the prevalence and importance of religion in families is clearly not reflected in family therapy journal literature. And if this literature accurately mirrors the real world of family therapy, then the religiousness of families appears to be underrepresented in practice and research.

It might be argued that the low occurrence of religion in family therapy is more in line with the lived value that families place on religion as distinct from self-reported value, with the former being substantially lower than the latter. If this be the case, then the modest appearance of religion in family therapy would be a truer gauge of genuine family religiousness than opinion surveys. This line of reasoning remains to be demonstrated. It might also be argued that family therapy is a legitimately secular enterprise that must focus on a large and complex set of factors of which religion is only one. In this case, although the low occurrence of religion in family therapy may not reflect its generally high valuation in families, it does reflect the extent to which it occurs in relation to the many other factors of family life. This, too, remains to be tested. A third possible explanation for religion's low occurrence in family therapy journals might be that many religiously oriented articles are submitted to journals that specialize in religious issues in mental health, thereby depressing the number that are published in family therapy journals. This information is outside the scope of this present research and is not otherwise currently available.

A fourth line of reasoning is that family therapy is rightly rooted in a secular, scientific, and non-religious point of view that is counter to the fundamentally delusional world of religion. In this case, religion is a bothersome phenomenon that ultimately impedes progress in family living and family therapy (Ellis, 1980). A valuation of religion as a delusion is primarily a philosophical and theological problem. From an empirical point of view, although current data are inconclusive, Bergin (1983) has shown that religious beliefs tend to be, on the average, associated with favorable attitudes and behaviors.

On the other hand, if, as current data strongly suggest, there is a significant gap between the place of religion in family life and its status in family therapy, several reasons may account for this. Perhaps family therapy, as a predominantly secular enterprise, attracts more secularly oriented families than religious families (Zuk, 1978). Or religiously oriented families may include a disproportionately large number of well integrated families who do not need family therapy (Pattison, 1982). Or, if family therapists have value systems similar to other therapeutic professionals, then they are far more likely than the general population to have personal life philosophies that exclude religion (Bergin, 1980), and this largely nonreligious orientation is mirrored in family therapy practice and research. Or, all three of these factors may be at work.

Without altering in the least the secular nature of family therapy, it is proposed that there are several ways of beneficially diminishing, in research and practice, the ostensible discrepancy between religion in family life and family therapy. One would be to have relevant religious factors included more frequently in the study of issues that are not directly religious. For example, religion would often be appropriate to studies whose primary focus is overall family functioning, values, intimate relationships, commitment, pre-marital preparation, sexual attitudes and practices, the care of children, family rules, divorce, alcoholism and drug addiction, cultural influences, serious illness and disability, and death and mourning, to mention only a few. Religion in the context of these studies could at the same time be clarified in its beneficial and detrimental aspects. The inclusion of religious factors in such studies might also entail increased references to pertinent studies in journals that focus on the conjunction of religion and the behavioral sciences, thereby further enhancing the understanding of religion in family therapy. Complementary to this indirect and careful integration of religious factors into family therapy research and practice, there could be a reasonable and modest increase in published studies and related practice whose primary focus is religion in family life and therapy. However, given the secular nature of family therapy and the need to investigate a large and complex array of factors, it can be expected that family therapy articles with a primarily religious orientation will remain relatively small.

The importance that so many families attach to religion, the advantages that mature religious practice can bring to family functioning, and the need to distinguish positive from negative effects of religion all point to the benefits that could accrue from a reasonable increase of attention on religion in family therapy research and practice.

REFERENCES

Ablon, J. 1980. The significance of cultural patterning for the "alcoholic family." *Family Process, 19*, 127-144.

Abroms, G.M. 1978. The place of values in psychotherapy. *Journal of Marriage and Family Counseling, 4*(4), 3-17.

Allman, L.R. 1982. The aesthetic preference: Overcoming the pragmatic error. *Family Process, 21*, 43-56.

Anonymous. 1982. Note from an adolescent who shot himself. *International Journal of Family Therapy, 4*, 67-68.

Bader, E., Microys, G., Sinclair, C., Willett, E., & Conway, B. 1980. Do marriage preparation programs really work?: A Canadian experiment. *Journal of Marital and Family Therapy, 6*, 171-179.

Bagarozzi, D.A. 1985. Family measurement techniques. *The American Journal of Family Therapy, 13*, 67-71.

Beach S.R.H. & Arias, I. 1983. Assessment of Perceptual Discrepancy: Utility of the primary communication inventory. *Family Process, 22*, 309-316.

Becnel, J. & Levy, L. 1983. A marriage enrichment program as a facilitator of focusing and finding meaning in life. *Family Therapy, 10*, 275-282.

Berenson, D. 1987. Alcoholics Anonymous: From surrender to transformation. *Family Therapy Networker, 11* (July-Aug.), 25-31.

Bergin, A.E. 1980. Psychotherapy and religious values. *Journal of Consulting and Clinical Psychology, 48*, 95-105.

Bergin, A.E. 1983. Religiosity and mental health: A critical reevaluation and meta-analysis. *Professional Psychology Research and Practice, 14*, 170-184.

Bernal, G. & Ysern, D. 1986. Family therapy and ideology. *Journal of Marital and Family Therapy, 12*, 129-135.

Bertman, S.L. 1980. Lingering terminal illness and the family: Insights from literature. *Family Process*, *19*, 341-348.

Bloom, B.L. 1985. A factor analysis of self-report measures of family functioning. *Family Process*, *24*, 225-239.

Bowlby-West, L. 1983. The impact of death on the family system. *Journal of Family Therapy*, *5*, 279-294.

Boverman, M. & Adams, J.R. 1964. Collaboration of psychiatrist and clergyman: A case report. *Family Process*, *3*, 251-272.

Bradley, J.E. 1988. The bittersweet life of Jimmy Holloran. *Family Therapy Networker*, *12* (Jan.-Feb.), 45-48, 50-51, 82-89.

Coleman, S.B., Kaplan, J.D., & Downing, R.W. 1986. Life cycle and loss — The spiritual vacuum of heroin addiction. *Family Process*, *25*, 5-23.

Coles, R. 1987. Moral purpose and the family. *Family Therapy Networker*, *11* (Nov.-Dec.), 45-53.

Cotroneo, M. & Krasner, B.F. 1977. A study of abortion and problems in decision-making. *Journal of Marriage and Family Counseling*, *3*(1), 69-76.

Dewaraja, F. & Money, J. 1986. Transcultural sexology: Formicophilia, a newly named paraphilia in a young Buddhist male. *Journal of Sex & Marital Therapy*, *12*, 139-145.

DeYoung, A.J. 1979. Marriage encounter: A critical examination. *Journal of Marital and Family Therapy*, *5*(2), 27-35.

Dinkmeyer, D. & Carlson, J. 1986. A systematic approach to marital enrichment. *The American Journal of Family Therapy*, *14*, 139-146.

Diskin, S. 1986. Marriage enrichment: Rationale and resources. *Journal of Psychotherapy and the Family*, *2*, 111-124.

Doherty, W.J., Lester, M.E., & Leigh, G. 1986. Marriage encounter weekends: Couples who win and couples who lose. *Journal of Marital and Family Therapy*, *12*, 49-61.

Doherty, W.J., McCabe, P., & Ryder, R.G. 1978. Marriage encounter: A critical appraisal. *Journal of Marriage and Family Counseling*, *4*(4), 99-107.

Doherty, W.J. & Walker, B.J. 1982. Marriage encounter casualties: A preliminary investigation. *American Journal of Family Therapy*, *10*, 15-25.

Easson, W.M. 1980. A child's death and the family. *International Journal of Family Therapy*, *1*, 401-412.

Elkaim, M. 1985. From general laws to singularities. *Family Process*, *24*, 151-164.

El-Islam, M.F. 1983. Cultural change and intergenerational relationships in Arabian families. *International Journal of Family Psychiatry*, *4*, 321-327.

Ellis, A. 1980. Psychotherapy and atheistic values: A response to A. E. Bergin's "Psychotherapy and religious values." *Journal of Consulting and Clinical Psychology*, *48*, 635-639.

Feldman, R.L. 1980. Tragedy and the common man: Existential analysis and Arthur Miller. *Family Therapy*, *7*, 1-58.

Forman, B.D. & Hagan, B.J. 1983. A comparative review of total family functioning measures. *The American Journal of Family Therapy*, *11*, 25-42.

Forman, B.D. & Hagan, B.J. 1984. Measures for evaluating total family functioning. *Family Therapy, 11,* 1-36.

Frederickson, J. 1983. Exorcism as a process of family projective identification and indigenous psychotherapy. *Family Therapy, 10,* 165-172.

Friedman, P.H. 1980. An integrative approach to the creation and alleviation of dis-ease within the family. *Family Therapy, 7,* 179-195.

Friedman, P.H. 1981. Integrative family therapy. *Family Therapy, 8,* 173-178.

Friedman, P.H. 1982. The multiple roles of the integrative marital psychotherapist. *Family Therapy, 9,* 109-118.

Gallup, G., Jr. 1987. *The Gallup Poll.* Wilmington, DE: Scholarly Resources.

Gardner, F.A. 1970. A four-day diagnostic-therapeutic home visit in Turkey. *Family Process, 9,* 301-325.

Gelcer, D. 1983. Mourning is a family affair. *Family Process, 22,* 501-516.

Giblin, P., Sprenkle, D.H., & Sheehan, R. 1985. Enrichment outcome research: A meta-analysis of premarital, marital and family interventions. *Journal of Marital and Family Therapy, 11,* 257-271.

Glicken, M.D. 1978. The child's view of death. *Journal of Marriage and Family Counseling, 4*(2), 75-81.

Griffith, J.L. 1986. Employing the God-family relationship in therapy with religious families. *Family Process, 25,* 609-618.

Huffer, V. 1973. Australian Aborigine: Transition in family grouping. *Family Process, 12,* 303-315.

Irving, H.H., Benjamin, M., & Trocme, N. 1984. Shared parenting: An empirical analysis utilizing a large data base. *Family Process, 23,* 561-569.

John Paul II. 1981. The parable of the prodigal son. *International Journal of Family Therapy, 3,* 153-159.

Jordan, J.F. 1985. Paradox and polarity: The Tao of family therapy. *Family Process, 24,* 165-174.

Juni, S. 1980. The stigma of mental illness as a cultural phenomenon: A study of schizophrenia in the Orthodox Jewish family. *Family Therapy, 7,* 223-236.

Kaslow, F.W. & Gingrich, G. 1977. The clergyman and the psychologist as marriage counselors: Differences in philosophy, referral patterns and treatment approaches to non-marital relationships. *Journal of Marriage and Family Counseling, 3*(3), 13-21.

Keeney, B.P. & Sprenkle, D.H. 1982. Ecosystemic epistemology: Critical implications for the aesthetics and pragmatics of family therapy. *Family Process, 21,* 1-19.

Kinzie, D., Sushama, P.C., & Lee, M. 1972. Cross-cultural family therapy – A Malaysian experience. *Family Process, 11,* 59-67.

Lantz, C.E. 1979. Strategies for counseling Protestant evangelical families. *International Journal of Family Therapy, 1,* 169-183.

Lau, A. 1984. Transcultural issues in family therapy. *Journal of Family Therapy, 6,* 91-112.

Lehtinen, M.W. & Smith, G.W. 1985. MATESIM: Computer assisted marriage analysis for family therapists. *Journal of Psychotherapy and the Family, 1,* 117-129.

Lester, M.E. & Doherty, W.J. 1983. Couples' long-term evaluations of their marriage encounter experience. *Journal of Marital and Family Therapy, 9,* 183-188.

Liddle, H.A. 1982. On the problems of eclecticism: A call for epistemologic clarification and human-scale theories. *Family Process, 21,* 243-250.

Luthman, S.G. 1978. The internalized emotional structure for unleashing creativity and expanding consciousness. *Family Therapy, 3,* 205-225.

Mace, D. & Mace, V. 1986. The history and present status of the marriage and family enrichment movement. *Journal of Psychotherapy and the Family, 2,* 7-18.

McConnell, L.G. 1977. The sexual value system. *Journal of Marriage and Family Counseling, 3,* 55-67.

McGoldrick, M., Hines, P., Lee, E., & Preto, N.G. 1986. Mourning rituals. *Family Therapy Networker, 10*(Nov.-Dec.), 28-34.

McGoldrick, M. & Pearce, J.K. 1981. Family therapy with Irish-Americans. *Family Process, 20,* 223-241.

McGoldrick, M. & Preto, N.G. 1984. Ethnic intermarriage: Implications for therapy. *Family Process, 23,* 347-364.

McGoldrick M. & Rohrbaugh, M. 1987. Researching ethnic family stereotypes. *Family Process, 26,* 89-99.

Midelfort, C.F. 1962. Use of member of the family in the treatment of schizophrenia. *Family Process, 1,* 114-118.

Milholland, T.A. & Avery, A.W. 1982. Effects of marriage encounter on self-disclosure, trust and marital satisfaction. *Journal of Marital and Family Therapy, 8,* 87-89.

Moos, R.H. & Moos, B.S. 1976. A typology of family social environments. *Family Process, 5,* 357-371.

Narain, D. 1964. Growing up in India. *Family Process, 3,* 127-139.

Notzer, N., Levran, D., Mashiach, S., & Soffer, S. 1984. Effect of religiosity on sex attitudes, experience and contraception among university students. *Journal of Sex & Marital Therapy, 10,* 57-62.

Oliveri, M.E. & Reiss, D. 1984. Family concepts and their measurement: Things are seldom what they seem. *Family Process, 23,* 33-48.

Olson, D.H. 1985. Microcomputers for couple and family assessment: ENRICH and other inventories. *Journal of Psychotherapy and the Family, 1,* 105-115.

Ostrov, S. 1978. Sex therapy with Orthodox Jewish couples. *Journal of Sex & Marital Therapy, 4,* 266-278.

Panitz, D.R., McConchie, R.D., Sauber, S.R., & Fonseca, J.A. 1983. The role of machismo and the Hispanic family in the etiology and treatment of alcoholism in Hispanic American males. *The American Journal of Family Therapy, 11,* 31-46.

Pattison, E.M. 1982. Management of religious issues in family therapy. *International Journal of Family Therapy, 4,* 140-163.

Penn, P. 1985. Feed-forward: Future questions, future maps. *Family Process*, *24*, 299-310.

Piercy, F., Hovestadt, A., Fenell, D., Franklin, E., & McKeon, D. 1982. A comprehensive training model for family therapists serving rural populations. *Family Therapy*, *11*, 237-249.

Pittman, F.S. 1985. Children of the rich. *Family Process*, *24*, 461-472.

Rait, D. 1987. Survey results. *Family Therapy Networker*, *11*(Jan.-Feb.), 53-57.

Sander, F.M. 1970. Family therapy or religion: A re-reading of T. S. Eliot's *The Cocktail Party*. *Family Process*, *9*, 179-296.

Schatzman, M. 1971. Paranoia of persecution: The case of Schreber. *Family Process*, *10*, 177-206.

Schiff, N.P. & Belson, R. 1988. The Ghandi technique: A new procedure for intractable problems. *Journal of Marital and Family Therapy*, *14*, 261-266.

Schumm, W.R. 1985. Beyond relationship characteristics of strong families: Constructing a model of family strengths. *Family Perspective*, *19*, 1-9.

Schumm, W.R. & Denton, W. 1979. Trends in premarital counseling. *Journal of Marital and Family Therapy*, *5*, 23-32.

Schwartz, L.L. & Kaslow, F.W. 1979. Religious cults, the individual and the family. *Journal of Marital and Family Therapy*, *5*(2), 15-26.

Schwartz, L.L. & Zemel, J.L. 1980. Religious cults: Family concerns and the law. *Journal of Marital and Family Therapy*, *6*, 301-308.

Singer, M. 1984. Spiritual healing and family therapy: Common approaches to the treatment of alcoholism. *Family Therapy*, *11*, 155-162.

Stein, A. & Kleiman, J. 1984. A self-report family data form for family therapy. *Journal of Family Therapy*, *6*, 63-67.

Stein, H.F. 1973. Cultural specificity in patterns of mental illness and health: A Slovak-American case study. *Family Process*, *12*, 69-81.

Stein, H.F. 1978. The Slovak-American "swaddling ethos": Homeostat for family dynamics and cultural continuity. *Family Process*, *17*, 31-45.

Stephen, T.D. & Markman, H.J. 1983. Assessing the development of relationships: A new measure. *Family Process*, *21*, 15-25.

Stierlin, J. 1973. Group fantasies and family myths — Some theoretical and practical aspects. *Family Process*, *12*, 111-125.

Taggart, M. 1980. Salvete et valete: On saying goodbye to a deceased former parent. *Journal of Marital and Family Therapy*, *6*, 117-122.

Trotzer, J.P. 1982. The centrality of values in families and family therapy. *International Journal of Family Therapy*, *3*, 42-55.

Ulrich's International Periodicals Directory: 1987-88 (26th ed.). 1987. New York: R.R. Bowker.

Walls, G.B. 1980. Values and psychotherapy: A comment on "Psychotherapy and religious values." *Journal of Consulting and Clinical Psychology*, *48*, 640-644.

Weltner, J.S. 1982. A structural approach to the single-parent family. *Family Process*, *21*, 203-210.

Wendorf, D.J. & Wendorf, R.J. 1985. A systemic view of family therapy ethics. *Family Process, 24*, 443-460.

Whipple, V. 1987. Counseling battered women from fundamentalist churches. *Journal of Marital and Family Therapy, 13*, 251-258.

Wilson, N.R. 1982. Family therapy in Kenya. *Journal of Family Therapy, 4*, 165-176.

Wolin, S.J. & Bennett, L.A. 1984. Family rituals. *Family Process, 23*, 401-420.

Yost, J.L. 1986. For God, country, and family: A personal tribute to Christian Fredrik Midelfort, M.D. *Family Process, 25*, 149-151.

Zuk, G.H. 1978. A therapist's perspective on Jewish family values. *Journal of Marriage and Family Counseling, 4*(1), 103-109.

Index

Acceptance, 49,50,51,56-57
Ackerman Institute, 142
Ackerman, Nathan 16
Aesthetical issues, 192
Agnostics, 110
American Psychological
  Association, 5
Andolphi, Maurizio, 94
Angelou, Maya, 42
Appreciation, 95
Association of Unitarian and
  Universalist churches, 117
Atheists, 110,148
Authority structures, Biblical
  references to, 144-45

Baptism, 115
Baptist families, 177
Bible, 140,151-52
  relationship principles in, 142-47
Black Baptist families, 177
Blaming behavior, 123-25
Boehme, Jacob, 51
Boundaries, surrounding families,
  176-79
Boundary profiles, of therapists, 8-9
Brain, evolutionary development,
  130-31
Buber, Martin, 22

Calvinists, 116,117
Case illustrations
  couples therapy, 20-22,30-33,71,
    96-100,152
  family of origin problems, 149-51
  family therapy, 87-88
  family types, 20-22

God construct, 64,67
  interfaith couples, 113,123-24,
    125-26,132
  psychodramatic techniques, 74-83
  relationship problems, 153-54,161
  systems therapy, 87-88,96-100
Casti Connubii, 172,173
Catholic Church, faith structure, 114
Change
  faith and, 158
  theory of, 44-46
Children
  embeddedness of belief systems,
    129-30
  God concept development, 65-67,
    83-84
  of interfaith marriages, 133-34
  organizational closure, 83
Choices, life, 43-44,49,50,51
Christianity
  compared to Judaism, 111-12,
    113,114-15
  denominational variations, 108-9,
    114,140
  faith structure, 136
  as meaning coordinate, 114-15
Christians
  as clients, 139-62
  model behavior, 152
Closed-type family, 20,25,167,
  169-71
Codependence, 156
Cognitive thinking, 130-31
Communication, in families, 92,175
Conflict resolution
  Biblical references to, 146-47
  in families, 175
Connectedness
  family, 91-92,95

in relationships, 160-61
  spirit and, 89-90
Constructivist-determinist split,
    16-17
Contextual therapy, 52-53
Couples therapy
  case illustrations, 20-22,30-33,71,
    96-100,152
  see also family therapy
Cults, 192-93
Cultural identity patterns, 113
Culture
  in family therapy journals, 190-91
  religion and, 17-18,106
Curing, healing vs., 47

Death, 191-92
Decentration, 130
Decision making, in families, 175
Deconstruction, 32-33
Denominational differences, 108-9,
    114,140
Determinists, 16-17
Discipline, Biblical references to,
    146
Distancing, in families, 92
Duhl, Fred, 94

*Educational Guidance in Human
    Love*, 172,173
Elkaim, Mony, 94
Embeddedness, in belief systems,
    129-31
Emotional bonding, 174
Emotional triangles, interfaith
    couples and, 124
Empathizing, by therapist, 54-55,56
Envisioning techniques, 161
Ephesians 4:5-6, 146
Ephesians 6, 146
Episcopal Church, faith structure,
    114
Equilibrium, in family systems,
    179-81

Ethics, study of, 7
Existentialism, 14
Exodus story, 32
Extrinsic religious orientation, 168,
    180

Faith
  adopting friend's faith, 149-50
  family of origin and, 147-49
  importance to therapist, 30,
    139-40,151-52,158,159-61
  traps, 151-52
Faith paradigms, 19
Faith relationships, 140-42,150-51,
    157-58
Faith structure, 105,106-11
  affect coordinate, 110-11,111-13
  culture and, 106
  defined, 106
  God in, 109-110
  influence on individual, 131-32
  in interfaith marriage, 122,135-36
  in life cycle situations, 128-29,
    131
  meaning coordinate, 110-11,
    114-15
  minister oriented, 107
  power coordinate, 108,109-11,
    114,115-18
Families
  communication in, 92,175
  distancing in, 92
  as meaning making system,
    118-22
  resources of, 156-59
  rituals, 180
Family boundaries, 176-79
Family connectedness, 91-92,95
Family functioning, religion and,
    165-81
Family histories, 27
Family life cycle, 91-92
Family loyalty, 119-20,122-27
Family of origin
  faith and, 147-49

problems relating to, 157
relationship attitudes and, 149-51
religious customs in, 113
view of God and, 149-51
Family paradigms, 19
Family stories, 33-35
Family structure
  influence of religion, 171-74
  Jewish views, 172
  Protestant views, 173
  Roman Catholic views, 172-73
Family style, religious commitment
  and, 169-71
Family systems
  boundaries, 176-79
  equilibrium, 179-81
  integration, 179-81
  theory, 91-92,119-20,166-68
Family therapy
  case illustrations, 20-22,87-88
  Christians as clients, 139-62
  clergy support, 199
  envisioning techniques, 161
  goals, 52-53,159-61
  hermeneutic model, 26-36
  interfaith families, 103-36
  models, 22-36,141-42
  practice, 53-56
  religious beliefs in, 196-200,
    201-2
  spiritually based, 41-59,63-84,
    94-96,139-62
  stance, 16-17
  systems therapy, 87-100
  values and, 22-26,177
Family therapy journals
  measurement methods, 194-95
  religion in, 185-203
  themes in, 188-94
Family therapy research, religion in,
  200-1
Family types
  case illustration, 20-22
  individualistic-random, 20,25,168

negotiating-open, 20,25,167,
  169-71
traditional-closed, 20,25,167,
  169-71
Fellowship communities, 157-58
Forgiveness, 49,50,51,56-57
Freud, Sigmund, 23,26,31
Fuller, Buckminster, 37
Fundamentalism, in family therapy
  journals, 192-93
Fundamentalist Protestants, 177,178

Galatians 4,143
Gender, power distribution and, 35
Generativity, 35-36
Genesis 2,145
Genesis 3:10, 22
Genograms, 141-42
God
  detriangling, 160
  development of belief in, 65-67
  in image of parent, 149-51
  relationship with, 63-84,147-48,
    159-61
  as scapegoat, 152-53
  views of, 42,110,144
God-construct, 63-84
  case illustrations, 64,67
  conversations with, 70-74
  defined, 65
  epigenesis, 64-69
  language systems approach, 70-74
  organizational closure, 68*il*, 69*il*
God-schemes, 65,66,68*il*,69*il*,83
Grace, contexts for, 57-58
Grand Unification Theory, 110
Grief, stages of, 49,50,51
Growth, cognitive impetus, 130

Healing, 47,56-58,151,157-58
Hebrews 12,146
Hermeneutics
  defined, 26
  models, 26-36

stages, 29-36
History taking, 27
Holy Spirit, 90
Hoover, Jackie, 7-8
Hospitality, 3
  defined, 29
  in therapy process, 29,30-31
Human life, interactive subsystems,
  17-18
Humanism, 6,110

Imagination, in family therapy,
  33-35
Individualistic-random family type,
  20,25,168
Individuality, Biblical references to,
  144
Information processing, in families,
  174-75
Injustice
  acceptance of, 45-46
  reaction to, 47-49
  as reason for therapy, 44-45
Integration, of family systems,
  179-81
Interfaith couples, 155-56,178
  case illustrations, 113,123-24,
    125-26,132
  children of, 133-34
  counseling, 103-36
  emotional triangles, 124
  grief work, 135-36
  guilt expressions, 123-24
  parents' reactions, 123-26,127
  religious issues, 122,132-35
  religious outsider problem, 123-25
Intergenerational connectedness,
  91-92,95
Interviewing
  God-construct in, 72-74
  interventive, 72-74
Intrinsic religious orientation,
  168-69,180
Irish Catholic families, 177

Jackson, Don, 16
Jewish families
  boundaries, 178
  structure of, 172
  values, 177-78
Joining processes, 29,54,55
Judaism
  as affect coordinate, 111-13
  compared to Christianity, 111-13,
    114-15
  faith structure, 136
  family structure, 172
  peoplehood ties, 111,112,113
  rituals of, 112

Language systems approaches,
  70-74
Leaving-cleaving cycle, Biblical
  references to, 145-46
Levine, Steven, 44
Life choices, 43-44,49,50,51,90
Life cycle issues, 91-92
  emotional reactions to, 129
  in religious identification, 127-32
Life stories, meaning, 95-96
Love
  Biblical references to, 143-44,
    146,146-47
  spiritual, 47-51
  unconditional, 55-56,57
Lutheran Church, 115

Mark 3:33, 146
Mark 7:10, 145
Marriage encounter, 193-94
Marriage enrichment, 193-94
Marriages, interfaith. *See* interfaith
  couples
Marx, Karl, 31
Matthew 18:15-16, 146
Matthew 5:23-24, 146
Mid-life cycle, religion in, 132
Milan group, 16-17
Ministry, demands of, 154-55

Minuchin, Salvador, 16
Mishnah, 172
Mourning, 191-92

Natural relationships, 140-42,147-56
Negotiating-open family type, 20,
    25,167,169-71
Nietzsche, Friedrich, 31

Open-family type, 20,25,167,169-71
Organizational closure, 66,68*il*,
    69*il*,83
Orthodoxy, 169,170

Palmer, Parker, 3
Paradigm shifts, 20
Parents, interfaith marriages and,
    123-26,127
Personal self, 51-52
Personality, religious commitment
    and, 168-69
Philosophical themes, in family
    therapy journals, 192
Piaget, Jean, 65,83,129,130
Pindar, 7
Power distribution
    in families, 35
    gender and, 35
Premarital counseling, 193-94
Prodigal son, 144
Protestant churches, faith structure,
    114
Protestant families, structure of, 173
Psychodramatic techniques, 72
    case illustration, 74-83
Psychologists
    desirability of religious beliefs
        and, 4-6,185,196-200
    spirituality of, 5
Psychotherapy
    religious reality and, 30
    spiritually based. *see* family
        therapy

Puritans, 116,117

Quest religious orientation, 169,180

Random family type, 20,25,168
Reality
    personal constitution of, 130
    perspectives on, 19-20
Recentration, 130
Reconstruction, 33-35
Relationship, with self, 46
Relationship problems
    case illustrations, 153-54,161
    God and, 160-61
    religious differences and, 119-22
    see also family therapy
Relationships
    connecting, 160-61
    models, 143-44
    natural, 140-42,147-56
    spiritual, 140-42,147-56
Religion, 19-20,112
    compared with spirituality, 13-14
    cultural systems and, 17-18
    defined, 15,18
    family functioning and, 156-59,
        165-81
    family structure and, 171-74
    in family therapy journals,
        185-203
    in family therapy research, 200-1
    importance to Americans, 185
    psychology and, 4-6,16
    sociological approach, 15-17
    theological approach, 16
    world view of, 106,107
Religious commitment, 168-71
Religious differences
    in families, 155-56
    relationship problems and, 119-22
    teaching children about, 133-34
Religious identification, life cycle
    issues and, 127-32

Religious orientation, 27-28,130, 168-69,180
Religious values
diversity of, 140
family values and, 177
understanding clients', 23,24-25
Risk, in therapy process, 28-29
Rituals, 180
Roman Catholic church, pre-Reformation, 117
Roman Catholic families, structure of, 172-73

Sacralization, 179-80
Sartre, Jean-Paul, 105
Schemes, as cognitive structures, 65
Self
conversations with God-construct, 70-74
integration of, 51-52
relationship with, 46
Self issues, therapists', 54
Self-in-relation, 14
Selfishness/selffulness relationship, 156
Sex, in family therapy journals, 195
Sex education, 173
Spirit, will and, 89-90
Spiritual awareness
of client, 44-46,50-51
of therapist, 41-44,45,46,50-51
Spiritual growth
defined, 53
opportunities for, 46
therapists, 55-56
Spiritual guidance, in systems therapy, 87-100
Spiritual love, 47-51
Spiritual relationships, 140-42, 147-56
Spiritual self, 51-52
Spiritual/religious orientation, 27-28, 130,168-69,180
Spiritualism, 192-93

Spirituality
compared with religion, 13-14
defined, 14-15,89
embodiment, 14-15
psychologists and, 5
systems therapy and, 87-100
Spiritually based therapy. *See* family therapy
Stories, meaning of, 95-96
St. Paul, 144
Support groups, 54-55
Suspicion, in family therapy, 31-32
Systems theory, 91-92,119-20, 166-68
Systems therapy
case illustrations, 87-88,96-100
spirituality and, 87-100
see also family therapy

Talmud, 172
Therapists
boundary profiles, 8-9
conversations with God-construct, 71-72
religious views of, 3-6,24,56-57, 198
self issues, 54
spiritual awareness, 3-6,41-44,45, 46,139-40
spiritual growth, 55-56
therapeutic neutrality, 56-57
training, 8-9
value systems of, 22-26
world views of, 6-9,10,20-22,121
Tillach, Paul, 18
I Timothy 3, 145
Torah, 172,177
Traditional-closed family type, 20, 25,167,169-71
Transitions, in family life cycle, 91-92
Trinitarian Congregationalists, 116
Trinity, 144
Truth, search for, 42-44

Truthfulness, Biblical references to, 146-47

Ultimate concerns, 17-18
Unbelievers, 67
Unconditional love, 55-56,57
Unconditionality, 43-44,46,50
Unitarian Universalism, 112,117-18
  faith structure, 136
  history of, 115-18
  as power coordinate, 115-18
Unitarian Universalist Association, 116
Unity, Biblical references to, 144

Universalist Church in America, 116-17

Values, 22-23,189-90

Weltanschauung, 6-9,19
Whitaker, Carl, 94
Wholeness, self-integration and, 51-52
Will, spirit and, 89-90
Williamson, Donald, 94
World view
  of client, 6-9,10,19
  of therapist, 6-9,10,19,121